THERMAGEDDON

THERMAGEDDON

COUNTDOWN TO 2030

ROBERT HUNTER

ARCADE PUBLISHING • NEW YORK

Copyright © 2002, 2003 by Robert Hunter

FIRST U.S. EDITION 2003

First published in 2002 in Canada under the title *2030: Confronting Thermageddon in Our Lifetime* by McClelland & Stewart Ltd and revised and updated for this edition

Extract from "Alaska, No Longer So Frigid, Starts to Crack, Burn and Sag" copyright © 2002 by the New York Times Co. Reprinted by permission

Library of Congress Cataloging-in-Publication Data

> Hunter, Robert, 1941–
>> Thermageddon : countdown to 2030 / Robert Hunter
> — 1st U.S. ed.
>>> p. cm.
>> Includes bibliographical references.
>> ISBN 1-55970-667-8
>>> 1. Global warming. 2. Climatic changes —
> Environmental aspects. I. Title.

> QC981.8.G56H87 2003
> 363.738'74 — dc21   2002038349

Published in the United States by Arcade Publishing, Inc., New York
Distributed by AOL Time Warner Book Group

Visit our Web site at www.arcadepub.com

10 9 8 7 6 5 4 3 2 1

Designed by Terri Nimmo

EB

PRINTED IN THE UNITED STATES OF AMERICA

For Emily Augustine Joan Hunter
whose world, after all, this is

CONTENTS

ACKNOWLEDGMENTS

The word "Thermageddon" was invented by my good friend, Royal Institute of International Affairs Associate Fellow Walter C. Patterson, during a conversation in the United Kingdom in 1999. Special thanks to Henry Hengeveld, Senior Science Advisor to Environment Canada, for his time. And again, many thanks to my wife, Roberta, for taming the computer, and to my talented and patient editor, Pat Kennedy, for taming the prose.

God gave us always some reason, some hope; but now a new terror has soiled us, which none can avert, none can avoid, flowing under our feet and over the sky.

— T. S. Eliot
Murder in the Cathedral

THERMAGEDDON

PROLOGUE

AFTER A DOZEN YEARS OF EERIE warmth, the snow fell relentlessly on Toronto through the winter of 2001. I had grown used to the sight of empty outdoor hockey rinks turned into dun-colored fields in January, with puddles instead of ice. Now I was out shoveling day after day, week after week, while mini-mountain-ranges grew along the driveway and sidewalks. For the first time in my life, I enjoyed it. It was the best snow I'd seen since I was a young man in Winnipeg. For a change, I didn't nag the kids to come and help. My wife thought I was being a saint, but I was actually being greedy, hogging the experience. Everything I had learned at the historic 1997 conference of the Intergovernmental Panel on Climate Change in Kyoto, Japan, had pointed to the fact that the mighty northern winter as we have known it — and as it has defined us — is on the endangered ecosystems list. Yet, look how the snow flowed boundlessly down one more time! The wind shaped it into drifts in the backyard, burying the lawn ornaments. Real icicles formed clear stalactites from the eaves to the drifts.

The snow falling through that long, beautiful winter seemed like a gift. Look upon it, I wanted to say to strangers. Isn't this wonderful? Whenever my oldest son, Conan, came over with his family, and I had my three grandchildren under my roof, we heaped the fire up, turned down the lights, and hunkered on the sofa and cushions looking out between the icicles at the moonlight glinting on the glassy blue-silver drifts in the yard. The high cedar hedge gave us the illusion of being perched on the edge of a forest. Our little poodle whined to be let out to howl, the wolf DNA stirred by genetic memories of man and dog surviving in the shadow lands of the glaciers.

As the snow fell, I looked down at my youngest grandson, Dexter Peregrine Hunter-Laroche, born in April a year before, one of the first children of the new millennium. Firelight and moonlight played upon his sweet, serious face as he gamely took his first steps. I wonder if he'll have even a dim memory of a classical winter like this one? Most likely, he'll be sweating it out in a Florida-like atmosphere, along with refugees *from* Florida. One thing seems unavoidable. By the time he's *my* age, approaching his sixtieth birthday, the world is going to be drastically, catastrophically, devastatingly different. Such "eternal" certainties as predictable weather patterns, reliable growing cycles, a temperate climate, seasons that stay the same, could all be lost: a paradise destroyed!

Those of us living now in the industrialized countries should be thankful that the barrier of time appears to be firmly locked, because if they could ever break through, the people of the future — starting with Dexter's people — will surely come back to strangle us, the ancestors from hell, in our sleep, for having squandered the Earth's legacy in a handful of generations.

This, then, is a document for Dexter's records, so that he will understand what we — what *I* — did to him. By a huge margin, I was one of the very *worst* culprits, right up there on the edge of being part of the actual jet-set culture.

Dexter will not need to be told that the glorious, fecund interglacial climate known as the Holocene was wrecked by uncontrolled pollution. That will be the most obvious thing in the world. How the disaster was allowed to happen, *despite the existence of an instantaneous global communications system*, will be of enormous interest to him, however. And, more to the point, he will want to know *who* allowed it. Were there no sentinels?

Why were the messengers ignored? Who was on watch? Who was in command?

We can be sure there will be climate-damage-related reparation actions in motion and/or completed by the time Dexter approaches his sixtieth birthday. The corporations and governments that today continue to profit from the flow of oil will have been found guilty of crimes against humanity, and Dexter, like billions of his generation, will doubtless appreciate any compensation he can get his hands on. But of this we can be certain: whatever the payment, it will not be enough to compensate for the loss of the "old" climate, the flooding of coastlines, the droughts, deluges, fires, and the frenzy of megastorms that will define the limits and possibilities of his life. Like his peers, he will know by then exactly how to measure Ecological Footprints. He will know *exactly* how brontosaurian his grandparents' appetite for resources was. He will be able to compare it down to the milligram against whatever meager resources he will be permitted to consume himself, the planet having been changed forever from an unparalleled beauty to a haunted hag of a world.

They will want to spit on our pictures, Dexter and his peers. Every one of us now living will be seen by their time as having been *the* problem. We will be unable to shake the future's conviction that we all knew what we were doing, even when we denied and closed our eyes, even when we told the pollsters that other issues, like taxes and health care (very concerned about *our* health, we are), were much more important to us than boring old global warming. And to the extent that we did nothing to prevent the disaster from happening, it will be said that we served the purposes of evil, and therefore we *were* evil. This is the perspective Dexter's generation cannot help but have. There is nothing I can write that will redeem those of us now living in the developed countries, most especially Canadians and Americans with cars, those of us who are frequent flyers, truckers, sports-utility-vehicle owners, all-terrain-vehicle operators, Ski-Dooers, Sea-Dooers, people with leaf blowers, snow blowers, power mowers, motor-cycles, outboards, inboards — everybody who adds to the green-house-gas load.

Let us admit this much to begin with: if brutal high-tech invaders from somewhere out in the galaxy had come here to loot the world's resources, they could scarcely have done a more thorough job of vandalism than we have done ourselves.

This book is an accounting of a pillaging, really: the Sack of Planet Earth. And there were many, *many* of us involved.

Once, when I was out on the Grand Banks on a chartered Newfoundland-based ship, a former dragger, covering the Turbot War, the captain of our ship invited me up to his quarters to share a Scotch. He was a courtly gentleman, handsome and dignified. We got to talking about the disappearance of the cod in the 1980s, and, to my astonishment, the captain admitted: "We knew we was overfishin'. We knew it couldn't go on. We did it anyway." My sympathy for the unfortunate East Coast fishermen who ended up jobless on the streets after the cod vanished was tempered from that point onward by the grim, shocked realization that perfectly rational human beings could make themselves behave as though they were oblivious to the consequences of their actions, even when they weren't. We lecture juvenile offenders over the issue of taking responsibility, yet here was a whole society, in a supposedly mature liberal democracy, closing its eyes to ecocide. People had mortgages, my good Newfoundland captain explained.

At first, I thought such appalling myopia must surely be a local phenomenon. But as Dexter will know only too well, what the captain admitted to having done — *having destroyed an entire fishery for immediate gain* — was in fact being done around the world by some ten thousand fishing boats, prowling the sea, drift netting and dragging, moving steadily down the food chain as one commercial species after another declines. They also know perfectly well what they are doing. The governments know about it. But everybody has mortgages. And governments, whatever they think, respond — if they respond at all — to electoral, not biological, cycles.

Polls indicate that most people at the turn of the twenty-first century would appear to be largely in denial about the scale and seriousness of the ecological damage being done right now. In North America, it seems we cannot be said to have an informed public. In Europe, there is a far higher level of awareness of the dangers ahead, partially because of the existence of powerful environmental lobbies and parties, but also because Europeans are not quite so blinded by infatuation with the automobile, which permits them to contemplate alternatives. North Americans are profoundly addicted, and worse, locked into suburban grids that were built on the assumption that everybody would have at least two cars.

By the summer of 2002, there was hardly any way to avoid facing the abyss. The new facts of ecological life had become overwhelming. A twenty-one-year satellite weather photo study of the appearance and falling of leaves had revealed that the growing season in North America had lengthened by twelve days in that period. In Maine, a thousand private wells fell empty after the driest winter in 108 years. At least fifty-seven rivers on the East Coast and the Great Plains were trickling along at record low water levels. Across the desiccated West, rats had emerged, driven into the open by a strangling drought. Rats overran the beaches of Ventura, California, crawled over the rooftops in Pasadena, and scampered down from the trees and in from the fields into Beverly Hills itself.

Yet, politically, hardly anthing moved! Denial was — and is — somehow still in vogue. Can apparent North American public blindness be blamed on the media? The answer is a partial yes. The mainstream media (and what else is there, really?) overwhelmingly continues to treat climate change and its causes as a "science" story, detached from any political and social context, virtually never worthy of the front page — or, in the case of

television and radio, not "time-sensitive" enough. In Russia, the
public has been virtually blinded, as post-Soviet energy oligarchs
have seized control of the media, buying up the television stations in particular, and shutting the windows on any opportunity for the average suffering Russian to glimpse what goes on
behind the scenes.

In the dictatorships of the Middle East, Africa, and Asia,
where money earned from export of oil and natural gas pays for
the armed muscle to enforce tyranny, there is of course no
freedom of the press. Ecology? The future? Climate? People
who are starving or trapped in some primitive theocratic political nightmare can't be blamed for being blind. But why is it that,
in the West, where there is little excuse for ignorance, the
general public seems to be clinging to an attitude that can only
be described as willfully ignorant? Enough of the real truth leaks
through between the lines of print in even the most right-wing
tabloid. There are enough flickering images on television screens
of a walrus perched precariously on an eaten-away sculpture of
ice here, of a skinny polar bear shivering in the cold there, of a
crack in the Antarctic, of more forests burning. People *know* the
ecostorm is coming, just as the Newfie captain knew about
the cod disappearing. He just found some way to block it from
his consciousness, to disconnect himself from the effects that he
himself caused, to shut down his adaptation reflex. Instead of
changing course or even slacking off, he followed the rest of the
fishing fleet, exactly like a lemming, except he was a lemming
with an awareness he decided *not to use.* In the end, his wonderful, highly evolved human consciousness proved useless; for all
intents and purposes it might as well not have existed, since it
played no role in the way the history of the world unfolded.

And this is what makes my blood run cold. Men who are
brave enough, smart enough, and organized enough to go to sea
and survive, and indeed, make a living, are not fools. They know
their environment, instruments, and equipment intimately. If, for

all their intelligence and accumulated knowledge and skills, men like these who are *leaders* somehow lacked the capacity to adapt in time to avoid wiping out their basic resource, what can we expect from society as a whole? Each man for himself, grabbing while he can, taking what he can get, head down, not looking ahead at all, scrambling, clawing, pocketing? What did the good captain leave for *his* grandchildren? An ocean one step closer to becoming a biological wasteland, thank you. The mortgage was always the excuse, the need to get by. And the poorer the man, the fiercer the logic of his refusal to consider the future.

As for those of us who are not poor, who are not enslaved, what is our excuse? Why do we turn our backs on our own progeny's fate? It is, I suspect, partially for reasons of emotional pragmatism. Because it makes us feel so terrible, we don't want to admit that there is a direct connection between our personal everyday lives and something awful and maybe even profoundly evil happening to the whole wide world. It is also very much to do with not wanting to *admit* to the grievous harm that will happen to our own grandchildren years from now through our present inaction. The strategy, cynical and effective and widespread (nearly universal, in fact), is to *feign ignorance now and hope to be able to claim it later.*

Yet we are anything but ignorant. At the level of the personal anecdote, the with-my-own-eyes stuff, at the time of this writing, I doubt that there is anyone who has not heard the wind blowing harder at odd times, or noted early flowerings, or low lake levels, or more mosquitoes, or else seen the tide surge across land that has never been flooded before. How many people this summer stared at toppled oaks that had stood for centuries? Or felt the dust stirring across the prairies? Or for the first time heard thunder over the permafrost?

Even if we can't see it, we can *hear* it: a roar, muted and distant, but growing louder, a vast "shivering," as the scientists call it, in the planetary climate's regulatory mechanism. It is a cacophony comprised of the booming of the Larsen ice shelf as it breaks off, the rumble of river torrents unleashed by glaciers melting from Kilimanjaro to Mount Everest, the pneumatic hiss of permafrost pressure ridges decrystallizing below the taiga flatlands, the crackle of forest fires raging from Brazil to northern Ontario, the whoosh of sand dunes from the Gobi Desert piling up against the gates of Beijing, the thud of shorelines along California collapsing, the howl of subtropical super-hurricanes, the gurgle of more floods in Asia than at any time in recorded history, the groan of Quebec's power lines bending under unforeseen burdens of ice, and the cries of environmental refugees who have become more numerous than victims of war.

The most obvious fact of life at this juncture of history, Dexter, is that if we continue to pollute, burn, overfish, clearcut, strip-mine, dam, drain, net, poison, dump, exterminate, develop, fly, drive, and procreate at our current rate, we will *inevitably* precipitate a global disaster. The tilting of the system has already begun. And all the high-tech gadgets in the world will be of little joy to us if the biosphere has collapsed and the survivors are either clinging to a threadbare existence on a ruined planet, or desperately trying not to make the same mistakes on other planets.

You will know. I can just guess. But it is just a matter of time before the Alps are snowless, the Arctic Ocean ice-free, the Amazon rainforests and the boreal canopy of the Canadian Shield burned, the salmon vanished, the coral reefs bleached away, the Everglades inundated by salt water, the Gulf Stream itself thrown out of whack. How long before the seasons as we know them have disappeared under a chemical shroud? There is no point in my generation kidding itself any longer about what we are allowing to happen in our lifetimes. There is no intellectually honest way to avoid facing the truth of our culpability.

The central characteristic of the new millennium is that all around us, above and below, the planetary life-support system is being degraded at a rate that leaves us very little maneuvering space. The paradise called Earth is being transformed into a fiery, storm-whipped Hieronymus Bosch–like ecological nightmare, with an even worse long-term possibility — a million-year ice age — looming on the horizon. A great gear is shifting that will affect the global climate mechanism throughout the rest of history.

No one could suspect that the doom of our civilization was to be found in these four separately benign words: *accelerated positive-feedback loops*. But this is the phrase that best describes the real threat confronting us, and nobody in any position of power in my time is factoring it in. This is like driving a car with a frosted windshield and a speed gauge that says you are barely moving, when in fact you are racing out of control. Our governments, and far too many scientists, even the good guys, are behaving as though climate change is something that is going to waltz into the lifetimes of our grandchildren at a stately pace. They perceive it as an evolutionary process, involving incremental changes stretched over a huge rack of time. But it might not be coming that way at all. It might be speeding up as it advances, like a storm gathering momentum. With each notch upward in temperature, more methane and carbon are released, the hydrological cycle turns a little faster, the albedo — the reflective power of the planet's surface, which plays a critical role in the absorption of warmth — lessens or intensifies, depending on evaporation rates, and suddenly the rate of permafrost melt is greater than indicated by purely linear projections. Moreover, what we cannot calculate is the cumulative effect. What we may in fact be seeing and hearing all around us are the early stages of a sudden lurch into an entirely new climate regime, probably another ice age, although in the short — which is to say the century-long — run, we will continue our descent into an inferno of heat surges, drought, flood, and desertification. The worst news, of course, is that paleontologists have uncovered proof from ice-core drilling that rapid, dramatic changes in climate have indeed occurred before, caused by changes in solar intensity and abrupt changes in ice sheets and/or ocean circulation — and the terrible truth seems to be that the massively disruptive shifts in climate that they caused took place within mere *decades*.

The point of no return could be reached within the next thirty years — a point no further away in time than the breakup of the Beatles. This will be the most obvious fact of life to you, Dexter. By then, the carbon dioxide in the atmosphere will be *double* what it was in preindustrial times, just two centuries ago. The Arctic ice cap will be on the verge of vanishing entirely during the summer, which will mean that its surface will change from white to black, making it absorb heat instead of reflecting it, and thus altering the planet's albedo. Beyond that moment of final polar dissolution, *there will be absolutely nothing we can do to stop or reverse the transformation set in motion*. We will have precipitated a temperature-induced *Götterdämmerung* so sweeping and destructive that I think we need a new word to describe it. The scientific term "radiative forcing" describes the process in which a change in the atmosphere drives a change in climate, but in order to properly convey the profundity of that process, we need stronger language by far.

I therefore submit a combination of *thermal*, meaning temperature, and *Armageddon*, the biblical world's-end, the final battle between good and evil. This gives us the hybrid word *Thermageddon*. (Interestingly, the Bible in the Book of Revelation 16 describes the battle of Armageddon, saying "men were scorched with great heat . . . the water thereof was dried up . . . and every island fled away . . .")

If our present sweet, gentle climate is envisioned as a field held or holding itself in an exquisitely beneficent balance, what has begun to happen can no longer be thought of in such pastel terms as a "warming" or simply a "change." The appropriate word for what is happening to our ten-thousand-year-old Holocene-era climate, as scientists call it, is a "crash."

It will seem incredible to you, Dexter, that the term "greenhouse effect" didn't enter the realm of pubic debate until nearly the end of the twentieth century. The concept had been proposed as early as the 1820s, when Jean-Baptiste-Joseph Fourier observed: "The atmosphere acts like a hothouse, because it lets through the light rays of the sun but retains the dark rays from the ground." It took a while for scientists to figure out the reason for this: the existence of gases that trap heat, the so-called greenhouse gases. Some of them occur naturally — like carbon dioxide, methane, and nitrous oxide — although over time they would be released in increasing volume by the burning of coal, oil, and gas and by leakage from pipelines and landfills. Some of them, the chlorofluorocarbons (CFCs) and halocarbons, were completely alien chemicals not introduced into the atmosphere until the 1930s, when they were first used for refrigeration, air conditioning, and insulation.

Eventually we came to understand that, relatively sparse as the greenhouse gases are — a few hundred parts in a million — they have an enormous effect. They are transparent to incoming sunlight, but when the heat of the sun is reradiated from the planet's surface, the energy is altered to long-wavelength infrared. At this new frequency, the rising heat is absorbed by the gases, which pass it on to the rest of the atmosphere. As early as 1896, while trying to explain ice ages, the Swedish scientist Svante August Arrhenius correlated changes in surface temperature with changes in atmospheric carbon dioxide, and a few years later became the first to suggest that industrial pollution could trigger major climate changes.

In truth, no one can predict exactly which way the climate will ultimately swing. One scenario has it going over the edge of a sudden superheating process that would lead to an extreme cooling correction, plunging our northern civilization into a new hemispheric ice age that could last for millions of years. Another has it spinning out of control down into a sulphurous Venusian-type hell, with all oxygen-based life at risk. Whichever form climate change takes, it seems virtually certain now that an epochal atmospheric oscillation looms just over the horizon, a radiative-forced nightmare of either fire or ice which will be the defining crisis of the twenty-first century.

Surely, my contemporaries will argue, the crisis cannot be compared to the threat of an all-out nuclear exchange, such as we faced until as recently as the 1989 collapse of the Soviet Union. Even by the late 1980s, there was nothing self-evident about the proposition that we would survive until the end of the century. For a long while, the odds seemed stacked against us. But we did *not* nuke ourselves, and thus it can be said that humanity has demonstrated a remarkable gift for last-minute salvation — or incredible luck. Either way, all history since the Cuban Missile Crisis of 1962 can rightly be described as borrowed time. Collectively, we had a near-death experience. We thought we had survived rather nicely, only to look up when the dust of the Cold War settled and see a climate cataclysm rumbling towards us that could have as devastating an impact on the northern hemisphere as a nuclear exchange.

And, if one can bear to think about it, this raises the even more soul-crushing question of how we are affecting the *millennial* cycle of climate. Contemplate that. Not just the next few generations affected, but generation after generation after generation. We won the struggle against those who would have nuked us all, but now it is *all of us* who are doing the nuking. It was a relatively simple business, in retrospect, avoiding nuclear destruction. All we had to do was make sure no one pushed The Button. What do you do to prevent half a billion vehicles' ignition keys from being turned on?

The military seemed so huge and powerful back in the sixties, Dexter. It was easy to be intimidated. How could disorganized bands of peaceniks ever prevail against the combined might of the Kremlin and the Pentagon? Yet the military in both superpowers bowed, in the crunch, to their political masters. On the climate-change front, it is not quite so simple. Politicians in both countries bow to other masters. Rather than controlling the oil interests who have brought us the climate crisis (and are as determined, for the most part, as the tobacco industry was to deny that their product causes widespread suffering, death, and destruction), it is clear that the Russian and American governments have been co-opted by oil. As, indeed, has my own government of Canada.

Vehicles with internal-combustion engines are coming off the assembly lines around the world at the rate of *one per minute*. How do you stem such a tide? In the 1970s and 1980s, when I was active in the Greenpeace movement, we discovered it was possible to get in the way of whaling and sealing ships, and stop them. Indeed, within a matter of just a few years, we helped get a ten-year moratorium on whaling, and closed down the harp-seal-pup fur industry. Likewise, we found we could interfere with nuclear tests, especially atmospheric ones, by dropping the anchors of our boats in the immediate downwind vicinity, or just offshore from Ground Zero, as I tried to do in 1971 in the Aleutian Islands, along with the crew of the original *Greenpeace* ship, as described in *Warriors of the Rainbow, To Save a Whale, The Greenpeace Chronicle, Greenpeace,* and *Greenpeace III: Journey into the Bomb*. But those actions were like sticking one's fingers, one hole at a time, into the cracks of a gigantic dike.

With climate change, we are looking at the whole dike collapsing at once.

In different times and situations, different actions become revolutionary. There was a time when the first act of a revolutionary was to raise a sword or pitchfork against his oppressor, and later it was to fire a musket or destroy a bridge. In my era, Dexter, it has involved everything from throwing Molotov cocktails at tanks to torching shopping malls to slow down urban sprawl. As the fossil fuel/renewable energy battle is joined, and the struggle to preserve a viable planet moves to stage center of the human and ecological drama, I think my generation will discover that the definition of "revolutionary" has changed yet again.

When we see Islamic fundamentalist regimes aligned with neo-communists, working behind the scenes with Texans, Albertans, and Russian "businessmen," we must accept that the basic geopolitical ground has shifted. Confronted with a true planetary crisis, can we really afford to tolerate the self-imposed ignorance of religious zealots or bottom-line-feeding corporate sharks if it involves continued damage of the biosphere? With the greatest, most dangerous climate interference coming from the burning of fossil fuels and the release of methane, the most important initial step is clearly to reduce emissions. Since energy demand is not going to lower itself voluntarily (barring the emergence of some sort of grassroots energy-reduction movement in the developed countries), the rapid production of substitute fuels and alternative energy sources becomes a primary objective.

Any step in that direction involves directly engaging the enemy, which at this point is the fossil-fuel industry and its flunkies and allies in politics and media. It cannot be stated much more clearly. And perhaps never until the arrival of George W. Bush in the presidency has the connection between Big Oil and the Republican Party been more transparent, or has the connection between Alberta Conservatives and Big Oil been more blatant.

The modern environmental movement's greatest prophet, Aldo Leopold, wrote in his 1949 classic, *A Sand County Almanac*, that he was pessimistic about the chances of the conservation movement achieving its goals because "no important change in ethics was ever accomplished without an internal change in our intellectual emphasis, loyalties, affection and convictions." Until now, there has been little reason for people in general to rethink such fundamental assumptions as those concerning our relation-ship to the world we inhabit. That we could reproduce ourselves endlessly was a given; that resources were ours for the taking, and that the air and water were limitless repositories for all our wastes and poisons, were also givens. But we are dimly coming to understand that these assumptions have to be stood on their head. Our values, based on the old assumptions, are dangerously out of date. They do not reflect eco-reality.

A person driving an SUV with a sign saying "Baby on Board" thinks he or she is displaying parental concern, yet the stuff spewing out of that fat tailpipe as they motor down to the shop-ping mall is in the process of devastating the world their child is going to inherit. For the moment, getting to the mall safely — and as quickly and effortlessly as possible — is the entire focus. The value of speed is unquestioned. The value of not having to walk is obvious. And the value of oil is implicit in these other two values. Oil makes us the modern sybarites that we are. It is the Fountain of Mobility. By association, *oil is good*. It is a mistake to underestimate the depth of the deep associations in our minds between oil and quality of life. Intellectual emphasis, loyalty, affection, and conviction all play a role. If one would make the case that oil, instead of being helpful, is worse than a narcotic like heroin (which after all only affects individuals, not systems), one must start by changing the basic perception of the role of oil in the modern world and its effect on the future.

Is it a drug? Yes. We don't mainline it, but our machines do. Is it a drug that kills? Yes, and not just individuals. It is *ecocidal*.

This is now so glaringly apparent that I believe the funda-mental question of our time has become: why are we doing so little to save ourselves? We're not stupid as individuals or even as some groups, but *en masse* we mill about uselessly as disaster envelops us, the voices of front men for the oil and coal indus-tries bellowing above the cries of environmental refugees. Money talks, of course, but surely the greater self-interest must prevail in the end? Or are we prisoners of a form of pack paralysis? Surely there is no one driving a car through rush-hour traffic under a pall of smog that doesn't know he or she is doing something ecologically *wrong*. But we are trapped, like bison herded down a chute over the edge of a cliff. And then, of course, it is one thing to have a sense that one is doing something wrong, but it is quite another to act upon it, especially if it seems like nearly everybody else in the world is doing the same "wrong" thing. It may be wrong but I can't personally be blamed. After all, look around! Are you suggesting *everyone* is wrong here? When it comes to fossil fuels, the masses refuse to move because they are under no serious peer pressure at all. On the contrary, we are exhorted at every advertising turn to get out there in a four-by-four and roar all over the place. Moreover, in the absence of cheap, fast mass transit, ownership of a vehicle is a question of survival for many.

In the years that I have been studying and writing about climate change, I have noticed a pattern of reaction when the subject is introduced — and the consistency of the pattern fills me with deep unease. I have seen it in many different countries. If I suggest to someone that the climate crisis could be upon us within thirty years — that is, around 2030 — instead of the century-or-so they have grown accustomed to hearing about, I see them immediately running one key calculation through their heads: how old will they be by then? Will they be around to face the music? If it happens to be a person fifty years or older, the automatic response, usually accompanied by an apologetic grin (but still a grin rather than a frown), is: *"I'll be gone by then."* I call this the NIML Syndrome, meaning Not In My Lifetime. Herein lies one of the greatest dangers, because this is one of our weaknesses. Unlike nuclear weapons or an approaching asteroid, climate change is still perceived as an event due to happen in "the future." In the television age, time has been folded into neat compartments. There is *today*, which is everything, *yesterday*, which is immediately consigned to history, and *tomorrow*, which never happens. As part of tomorrow, climate change is barely more than a smudge off to the side of the infomercial screen of our public attention.

The climate-change story has so far suffered from a dislocation of cause and effect. In fact, it has not really been a story. We only get glimpses of it. "Global warming" itself has earned grudging recognition as a fact of life, but with no sense of imminent doom. As a result, there is unease, but a nearly total absence of panic. The collective flight-or-fight response has not been triggered the way it was in the "old days" of the sixties and seventies, when we knew nuclear weapons meant possible oblivion by the weekend. Whales were about to go extinct any minute. The last great Douglas fir was due to be chainsawed in the next second. Climate change? Someday! Effective action on this front has been stymied by a combination of factors, including the stalling and disinformation tactics of the oil, coal, gas, and automotive interests, but the main problem has been the public perception that there is no immediate survival issue involved. Sea levels rising over the next hundred years? Yawn.

So far, the deadlines proposed by the scientific establishment — time frames of centuries — have been totally beyond the attention span of daily newsmongers. Another major problem has been the excessive caution and timidity of the scientific community, its dangerous reliance on very conservative models. This may make for "good science," but it tends to flatten the spikes, and is unlikely to prove any more accurate, in the end, than the daily weather forecasts.

This is heresy, but I think we should all be skeptical about the veracity of the findings of the Intergovernmental Panel on Climate Change (IPCC), not for the reasons cited by the petroleum hustlers — that scientists *overstate* the case — rather that they may be vastly *understating* it right now. So while their instruments tell them something *huge* is coming this way, they stick resolutely to the manual, waiting until *it* — whatever it is — actually comes into view before shouting the alarm. By that time it will very likely be too damn late. There have been plenty of examples in the past of scientists being overly conservative and thus forfeiting an opportunity to warn people of a coming natural disaster. It is worth keeping in mind a minor piece of history: back at the start of the anti-whaling campaigns in the mid-1970s, we were assured that the computer models used by the International Whaling Commission (IWC) showed *plenty* of whales still surviving, no problem. Of course, the models didn't include the fact that the Soviet fleet was turning in false reports while actually ignoring quotas, or that there was much more piracy than thought. Certainly none of the industry and government scientists who were constructing the models were factoring in the effects of polychlorinated biphenyls, kills by fishnet of various kinds up to drift nets, increased ultraviolet radiation exposure, loss of food sources, etc. Yet it was on these computations that the IWC based its go-slow, everything-is-all-right policy! While this is not an exact parallel, I greatly fear this basic situation is repeating itself in the case of climate change. Things are almost undoubtedly much worse than the computer models tell us. In retrospect, it was a good thing Greenpeace ignored what the whale population models were saying. We assumed the worst, not the best, and reacted with appropriate do-or-die urgency.

With the climate crashing, this should be the basic assumption. I am afraid, Dexter — as you will know all too well — that a sense of urgency in my time has been almost utterly lacking. In fact, in terms of *my* life, we have seen the opposite reaction.

I was taught to view oil as beautiful.

A PASSION FOR WHEELS

IT GREW ON ME SLOWLY: THE awareness that my life had been fundamentally shaped by the burning of the dead. By that, I mean the rotted, fossilized bodies of extinct plants and animals. Three hundred million years after they ceased to spread their pollen on the wind or shamble through swamps, the plants and creatures of the Paleozoic were being converted into less than ash, as though a mass cemetery had been opened and set aflame.

From the beginning, petroleum was so much a part of my life that it was like blood. Without it, life, as I have known it, would have been utterly impossible.

Its *smell* saturated my childhood. It was almost sickeningly sweet. There were empty oil drums piled up in the backyard, and my brother and I would sneak out, unscrew the caps, and take turns sniffing the fumes. It teased the nostrils in a weirdly seductive way, got into our sinuses, gave us a body-high, making us want to wiggle out of our skins from the sheer pleasure of it. We'd be giddy afterwards.

It was my first, deadliest, and most profound addiction, while likewise being the addiction of our entire civilization, even though there didn't seem to be anything wrong with it at the time. In a small way, I helped get civilization hooked. My first memory of being involved, apart from sniffing gasoline, goes back to 1948. That was the summer Dad took me out with him on the road in his North Star Oil Company truck.

It was just before they started spreading blacktop everywhere. Prairie chickens, now gone the way of the bison and the grasshoppers, burst from fields of flax and sunflowers, rocketing down the road, leaving a delicate trail of dust, nothing compared, especially, to ours: a permanent fog behind us, except when it rained. We headed northwest from Winnipeg, leaving the two lanes of gravel on the Trans-Canada Highway at Portage la Prairie, following mud roads from there through places like Neepawa, Dauphin, Souris, and Weyburn. By the time we reached northern Saskatchewan, it seemed we had pushed to the edge of the human world. We'd drive for hours at a time without seeing another vehicle or even anyone out in the fields. The absence of people and other trucks seemed to make Dad almost blissful. "This is it," he told me. "The freedom of the road." It was a precious thing. Most people didn't have it. Didn't even know it *existed*. Out here, we were away. We had escaped.

There were no diners or motels along the way, only hotels in the middle of towns, so when we stopped to pee, we stole corn and ate it raw, helped ourselves to sunflower seeds, climbed down into ditches filled with cattails to wash the dust from the last couple of hundred miles off our faces and arms — and even cupped the water in our hands and drank it.

It did not take much rain before the shallow ditches overflowed into the ruts in the road, hiding them beneath a murky clay-colored surface that spread out over the fields. The only way Dad could be sure we were still on the road at all was by gauging the distance between the storm fences marking off the quarter-section farms that were still common then. Other times, we bumped over dunes where the sands of the lost primeval sea had drifted across the road. We rolled past gray ruins of farms that had failed during the Depression. Just when the heat and the sun started to get unbearable, we'd drop down into cool valleys rippling with poplar and oak leaves, and find a creek to throw ourselves into with all our clothes on.

I sat for hours at a time, straddling Dad's bony knees, barely able to see over the hood of the engine, steering, while he worked the brake and gas pedals. Not once did he bother with the clutch. He would get us up to the right speed, slip out of gear, touch the gas pedal, and then slip into the next gear without moving his left foot an inch. He had a bottle of beer in one hand and a rolled cigarette in the other. I was seven years old, struggling just to reach both sides of the wheel, let alone control its spin, trying to steer a two-and-a-half-ton International KB-3 flatbed with two sixteen-thousand-gallon oil tanks weighing two tons each mounted on the stake box. If we had run into another rig, similarly loaded, on any of those clay-rutted prairie roads, we wouldn't have been able to pass. But it never happened. The tiny towns were, as yet, without the benefit of oil-storage facilities. And until they had a set of those big "Sixteen" tanks buried along Main Street, they were not fit to enter the new petroleum-dependent world Lorne Hunter and his firstborn son were bringing them on the back of our gasoline-powered tandem straight job, the biggest truck on the road, so close to being overloaded that the wheels were almost touching the bottom of the box.

Except for the trains, little prairie towns still enjoyed the isolation that feudal villages must have known. Some of them didn't have electricity yet, which meant that the construction crew that Dad would hire had to use dies to cut the threads for the screw pipes, turning with ratchet handles. It took three-quarters of an hour to put one thread in the pipe. It took about a week, in all, to set up an oil installation, and it was a major event. No sooner would we arrive in town than farmers started asking Dad what day he planned to hoist the Sixteens into place. Each tank was twelve feet in diameter and twenty feet long. He had to get them on top of ten-foot-high angle-iron stands mounted in cement. On the appointed day, farmers brought their families from miles around to watch. The atmosphere was like a circus, or at least a daredevil act. Business in town came to a halt as everyone gathered — at a respectful distance.

The tanks weighed two tons each. Dad had an elaborate boom system rigged on the truck. He maneuvered on one side of the angle-iron stand, pulling the tank upward from the other side. Everyone expected that, when it reached the top, it would keep going, falling on top of Dad and the truck, crushing both completely. But Dad had it all figured out. With a fantastic echoing sound, the tank clanged neatly into place, making me think of a black, headless Trojan Horse. There was a polite round of applause, as though a pianist had just given a concert. Dad took a bow.

Being out on the road with Dad, I sensed, even then, the ephemeral nature of existence. This was surely not a wisdom I had been taught at catechism classes, but I knew with an aching certainty that each and every scene in life is transitory, never to be experienced again. So I soaked everything in. The prairie radiated limitless space. It was like being out in the middle of forever and ever. Feeling the wind through the open window, sensing the enormousness of the world; enough to turn a boy inside out with ecstasy.

Owls *hoo-hoo*ed. Coyotes yowled. Infinitely far away you could hear a train moaning through the night. It was too good to be true. On Sundays, I didn't have to get up and go to church. I could wander wherever or sleep whenever I wanted. Dad might as well have given me drugs. The same thing held true for my brother when he got his chance to go out with the old man. Wanderlust was drilled into our souls. *Freedom. The Road.* And the promise of the sky.

Dad gave us a taste of that too, not long afterwards. He had a buddy who'd been a pilot in the war take my brother and me up in a Cessna from Station Winnipeg, the last big western Royal Canadian Air Force base. It was our moment of sharing, the passing on of the desire. The buddy did a loop-the-loop, then flipped us upside down and flew like that, while Don and I screamed in joyous terror. Dad laughed until he was almost sick, but he held on firmly to both of us, and that was as close as we ever got. After that, he basically disappeared from our lives, running off, as the expression goes, with another woman.

Still, he had done something to our psyches. My brother and I were now both hooked on the road and the sky. Having handled the wheel of the big KB-3, roaring across the dead sea bottom, and having stared *straight down* at the checkerboard plain by the time I was just eight years old, I had broken with the evolutionary limits set by gravity and muscle power. My grandfather had never flown, as, of course, none had before him. My father got up there only a few times, often enough to get a taste for it, but that was all. For me and my brother, the great Sky Gates being built all around the world were set to swing wide open, putting any destination on the planet within reach. Nobody in our lineage had ever been able to hop whole oceans in hours. Nobody had ever looked down from seven miles up. We should, by rights, have died of fright. Our instincts should have been completely against it. Instead, after that first flight, like just about everybody else, we were virtually immune to fear. We adapted to flying so easily, we humans, overriding millions of years of being glued to the land, that it seemed almost natural, as though we had been *intended* for something like this. Over at the Boeing hangars outside of Seattle, the first great jetliners were trundling off the assembly line. Humanity was bracing itself for the quantum leap to mass transportation above the clouds.

All at a price, of course. The price was a quantum leap in the amount of oil being burned and vomited like crematorium smoke into the atmosphere.

This absolutely did not matter to me. It had no relevance in any way. All I knew was that the two sweetest rushes in the world were to be hurtling with the power of hundreds of horses along an open highway across the boundless prairie, and to be streaking with the power of thousands of horses through the open sky above.

So, from very early, what I wanted in life, more than anything else, was a *car*.

By the time I was fifteen, I had it: a 1949 two-door Chevrolet. You had to be sixteen to qualify for a driver's license, but there was no law against owning a car. There were no laws about having to have insurance, either. In due course, I got both, but not before a six-month stint as an illegal underage driver. My Chevy had a 1950 Ford grille in place of the original. There was a fake dual-exhaust pipe, and I immediately punched a nail through the real pipe so the car made a noise like a motorcycle. She had fairy balls, as we called them for some reason, around the windows, and huge furry dice dangling from the rearview mirror. My possession of a car coincided with the peak period of the legendary drive-in theaters that started appearing on the outskirts of cities in the late forties. They loomed like giant TV sets. They were the epitome of the future, bringing *oohs* and *aahs* from kids and adults alike when they first stood at the base of one of these monoliths and looked up. The drive-ins later evolved into family-entertainment parks, with swings and slides and sandboxes. But in the fifties, they were mainly Passion Pits. You parked with your front wheels just over the little gravel hump next to a steel pole with a toaster-sized hard-wired speaker that you hooked over the top of your side window pane, and you'd put the sound on full blast to cover up all the moaning and groaning you intended to be doing. It was pretty much the same along row after row of parked cars, lights off, engines all facing the cliff-face of a screen, as though some religious ritual was taking place. You couldn't see inside most of the cars because the windows were all steamed up. At intermission, when the floodlights came on, everyone was instructed by a truly irritating black-and-white cartoon character to hurry to the concession building, while a ten-minute countdown began. It was a chance for the girls to go to the washroom to reapply their makeup, and for the boys to line up for popcorn and pop, wearing our lipstick smears with pride. It seemed the most natural thing in the world for hundreds of us to be arranged in concentric half-circles around a ten-story screen in our big American cars, with our American hairdos (ducktails and bouffant swirls), and our American styles (blue jeans and crinolines), watching American movies. At the beginning, they'd play "O Canada," and if you happened to be at the concession or even in the men's room when it blared over the loudspeakers, you were expected to stop and stand at attention, even if it was a restless slouch. As we were leaving, it was to the stirring strains of "God Save the Queen," a reminder of the old British Empire, while the new American one engulfed us.

Any time before June and after September, our engines would be idling, to keep the heaters going, and nobody would think twice. It was just plain logical. If all the attendance records of drive-ins from the time they first appeared on the North American landscape until now were compiled, the total emissions of CO_2 released while my generation *watched movies in our cars* could be calculated, and I am sure it would equal something like the combined burn from all the oil wells of Kuwait during the Gulf War.

After the show, of course, we'd drive to a burger place. There used to be plenty of independent mom-and-pop places, but by the time I had acquired my own wheels, the vast A&W chain had wiped most of them out. Having worked as a carhop, I was always polite when we were being served, but that wasn't the case with most of the other young guys docked in their various jalopies and hot rods at the rows of concrete bays, each of them thinking of himself as the hottest stud extant. Nobody simply drove in and stopped. You had to lay a bit of rubber down. And you didn't just leave, you peeled out. Engines rumbled and exhausts backfired. Radios rocked. People shouted over the noise. All we were doing, once settled in, was *sitting and eating*. No one cared that we were chomping down on our fries and burgers amid blue fumes. If anything, carbon dioxide was part of the ambience. And that seemed natural, too. It was not just that nearly everyone idled. They revved. *Vroom. Vroom. Vroom.* They slammed doors. They leaned on their horns. They cranked open engine hoods and trunks just so they could crash them shut again. The hierarchy was partially based on noise. Much as barbarians must once have banged their shields and axes around to enhance their general aura of ferocity, the car culture's first mass generation of motorized kids made noise in a decibel range which had not hitherto been possible.

Back then, with the Cadillac tail fin still inching toward its apogee, about a quarter of the cars were custom jobs. There were enough garages by then, enough machinery, enough mechanics and body makers, and, most importantly, enough money going around for the car culture to begin spinning off highly individualized self-mutating units. Like every greasy-haired young car owner, I bought copies of car magazines and looked at the glossy pictures of vehicles that must have popped in from another dimension. *This* was Manhood. To be able to create your own car! To mold it out of steel and glass! The guys who could actually do this tended to work in garages. Guys like me who had jobs as busboys and waiters could only drool. But drool we did, admiring the foldouts of customs jobs almost as much as those of *Playboy* nudes.

It must have been 1957 when we started drag racing. You could get away with short bursts of speed up to maybe eighty miles an hour in the city itself, before having to cool it, and you could run flat-out forever over country roads, but there was no point trying to race over open fields, which would either have been plowed or riddled with groundhog holes, and would shake your car apart in no time, even if you didn't get stuck. Places where you could formally race, that is, take off side-by-side and put your foot to the floor for as long as you dared, were few and far between. That is, until they started building the Perimeter Highway.

This type of "ring road" was being built around every city of over a quarter of a million people everywhere on the continent. The one around Winnipeg probably had more open space between it and the outer layer of suburbs than most places, but that was because there was so much land to spare. The road was a monstrously huge government project and it proceeded at a glacial place. While heavy earthmoving machines kicked up thunderheads of dust all through the day, the moment the five-o'clock whistle went and the cars and pickups erupted from the site, the wind began to disperse the ground-level clouds. By the time we drove with our headlights off across an abandoned field, and up onto the graded gravel tarmac, an incredible *four lanes wide*, we could see from horizon to horizon. So wide was the circle of road they were building that you couldn't detect its curve. Most amazing of all, there appeared to be some kind of jurisdictional vacuum. Because it was still under construction, it was treated like private property, and therefore ignored by the Mounties unless they got called. It was way outside of the juris-diction of the Winnipeg police, and I don't think the builders cared about us being out there. It probably helped to pack down the gravel.

Within a few years, I was reading Jack Kerouac, and had adopted the image of the Buddha-seeking hitchhiker/mad driver/existential loner as my kind of hero. The burning of fossil fuels in copious quantities was central to this new mythology, and angst-ridden young artists like myself bought into it by the tens if not hundreds of thousands. To be on the road in the *On the Road* sense was as cool as it could possibly get. Hitchhiking had literary virtue, although, one had to admit, no box office yet. Kerouac wrote about roaring back and forth across America in cars that he and his buddy pushed so hard they sometimes had to be abandoned. The wind rushes through the open window. They hurtle through the eternal night. Headlights blast across deserts. He is always leaving one situation by driving away, moving on to the next situation via the same device. Rather than being boring, the repetition of the transitions gave the trips, as they piled up, the character of a saga. I lost track of how many pilgrimages old Jack and his buddy Dean Moriarty, based on the legendary Neal Cassady, took back and forth between New York and Frisco and down to Mexico and up through Denver, but they left me spinning. Here was something *written* that confirmed my sense that to move was to live, stasis was death. Themes of transportation had shaped literature before, to be sure, from the *Iliad* to *The Grapes of Wrath*, and almost all of science fiction, but this was the first that spoke to my condition. In fact, Kerouac was about twenty years ahead of me, but we were of the same generation — he from the first decade roughly, and me coming in near the end, just before the arrival *en masse* of the Boomers. We caught the same wave of technological feedback from the war effort, with all its inventions, including The Bomb.

Years later, it occurred to me that my instant empathy with Kerouac's writings had something to do with an instinctive urge to race about like a blind insect in a frenzied effort to get out from under something that was coming slowly but steadily down, namely the end of the world. I don't recall a single word about The Bomb in any of Kerouac's books. It wasn't part of the spontaneous bop prose-flow. What Jack wrote about was the *scurrying*, the head-down *flight*, first this direction, then that. If it was the flight response that seized you, The Road was the place to be. You were a moving target. You didn't truly drive so much as duck and weave and dodge. Nothing less than evolution itself, I suspect, dictated that some of us, at least, kept leapfrogging around, slipping around, changing location, hoping to be out there on the road when the cities went up, which could be any day.

My own pattern of movement was frenetic, maybe even obsessive. "Seeing the world" wasn't a matter of a vacation or holiday. It was the primary purpose of sentient consciousness. Of this I was absolutely convinced. This was what had been passed on to me. Only once was I able to connect the urge to travel with the need to earn cash. I signed on with *Encyclopaedia Britannica*, and drove with a group of salesmen in a convoy of three cars all over western and northern Manitoba, as far as Flin Flon, getting out in each little town or village and sometimes at farms along the way to go knocking on doors, offering "free books." Some of the places I recognized, but mostly it was brand new territory. I wasn't "placing" any books, but I was ranging further afield, and that was what counted. I was *moving*.

The truth was, however, I hadn't gone anywhere yet on my own that my dad hadn't gone, and in this regard, I was like almost every other son in history, save the few who ventured out on genuinely original voyages or were shipped overseas against their will. In the late fifties on Planet Earth, despite the motorization of North America and Western Europe, the average human being still lived and died within forty miles of the place he or she was born. And they didn't travel much beyond that. Indeed, for the overwhelming majority of people through every epoch until now, existence had been a short-leashed experience. They had been bound tightly to the little plots of land that sustained them. By the time I was eighteen, I had already traveled thousands of miles in my car, in buddies' cars, and on buses and trucks. My dad's trucking years on the prairies had racked up his total mileage to something way above normal. As for *his* father, well, a single transatlantic flight lasting five hours covers the distance Grandpa Hunter traveled on his one major voyage in life, from Dublin to Montreal by boat and from there to Winnipeg by train. I have crossed the Atlantic roughly a hundred times. My grandfather's brother also set out from County Cork, but sailed to New Zealand instead, crossing the Pacific. I've done that a dozen times. Prior to those two venturesome brothers, members of Clan Hunter had pretty much stuck around Hunterston Castle in Ayrshire for eight hundred years, venturing out for the occasional battle. On my mother's side (the Gauvreaus), apart from a voyage by sail from Normandy to Quebec in the 1700s, and a few generations of canoeing, the genes were happy to take root in New France and multiply. I believe I have a bit of Huron blood, which may have meant roaming about in the woods, but essentially in the same Central Canadian Shield area, for at least nine thousand years. None of these ancestors were skyfarers, that's for sure. Their sagas were based on journeys that would barely rate as a weekend holiday tour today. And if you go back, say, a thousand years, both my French and Scottish ancestors were coexisting in Normandy. How they got there is a story covering tens of thousands, ultimately millions of years of evolution, starting either in Africa or Australia.

In terms of distance covered in a lifetime, nearly all of history would be a virtual flat line for our ancestors until the invention of the wheel and the sail. Even after the building of the first roads, the masses of humanity moved maybe only a valley along per generation, if that. Even the nomads had fixed, limited routes. It has only been in *my* lifetime that our species could be airlifted around the planet by the millions upon millions, a feat that stands as the crowning technological (and in a sense political) accomplishment of the human race thus far. Having in one trip alone circled the planet by flying from Vancouver to San Francisco to Honolulu to Sydney and from Perth to New Delhi and on to London before heading over the pole back home, I more than covered all the distance my ancestors had traveled in the millions of years of the journey up from apehood — and I did it *in six giant steps*. That's all. How can anyone take that for granted? I have a sense now of the actual size of the world.

I speak as someone who *worshipped* jets for nearly six decades before admitting they serve the forces of chaos. As an activist, travel writer, lecturer, author-on-tour, scriptwriter, tourist, and television reporter, I believe I have taken about one thousand flights. This is nothing by certain authentic jet-set standards. Yet it represents at the very least a thousandfold increase in distance logged in just three generations. By any historical standard of distances covered by people, my life has been *abnormal*. Yet, since it has been my subjective experience, to me it is quite ordinary. And precisely because I take fantastic mobility for granted, as does every flyer and driver in the world, the idea of giving it up is almost unthinkable.

A couple of years ago, in a paper commissioned by an environmental group, I wrote:

> In terms of getting on with the broad climate change campaign, I think directly inconveniencing the driving public is hugely counterproductive. Such behavior puts us in conflict with an enemy we don't need, and don't want to engage. Rather than fighting on that front, we must turn the spotlight on the real enemy, who operates mostly out of sight, out of mind. Politically, we should make every effort to avoid the public opinion "killing ground" of anticar activism where the enemy has no choice but to fight to the last man. The real enemy is fossil fuels, not the act of driving. Don't be distracted or lured into fighting on the wrong turf. Keep in mind that what an army doesn't do is every bit as important as what it *does*. Deciding where to attack involves avoiding unfavorable terrain as much as it does finding a weak spot.

This came perilously close to being soft on the demon car. It might, in fact, be that I am subconsciously still loyal to the freedom-of-the-road-and-sky culture, hang the consequences! Meaning hang the consequences for my grandson, Dexter. That's not good enough, is it? I just fear that if *I* — a good ol' green boy — am unable to break out of my addiction to life in the fossil-fuel fast lane, there isn't much hope for a mass movement in the immediate future, at least not in this country.

We don't have to look to the future to see that the use of oil has already had catastrophic effects on humanity, and I am not talking about oil spills or even the huge increase in weather-related disasters which have been measured in the last few decades. In purely *political* terms, oil has unleashed massacres, fortified criminal rulers, spawned atrocities, and served terrorism just about everywhere you look.

Historian and activist John Bacher's *Petrotyranny* reveals the full horror of political and ecological nightmare created by oil. Entirely apart from its devastating impact on the environment, the money from oil profits plays an enormous role in propping up dictatorships, with all the resulting human-rights violations, repression, and outright slaughter. Bacher throws a brilliant academic light on the backroom machinations that create the deadly trinity of oil, war, and dictatorship. His sweeping examination provides an overview of oil-driven politics around the world.

"Oil is critical to the support of dictatorships since it provides the most abundant form of wealth for a repressive government — income that does not have to be obtained through taxation," he writes.

The collection of taxes compels a higher degree of consent from citizens than a misappropriation of oil rents (what accountants call royalties) when big money is needed for the repressive apparatus of despotism. While repression is generally in retreat in the post–Cold War world, the remaining havens of dictatorship are concentrated in oil-rich states, many of which export war and repression beyond their borders. Such mischief is encouraged by the two Congos, the tiny but oil-rich Sultanate of Brunei, Angola and almost every oil-producing state in the Middle East.

Among the "super oil dictatorships" he lists: Algeria, Yemen, Oman, the United Arab Emirates, Iran, Iraq, Saudi Arabia, Equatorial Guinea, China, Turkmenistan, Sudan, Syria, Libya, Myanmar, Papua New Guinea, Sierra Leone. There *are* dictatorships without oil reserves, such as Somalia and Burundi, but they have foreign aid flowing in from Saudi Arabia and Iran. The very most repressive dictatorship of the lot, North Korea, receives substantial economic assistance from oil-rich states. Afghanistan, under the Taliban, was likewise propped up by oil wealth, mainly Saudi Arabian. How dramatically this will change in the months and years to come as the new U.S.-backed regime attempts to strengthen its tenuous hold on the Afghan countryside remains to be seen. In any event, the promise of oil pipelines plays a major background role in the political machinations.

While free labor movements have been vital in the struggle against despotism from South Africa to Poland, Bacher points out that

oil wealth now keeps such movements out of the Persian Gulf, where labor organizing died out in the late 1970s. At that time a flood of money was obtained from the sudden price increases achieved by the Organization of Petroleum Exporting Countries (OPEC). This made it possible for the super oil states to buy off labor demands without recognizing the democratizing principles of free collective bargains. . . . In addition to providing a carrot, oil wealth gave the super oil states a big stick, used with special severity against groups in the state not represented in their country's ruling elite. These states have maintained the most wide-ranging religious persecution of the post–Cold War period, except for Myanmar. All these tyrannies continue to practice capital punishment and use torture. Some make mutilations part of normal sentencing. Dissidents in the super oil states are threatened by the world's most ruthless security services.

Petroleum exports are the most lucrative form of wealth stemming from locational advantage rather than hard work or creativity, Bacher writes. In the grand tradition of feudal barons who extracted tolls from travelers along a river, the petrotyrants exploit everyone they can, and in the process they hold the industrialized world hostage to its own appetites. Control of resources in the ground in turn pays for repression within a state, the very opposite of a formula for peace, let alone ecology.

We might be too corrupted, too dependent, too selfish, too unwilling to face the truth. And where does that leave *you?*

To understand, of course, we must go back further than my lifetime — although not that much further. From an evolutionary point of view, the horror of the climate crisis is that it has been sprung upon us so quickly.

CHAPTER 2

HOW IT HAPPENED

AN ITALIAN MAN OF LETTERS, Antonio Stoppani (1824–94), expressed a giddy new viewpoint when he wrote "the creation of man was the introduction of a new element into nature, of a force wholly unknown to earlier periods." He argued that "man" is a new force on the earth, which might be compared in power and universality with the greater natural forces. This seemed like a nineteenth-century vanity to many, a gross Industrial Revolutionary megalomania to others. Measured against the mind-stretching vistas of entire ages with names like the Devonian, the Triassic, the Cretaceous, and the Pleistocene, what a claim for a species barely a million years old to make — moreover, a species which has done well only during a brief interglacial period called the Holocene. Yet Stoppani was right. In that short, spectacular period, we have indeed become a force capable of altering the biosphere, which might be good news if we knew what we were doing, or if we were improving anything. But this power came to us inadvertently. We are a force, but whether a force for good or profound ecological evil very much remains to be seen. Until the Industrial Revolution, we simply didn't have the physical or mechanical

muscle to start moving mountains. We were, of course, capable
of mass extinctions, involving the wiping out of lions and ante-
lope in southern France (with pointed sticks, before even spears)
and are now credited with doing in a whole level of large land
mammals in North America. We turned the Syrian cedar forest
to desert, denuded much of Europe and Africa, reduced the
Greek isles from forest to scrub brush, but our impact was
mainly a fleeting thing. Jungles, for the most part, closed in
behind us as we migrated. The damage we did, at worst, was on
a *regional* scale, and it only applied to a few megafauna. Overall,
we barely scratched the surface.

The beginning of our change from a source of food for larger
predators to a planetary force in our own right can be traced to
the day our ancestors captured fire. By the time we domesticated
animals, about ten thousand years ago, we could wield the power
of flame virtually at will — although not without consequences.
Blackened lungs characterize mummified corpses from the
Paleolithic era. Even when we began building adobe huts, ven-
tilation was nonexistent. Whether it was because people wanted
to escape from mosquitoes by filling their huts with smoke or
just plain poor design, our ancestors spent much of their lives in
a pall of indoor smoke. Outdoor pollution didn't appear until
the advent of cities. As early as the time of the Roman poet
Horace, magnificent marble temples were being smudged by
smoke. Regional pollution makes no appearance until the
introduction of coins in the ancient Mediterranean and Chinese
cultures, thanks to the smelting of copper and silver. Indeed, by
about 2,500 years ago, there was enough pollution that
Greenland ice-core samples reveal traces of copper emissions.
There were odd surges of pollution here and there — copper
and lead emissions rose sharply, for instance, in the Sumava
Mountains of the Czech Republic after 1640, and in the
eleventh century, coal use in iron forges in northern China
became common. But mainly our ancestors burned wood, at

least until Elizabethan times, when climate and the scientific method came together to transform everything.

In his excellent summary of the spread of industrialization, titled *Greenhouse: The 200-Year Story of Global Warming*, historian Gale E. Christianson notes that coal was burned in London during the late Middle Ages and Renaissance, but fireplaces and chimneys were too primitive to effectively handle the intensity of the heat. The preferred source of warmth was charcoal, made by piling wood into stacks covered with mud and set aflame. Charcoal had the virtue of being smokeless, but it still required trees — and as the Little Ice Age (a strictly regional event, it now appears) set in, the forests around London began to disappear, hacked down to produce fuel and make way for more agriculture to feed the burgeoning population. The huge kilns in which the charcoal was produced were burned at first on the outskirts of the city, but were pushed back like the forest, not to make way for anything but to bring some relief from the darkening of the skies and the blackening of rooftops and monuments. As temperatures plunged, demand for fuel soared. With both the wood and the charcoal growing more expensive because of the distances they now had to be transported, Londoners turned increasingly to coal. By the dawn of the eighteenth century, London had changed from a wood-burning city into one that depended on imported coal. There was opposition, to be sure, especially from craftsmen who wanted the "noxious vapours" banned, but the corner had been turned and there were suddenly thousands of miners — then hundreds of thousands, many of them children — toiling under horrendous conditions to bring the "black diamond" up to the surface to be burned. Seen from space, it would have looked like a black hole opening on the surface of the planet.

We can see it expanding ever so slightly but significantly to other British cities like Manchester, where a giant cloud formed, making travelers think it was raining. In fact, they were

seeing soot from the city's industrial furnaces. Places like
Durham, Cornwall, and Lancashire were soon the sites of
massive collieries, which were frequently lost to the sea as the
miners burrowed under it. Indeed, it was specifically for the
purpose of draining those flooded mineshafts that Thomas
Newcomen designed the first successful steam engine. By 1720,
similar engines were at work all over Europe. Half a century
later, Richard Arkwright invented the spinning jenny, which
revolutionized the textile trade and gave birth to the modern
factory system. By the last decades of the 1700s, factories big
enough to contain five hundred power looms had been erected,
and by then Newcomen's engine had been redesigned by James
Watt, who created a machine so unlimited in its potential power
that a new unit of measurement, "horsepower," had to be
coined. Henceforth, factories could be constructed around these
incredibly versatile devices in the very midst of cities, which was
to have huge consequences for everyone. Unfortunately, Watts's
mighty machine fed upon burning coal.

To make things much worse, there was a sudden mush-
rooming of tall chimneys on the horizon. To maximize the
power of the new steam engine, the chimneys were raised, stone
by stone, brick by brick, so that the coal would burn at a higher
temperature, thanks to powerful mechanical blowers placed
between the boilers and the chimney flue. The higher the
chimney, the more efficient it became. Owners could use cheap
high-sulphur slack, as it was called, so long as they built their
chimneys at least ninety feet high, that being the rather arbitrary
height at which local councils had decided the smoke would
disperse harmlessly into the air about the countryside. The
common wisdom that this took care of the stuff thus fitted in
with the emerging pattern of industrial capitalism. The monster
chimneys were erected, initially, in Britain, but soon after in
North America and Europe. Despite the risk of "falls," especially
in the early years, when stones and brick were used and the great

storms sweeping in from the Atlantic could sometimes topple them, the colossal monoliths were soon so numerous that John Ruskin predicted "from shore to shore the whole of the island is to be set as thick with columns as the masts stand in the docks of Liverpool . . . no acre of English ground shall be without its shaft and its engine." Architects made every effort to turn the chimneys into art objects, going to such absurd lengths as copying Cleopatra's Needle, as originally built by the Egyptians, so that the "supremely ugly" smokestacks could be disguised as slender, tapering obelisks. By 1841, a chimney passed the four-hundred-foot mark in Glasgow, making it only slightly shorter than the Great Pyramid of Cheops.

By then, they were being raised at the rate of a hundred per year in London alone. From that point onward, the amount of carbon dioxide being dispersed into the atmosphere began its tide-like rise, starting from the global baseline of roughly 280 parts per million (ppm).

The great polluting towers were still in their infancy, of course, compared to the thousand-foot behemoths to come, which would make use of new techniques involving steel and cement to make them bigger, taller, with a larger maw out of which the fumes could pour in clouds that did not disperse quite as quickly, that began to linger in valleys like scabs over festering urban sores. Around their edges, like gangrene, were the slag heaps and forges and mountains of burning coal. Then came the discovery that, by piling coal high enough, intense heat could be generated to drive the natural gases from the coal, leaving a nearly pure residue called coke, making the production of iron possible on a scale never imagined before. By the end of the 1700s, the amount of coke being burned had gone from zero to more than 100 million tons a year. And that was just the beginning.

As small mountain ranges of slag and cinders began to pile up in Britain, coal miners got busy burrowing into the ground in the

United States, Russia, and China. By 1820, the transition to a worldwide fossil-fuel regime was well under way. By then, there were thousands of mines scattered around the world — and the city-dwellers began to die prematurely from a new pestilence. London's air quickly became so bad that by 1879–80, some three thousand were killed by aggravated lung conditions. Indeed, by the time the political will was found to ban coal-burning domestic hearths in the mid-1950s, lung ailments had killed more Londoners than even the 1918 influenza pandemic. In the United States, cities began to build their energy systems around coal in a big way, starting in the middle of the 1800s. Chicago, Cincinnati, and Pittsburgh had the huge deposits of bituminous coal from southern Illinois to draw upon, with the result that, by 1866, one visitor described Pittsburgh as "Hell with the lid taken off." By the time the second Industrial Revolution had gotten under way with the launching of the steel industry, Pittsburgh was burning 3 million tons of coal a year, which was then 5 percent of the American total. Elsewhere, smokestack industries fired by coal were lurching to their feet in Germany and Belgium; Czarist Russia, mainly in the Ukraine; and in Japan, around Osaka. Smaller clusters of coal-fired steel, iron, and chemical industries took root in South Africa, India, and Australia.

The most far-reaching spinoff effect of the new method of forging iron was that it made the mass production of an entirely new kind of machine possible — the iron horse, invented, incestuously enough, to make the transport of ore easier. By 1822, an eight-mile-long track was in place to a colliery, and a mere nine years later the Liverpool and Manchester Railway was regularly sending a gangly boiler mounted on two sets of wheels, with two huge cylinders and an eight-foot-high stovepipe, somewhat prematurely called the *Rocket*, chugging along at twelve miles per hour. The world now had a truly self-propelled vehicle. Within a decade, some 1,300 miles of tracks were radiating outward from London.

The next major technological breakthrough came in the mid-1800s, when Henry Bessemer figured out a way to convert pig iron directly into steel in a matter of minutes. Forty-foot-long rails could now be built, along with large-caliber artillery pieces and locomotive boiler-tube plates. Steel production took a swift exponential leap. Steel-manufacturing towns sprang up around the world, but particularly in the United States, where ruthless entrepreneurs like Andrew Carnegie led the way, eventually moving beyond the Bessemer converters to an open-hearth method that permitted the production of sixty-five tons of steel at a time. By 1890, the skies over steel towns like Pittsburgh were every bit as soot-laden as those over Manchester.

The phenomenon of blackened skies and soot-encrusted landscapes was now something that could be observed in places like Magnitogorsk, Russia, and Donetsk, Ukraine; Germany's Ruhr Valley; and the Osaka–Kobe area, as well as the English Midlands. The Ruhr was an agricultural area until 1850. Within the following half-century it rose to political prominence by virtue of the fact that it was producing 110 million tons of high-sulphur coal per year, employing four hundred thousand miners, and providing the nascent German military-industrial complex with the gigantic steel- and ironworks of the Krupp and Thyssen companies. By 1900, the Ruhr was the biggest, most polluted industrial complex in Europe, making it possible for Germany to fight the First World War. In the Polish Silesia area, bounded by Prague, Krakow, and Dresden, the first European blast furnace had opened in 1796, initiating an era of steel, iron, and coal production that at various times served the purposes of Nazis and Communists alike, causing so much pollution that it became known as the Sulphuric Triangle. Over in Japan, starting about 1880, the Hanshin region between Kyoto, Kobe, and Osaka became the biggest Asian nexus of heavy industry, with sulphur dioxide pouring out of thousands of smokestacks, pitting industrial laborers against local farmers, raising the level of pollution in Osaka to the point where it rivaled

Pittsburgh and London. In 1800, the world's output of coal was about 10 million metric tons. By 1850, it had soared to 76 million metric tons. By 1900, it was 762 million metric tons. And by 1995, it was 5,000 million tons.

It was in the United States — not far from poor, befouled Pittsburgh — that the next stage of the Industrial Revolution was launched, a period referred to in oil-industry literature as "the unfolding of a new and wonderful opportunity for individual endeavor." A dark green, evil-smelling substance known as rock oil had been found at various locations around Kentucky, West Virginia, Ohio, and Pennsylvania. It was used as a medicine by the natives, as well as a vegetable dye and as waterproofing for wigwams. As a bottled "cure-all" the rock oil became snake oil, peddled far and wide by unscrupulous salesmen. It was recommended for liver complaints, bronchitis, consumption, and cholera morbus. Otherwise, the stuff was strictly a nuisance, getting in the way of other entrepreneurs who were drilling for brine in order to produce salt. It burned fiercely when ignited, often erupting in flame. Although some mill-owners in districts where oil had been found discovered for themselves that it could be used for lubricating machines and even lighting lamps, it wasn't until 1849 that one snake-oil salesman, Samuel K. Kier, thought to have the strange liquid analyzed to see if it could be refined. Indeed, the report came back saying that rock oil might make as good an illuminant as any the world had ever seen. It also yielded gas, paraffin, and lubricating oil. Seizing on part of the chance, within a decade Kier was shipping "carbon oil" all over the country to be used in coal-oil lamps.

In the meantime, grasping the larger picture, journalist and teacher George H. Bissell organized a company, the Pennsylvania Rock-Oil Company, and leased lands on which oil springs were located. He was the first to hit upon the idea of actually *drilling* for oil, instead of skimming it off the surface. To this end, he sent a stockholder in the company, named Edwin L. Drake, to Titusville, Pennsylvania. There, Drake entered the history books — not without considerable effort and repeated failures — by finally drilling the first successful artesian oil well. One day in late August 1859, the people of Titusville awoke to the stunning news that "Drake's Folly" had justified itself, and a day later the first twenty-five barrels of oil were filled. From farms and towns all over the country, opportunists and hustlers began to converge on Titusville, most of them with little to offer but strong backs and a willingness to do the dirty work. At the same time, from New York, came men with money and business experience, who were soon forming stock companies, buying up parcels of land, and drilling wells along every rocky run and creek, as well as on the slopes of steep hills. At first, pumping was hardly required. The wells flowed like blood, producing up to four thousand barrels a day. In fact, there weren't enough barrels in America to contain the bonanza. Every available whiskey barrel, molasses barrel, and turpentine barrel was rounded up and shipped to what was now being called the Oil Regions.

Soon, caravans of hundreds of heavily freighted wagons were forming along nearly impassable roads, trying to get the new product out to the nearest railway, in Pittsburgh, 132 miles away. Flatboats loaded with barrels were floated down the Allegheny River. Before long, river traffic was so heavy that a fleet of a thousand boats and some thirty steamers, crewed by four thousand men, could be seen riding floods and freshets caused by the opening of mill dams to make the river passable. It was a perilous journey. "Rare indeed," according to *A History of Standard Oil Company*, "was the freshet when a few wrecks did not lie somewhere along the creek, and often scores lay piled high on the banks, a hopeless jam of broken boats and barrels, the whole soaked in petroleum and reeking with gas and profanity." Before long, refineries were being constructed by the score in the northeastern cities of Boston, New York, Philadelphia, Baltimore, and Pittsburgh. In a single year, 1865–66, some fifty refineries were built in Cleveland alone.

From the beginning, oil wealth — or its promise — produced violence. Teamsters, whose number swelled as the demand for oil grew, were the masters of the situation for a while, controlling both the horse teams and the boats. When Samuel Van Syckel built the first pipeline — two inches wide — to move oil directly from his drilling rig to the railway shipping point, the teamsters responded by digging the buried pipe up and cutting it open so the oil would be lost. They also burned storage tanks and terrorized oil-company employees. Armed guards had to be stationed along the pipeline. In the end, the teamsters had no more luck trying to stop the tide than the unfortunate textile workers who had attempted to resist the spinning jenny. And now the refineries began to spring up. By 1880, oil could be said to have caught up with coal as the second great energy source of the Industrial Revolution. It also became the means of acquiring fortunes, providing you had the right capitalist instincts, which was certainly the case with John Davison Rockefeller, whose Standard Oil Company quickly learned the new tricks of vertical integration, assuming tentacle-like control over railways, pipelines, refineries, and wells.

"It was a classic case of the new pseudoscientific doctrine of social Darwinism at work, which Rockefeller and his fellow industrialists embraced with the fervor of the anointed," writes Dale E. Christianson.

> As with life-forms inhabiting the wild, society must either adapt or become extinct. And no artificial impediment (meaning government regulation) must be allowed to interfere with the struggle for survival. The ideal society would be one presided over by a natural aristocracy of strivers — Rockefeller, John Pierpont Morgan, Jay

Gould, Cornelius Vanderbilt, and not least, Andrew Carnegie — industrialists and financiers whose habits of thrift and hard work are a model to others.

Christianson notes that Carnegie even added a pious religious gloss, standing traditional Christianity on its head by invoking what he called the "Gospel of Wealth," according to which, he wrote in 1889: "Those who would administer wisely must, indeed, be wise, for one of the serious obstacles to the improvement of our race is indiscriminate charity." In canonizing the great rugged individuals like himself — the "captains of industry," as the historian Thomas Carlyle was the first to call them — Carnegie also canonized ruthlessness, justifying his right to exploit the uneducated, the downtrodden, and the environment "with an equable heart and a clear conscience, a self-styled variation of Manifest Destiny."

While the Americans were the first to make the shift from coal to oil, however, the first really big gushers erupted in Baku on the Caspian Sea in the 1870s. By the turn of the century, the Russians actually led the world in oil production. Derricks also began to rear their ugly heads in Romania and the Dutch East Indies. The first truly massive oil strike in the United States didn't come until a few days after the turn of the century, at Spindletop in Texas, followed quickly by major strikes in Oklahoma and California. Oil was also discovered under the verdant rainforests of Veracruz on the shores of the Gulf of Mexico — bad news for the local Totonac and Huastec Indians. At first, the area was exploited by British and American capital, using equipment developed in Texas, but with the coming of the Mexican revolution in 1910, oil became a political issue. Over in Russia, another revolution led to so much chaos that oil production there temporarily faltered, thrusting Mexico into the position of the second-largest oil producer, a status it enjoyed until Venezuela took over the spot in 1928. Spills, leaks, fires, and blowouts were common, and the land was quickly ruined. By 1930, oil had replaced coal as the main fuel in transportation, and by the late 1950s it had overtaken coal as the driving energy behind industry.

Back at the dawn, while Americans had dramatically taken the lead in the development of an oil industry, Europeans were pressing ahead with ways to increase the horsepower of their shiny new machines. As early as 1860, a young Belgian inventor named Étienne Lenoir discovered that, if he pumped air and gasoline into a small chamber, an electrical spark would cause the mixture to explode. The design was not that different from the steam engines of the day, except that the piston was driven by internal combustion as opposed to pressure generated externally. Altogether, about six hundred of the revolutionary new engines were produced in Paris and London, but the ignition system was unreliable, and factory workers and owners feared that the endless explosions would sooner or later blow the engines apart. It took two Germans, Nikolaus August Otto and Gottlieb Daimler, to come up with a smooth-firing engine that depended on the right combination of fuel and air, along with a "stratified charge" system that caused a mechanical linkage to operate a rotating cam. Their first successful prototype weighed some 1,200 pounds and could generate only two horsepower, but it ran nicely and used much less fuel than the original Lenoir engine. It was Daimler, of course, who had the vision of a lightweight high-speed engine that could be mounted on a vehicle. In November 1885, the first Daimler four-wheel road vehicle, driven by a one-cylinder engine, rolled out onto the cobbles of Stuttgart. It had been preceded by a three-wheeler with a two-cylinder engine that had been tested a year earlier by another German, Karl Benz, but it was Daimler's four-wheeler that became known as the horseless carriage, and is recognized as the first true automobile.

Within a few years, the release of carbon dioxide into the atmosphere accelerated almost as quickly as the cars themselves. Sources of pollution, for the first time, were mobile. It took only two decades for the horseless carriage to become the largest single reason for the production of oil, which was well on its way to becoming the world's foremost energy source. To the enormous black clouds pouring out of the great stacks of the steel mills and factories could now be added the blue fumes coming from tailpipes, destined to cast a toxic pall of their own in the countryside as well as the cities. Daimler's engine was also powering small boats, fire-engine pumps, scaled-down locomotives, and the first Zeppelin airships.

Henry Ford was a bit late out of the gate, not test-driving his first car until 1892. By the time he set up his own company, the tiny market was crowded. But he had an idea.

Automobiles were still basically handmade. The parts involved had short production runs, making the shiny new gadgets the playthings of only the very wealthy. Ford's idea was to move to mass production, using standardized parts that could be easily installed and replaced. He also thought to grab control of the raw materials and the means of distribution. Thus, in 1908, the first "Tin Lizzie," or Model T, rolled off the assembly line, to be followed quickly by 15 million more. The automobile curve was now exponential. By 1920, half the cars on the planet were Model Ts. By 1929, there were 26.7 million cars on the roads of America, a swarm that buzzed noisily around cities at first, but quickly pushed out over the mud roads across the country. Indeed, the automobile demanded more and better roads, and so more land fell to the beginnings of the great freeway systems to come.

In *Something New under the Sun: An Environmental History of the Twentieth-Century World*, J. R. McNeill writes:

Making room for cars took a lot of space. The United
States built a road network from a very modest start in
1900 to 5.5 million kilometers [3.1 million miles] of sur-
faced roads by 1990, exceeding the length of railways at
their maximum by 10 or 15 times. Most of the road-
building spree happened from 1920 to 1980, partly because
the federal government subsidized road building from 1916
onward. In the 1930s, Franklin Roosevelt's New Deal put
thousands of unemployed Americans to work on road construction. The fastest growth in the road network occurred
in the late 1940s. The interstate system that now crisscrosses
America dates from 1956. All these roads, especially the
interstates, attracted people, settlement, and business like
iron filings to a magnet, reorganizing America's broad
spaces into new patterns, which, in turn, made car ownership almost essential for most adults. No other country
achieved the same automobile saturation as the United
States, although some small countries have far higher road
densities. All in all, in North America, Europe and Japan,
auto space took about 5 to 10 percent of the land surface
by 1990. Worldwide it took perhaps 1 to 2 percent, match-
ing the space taken by cities (and overlapping with it). . . .
The automobile is a strong candidate for the title of the
most socially and environmentally consequential technology of the twentieth century. Cars in 1896 were such a
curiosity that they performed in circuses along with
dancing bears; by 1995 the world had half a billion cars.

The automobile was superbly suited to the demands of a vast,
still mainly uninhabited land and an immigrant population
genetically predisposed to mobility. Cars did not become anywhere near as common in Western Europe until the 1950s, and
the switch to individual vehicles did not really get under way in
East Asia until the sixties. It continues at an ever-accelerating

pace, with China having amassed "only" 2 million cars by 1997—a mere beginning, but enough to result in almost one hundred thousand accidents a year by 2001. A report in the *Daily Telegraph* notes that China is rapidly turning to the automobile. Communist officials and ordinary people alike dream of a land crisscrossed by wide expressways.

> At the moment, the nation is in a terrifying transition. Inexperienced drivers speed down new highways, honking at terrified pedestrians scuttling across what used to be their local street. Many pedestrians, especially the old or migrant workers, have no idea how fast cars can go or how hard it is for them to brake. Pedestrians often clamber over high barriers to cross expressways or wheel carts laden with vegetables across eight lanes of traffic. Drivers, on the other hand, see no reason to stop for a mere pedestrian or cyclist, even in a designated crossing point.

> Police have begun a crackdown — but not on motorists. It is the pedestrians who are being hit with fines. Indeed, people who walk are dismissed as those who "take route 11," a visual pun on a pair of legs.

It is difficult to resist seeing an organic shape to the spectacular growth of the automobile. Ecological succession would seem to have taken a dark, science-fiction turn. Where dinosaurs laid their eggs, trucks were now parked. It was as if machines had arisen to fill the vast niche left by the vanished herds of bison. They came in the form of cars, trucks, buses, combines, tractors, tanks, snowplows, bulldozers, graders, cranes, motorcycles, and later, snowmobiles and all-terrain vehicles. And from the skies, where clouds of passenger pigeons once passed, came the deep roar of the jetliners. Flesh had morphed into contraptions with steel exoskeletons. Looking back on the history of these machines, it seems they came up out of the earth like shiny insects, breaking surface in a few places but not getting far from their European burrows until suddenly there was an eruption of them through a large hole called Detroit, and now they are breaking through *everywhere*.

Yet, for all the appearance of a natural phenomenon, the advance of the car was as deliberate as a military campaign. It didn't just "happen." The human race had survived and done fairly well without the horseless carriage. Its ascension was plotted and orchestrated by a handful of powerful men, aided and abetted by corrupt politicians.

By the 1920s, General Motors had overtaken Ford by adopting his methods and going one further, bringing out new models every year. Seeking to expand its advantage, GM decided to crush all alternative transportation competition, starting in Fresno, California, and moving into Los Angeles. It was a literal scorched-earth policy. Through a series of holding companies, GM, in league with Firestone Tire and Standard Oil of California, grabbed control of the state's largest interurban electric rail-transit system, the Pacific Electric Railway Company, replacing three thousand quiet, high-speed trolleys with unreliable, noisy, stinking diesel-powered buses. It seemed like utter madness to the infuriated commuters, but it was all going according to plan. Frustrated and desperate, commuters turned *en masse* to the family car, which was conveniently being offered at affordable prices, very little money down. Thus, in a period of twenty years, the L.A. Basin went from being a smog-free paradise to a gray twilight zone, so choked with petrochemical clouds that the stars could not be seen at night. In all, GM and its allies broke the backs of more than one hundred trolley systems in forty-five North American cities. Impressed by the success of the GM campaign (and equally indifferent to its ecological effects), Ford and Chrysler went into action, mainly as part of a mop-up operation, hunting down and destroying any remaining electric carriers. Sales of gas-gobbling cars soared across the continent. The strategy had worked brilliantly. The growth in the number of auto-mobiles worldwide has been dizzying: from less than a million in 1910 to 100 million by 1955 and half a billion by 1995.

Along the way, some 700 billion barrels of oil have been burned.

By 2001, the view from space said it all. James Drummond, a physics professor from the University of Toronto, was able to report the findings of a device fitted onto one of NASA's Terra Earth-observing satellites, which gave scientists an unprece-dented view of pollution wafting across the world's oceans and continents. Called MOPITT (Measurements of Pollution in the Troposphere), the device tracks carbon monoxide in the lower atmosphere using a method called correlation radiometry, which detects infrared radiation coming off the planet. From this it is possible to detect the distinct signature of carbon monoxide, which is both a toxin itself and a tracer of other types of pollu-tion. The data revealed "spectacular" and immense clouds of carbon monoxide from forest and grass fires in South America and Africa circling the southern hemisphere in high concentra-tions, while "huge plumes" of pollution, coming from fires and industrial sources in Asia, could be seen spreading across the Pacific Ocean to North America.

A mosaic of night photos taken by U.S. weather satellites, repre-senting a north-to-south transect from Europe to Africa, offers another window from above onto the tormented landscape. In *Planet under Stress: The Challenge of Global Change*, William S. Fyfe describes the spectacle:

> Much of Africa is dark. The major sources of light are from controlled fires, the result of grassland burning, slash-and-burn agriculture, and the clearing of forests. These fires are prominent throughout the highlands of the sub-Sahara savannas and East Africa. The giant bright

spots in the Persian Gulf are also from burning, the flaring-off of natural gas from the great oil–gas fields — an image of waste. Ironically, we see the same phenomenon in the Niger Delta region of energy-poor Nigeria. The North is alight with the developed technology that provides its population with a high material standard of living. In the energy- and technology-poor South, poverty and hunger abound.

A mere two centuries earlier, there would barely have been flickers of light to break the darkness of the planetary night — and that was scarcely more than four or five lifetimes ago. In that period, we have managed to substantially alter the earth's atmosphere. The pace has been accelerative. The curves look exponential. It would be pathological, from this point onward, to refuse to face the reality that we have joined in nature's game of transformation completely. The only question is: what will our move be? If we don't make any move at all, other than letting everything smolder and combust, the great plumes and the fires will eventually consume everything.

THE FINGERPRINT

Dᴇꜱᴘɪᴛᴇ ᴛʜᴇ ᴏʙᴠɪᴏᴜꜱɴᴇꜱꜱ ᴏꜰ the physical changes to the biosphere and their correlation to rising greenhouse-gas emissions, scientists have felt compelled to play according to the rules of an elaborate game. By definition, they cannot agree among themselves, and so there will be — and *must* always be — scientists who challenge other scientists' assertions. This will always have political repercussions, with one side or another in a social power struggle seizing upon the particular argument in a scientific debate that suits their purposes. Nowhere has this ever been more the case than when it comes to climate change. Because there is so much at stake, with such huge financial rewards and geopolitical points to be made or lost, scientists have felt compelled to bend over backwards to prove their case — or at least to avoid being caught out on a speculative limb by the corporate sponsors of so many of their activities.

Thus, *evidence* of humanity's role in climate change has become central to the public debate about whether to do anything or not, as opposed to *proof* that the disaster is *not* happening. This particular rearguard action has involved a persistent search for a "human footprint" connecting *my* (and your) behavior to the phenomenon of global warming. The exercise, while useful to the extent that it tended to focus resources on the big picture, was also adroitly used by Big Oil to delay, and delay, and delay.

The effort has been seriously under way since 1990, when the IPCC offered its first Assessment, warning that it might not be possible to detect the "fingerprint" for at least a decade. "Our ability to quantify the human influence on global climate is currently limited because the expected signal is still emerging from the noise of natural variability and because there are uncertainties in key factors." In fact, by the time the Second Assessment was released in 1995, scientists had uncovered enough new evidence to say that the warming since pre-industrial times "is unlikely to be entirely natural in origin" and that "the balance of evidence . . . suggests a discernible human influence on global climate."

The stronger assertion was based on findings from "pattern-based" studies that attempted to establish a cause-and-effect relationship between human activities and observed climate changes. According to the new premise, the Earth's temperature changes in different ways, according to different causes. The search for recognizable patterns that would reveal these causes produced a distinct correlation between the patterns the computer models said should occur if human activities were causing the changes and what indeed was being observed happening in the real world. As Environment Canada chief science advisor Henry Hengeveld explained, "The evidence clearly suggests that recent climate behavior is increasingly unusual relative to past climates and that human interference with the climate system is the most plausible explanation."

In May 1995, the U.S. National Data Center (NDC) exhaustively examined measurements from balloons, ships, satellites, and land stations concerning glacial melt, rising sea levels, and changes in precipitation patterns, and concluded: "Only by looking at the aggregated field of evidence can some level of confidence be placed in the results. . . . But the preponderance

of evidence supports the notion of a real man–made climate variation in the record." Over the previous fifteen years, a "pattern"
had emerged across the United States of higher-than-normal
daily minimum temperatures, extreme or severe droughts in
warm months, and higher-than-average precipitation in cool
months. They were able to calculate a "greenhouse climate
response index" to quantify any persistent trends. The index,
they found, had been consistently high since the late 1970s, in
contrast to earlier patterns. The probability of this change representing natural fluctuation in a stable climate was about 5
percent, they estimated. A year later, one of the top officers of
the U.S. National Oceanic and Atmospheric Administration
(NOAA) was quoted in newspapers as saying: "For the first time,
I feel confident in saying there's a human component."

In June that year, two more heavyweight studies came out. A
team from the Max Planck Institute for Meteorology concluded
there was only a one-in-forty chance that the warming seen in
the last thirty years could be caused by natural variability.
Scientists at the Lawrence Livermore Laboratory factored the
cooling influence of sulphate aerosols, mainly from the burning
of coal, into the temperature record. Looked at seasonally, ver-
tically in the atmosphere, and geographically, the model and
actual temperatures corresponded. About 1950, when the
growth of carbon-dioxide emissions leapt dramatically, so did
temperatures. If this wasn't a greenhouse fingerprint, what was?
In August, researchers at the United Kingdom's Meteorological
Office published the results of the most sophisticated climate-
model experiments yet. Using a "coupled model," which links
both oceanic and atmospheric components and includes sulphate aerosol effects, they were able to boost the levels of
confidence in the accuracy of the models — "a turning point,"
as one scientist put it, "in our ability to understand past changes
and predict the future."

In her excellent overview of the dilemma, *Storm Warning:*

Gambling with the Climate of Our Planet, science writer Lydia
Dotto writes:

> The obsession with whether we've already seen the
> human signature is puzzling in some ways. After all, there
> is *no question* that human activities emit greenhouse gases
> into the atmosphere, or that atmospheric concentrations
> of greenhouse gases are increasing as a result, or that
> greenhouse gases cause warming. Therefore, logically,
> there is *no question* that human activities contribute to
> warming the climate. And since there is also *no question*
> that greenhouse gas emissions from human activities are
> currently increasing every year, we know that their
> climate influence is bound to grow.

The hard numbers are as follows: Since the Industrial Revolution, the amount of carbon dioxide in the atmosphere has
increased by almost 30 percent, from 280 parts per million by
volume (ppmv) to more than 360 ppmv today, which, according
to ice-core readings, is higher than any level of CO_2 in the last
220,000 years. Prior to the late 1700s, CO_2 levels had remained
stable for as long as the climate had remained stable, nearly 10,000
years. The amount of methane being added to the atmosphere
since preindustrial times has risen from 700 parts per billion by
volume (ppbv) to 1,720 ppbv, an increase of 146 percent! One of
the IPCC's first general observations was that there is *no doubt* that
increases in greenhouse gases like these are mainly due to human
activities such as fossil-fuel burning, deforestation, and agriculture. In fact, the IPCC offered an early estimate that 80 percent of
greenhouse warming is caused by human activity, with CO_2
weighing in as the biggest factor, causing 60 percent of the
warming by itself, followed closely by halocarbons, which did not
even *exist* until the Industrial Revolution. Their mere presence
in the atmosphere objectively constitutes an anthropogenic

"fingerprint." If human beings had not existed, there would be no halocarbons in the atmosphere, period!

The role of halocarbons — used in everything from refrigeration to aerosols — in global temperature rise has until recently been underestimated, but it is now clear that, while their concentrations are much lower than the major greenhouse gases, they are much more powerful "heat-trappers," so their effect transmitting light but blocking heat as it tries to escape is magnified. Worse, so armor-plated are these man-made ozone-eaters that nature can do little to dissipate them for decades, centuries, and in some cases possibly millennia. They have been destroying the stratospheric ozone layer at a rate of nearly 5 percent per decade since the 1970s. A fingerprint? This is more like a claw mark.

Looking ahead, the IPCC's supercomputers see fingerprints and footprints and signals everywhere, although for the most part they are magnifications of processes that are normal, and thus do not bear the indelible stamp of a climate event emerging from the noise. The IPCC predicts higher maximum temperatures and more hot days in nearly all land areas, an increase in the heat index, more "intense precipitation events" (read: storms), fewer colder days, fewer frost days, reduced diurnal temperature range and summer continental drying (drought), increase in tropical cyclone peak wind intensities, and increase in tropical cyclone mean and peak precipitation events (super-hurricanes). Glaciers and ice caps will continue their widespread retreat. The major footprint — more of a smudge, really — among all these others, will continue to be the amount of anthropogenic greenhouse gases building up in the atmosphere. In its *Special Report on Emissions Scenarios*, the panel notes that

> emissions of CO_2 due to fossil-fuel burning are virtually certain to be the dominant influence on the trends in atmospheric CO_2 concentration during the 21st century.

As CO_2 concentration increases and climate changes,
ocean and land will take up a progressively decreasing
proportion of anthropogenic CO_2 emissions. By the end of
the century, models project CO_2 concentrations of 540 to
970 ppm (compared to the preindustrial concentration of
280 ppm, and about 367 ppm today). . . . The sequestration
of carbon by changing land use could influence atmospheric CO_2 concentrations. However, even if all of the
carbon so far released by land use changes could be restored
to the terrestrial biosphere (e.g. by reforestation), CO_2 concentration would be reduced by only 40 to 70 ppm.

I suggest there is a rather striking symmetry here. It is my
observation that, while the Antarctic ozone hole is a matter of
radiation working from the outside inward — that is, *from
above* — in order to eat away at the deflective ozone shield, at
the opposite pole the Arctic ice cap is decaying, as trapped heat
eats away at a reflective ice shield from within — that is, *from
below*. We are looking at huge bites being taken out of the biosphere, like an apple.

Still, the question persists in one form or another: When will
a "climate domino effect" kick in? When will a climate change
"trigger mechanism" go off? When will we see a "smoking
gun" or a clear "greenhouse signal"?

The question has in all likelihood already been answered.
Since November 1999, the signal that scientists have been
looking for has been staring us in the face. It came in the form
of sonar measurements of Arctic ice thickness conducted by
nuclear submarines during the Cold War and finally declassified
by the U.S. and British navies. Dr. Drew Rothrock of the
University of Washington in Seattle analyzed the data, compar-
ing findings from between 1958 and 1976 with findings from
1993 to 1997, and determined that the thickness of the ice
decreased from 10.2 feet in the earlier period to 5.9 feet in the

1990s. "This is not a case of thicker ice appearing in one region simultaneously with thinner ice appearing in another, induced perhaps by a change in surface winds or other transient conditions," Dr. Rothrock said, noting that the decrease was widespread in the central Arctic Ocean, and most pronounced in the eastern Arctic.

According to Dr. Peter Wadhams of the Scott Polar Research Institute at Cambridge, quoted in an August 25, 2000, article in the *Guardian*,

> The average ice thickness in summer has decreased by 40 percent between the Seventies and now. That's a pretty major decrease. And we're looking at satellite images showing the *area* of ice to be shrinking too. That's been going down by 5 percent a decade. At that rate, it will have vanished in 50 years.

Dr. Wadhams said he was convinced that global warming is the cause. In particular, he observed, the ice was being undermined from below by warmer seas. He firmly rejected any suggestion that a natural adjustment, such as a change in winds, would flip the cycle back to rethicken the ice. "The balance of the probability is that this is a real global-warming effect, and it's not going to go back." Average Arctic temperatures in the winter have risen 11 degrees over the past 30 years, which makes it warmer than any time in the last four centuries. Directly, the loss of the shiny white ice at the pole means the loss of a huge reflector that beams the sun's heat back out into space. Open water, which is darker, absorbs heat better. The loss of ice would create a positive-feedback loop, speeding up the general heating of the planet.

In a July 2000 article in the Norwegian science journal *Cicerone*, polar researcher Tore Furevik predicted that such creatures as polar bears and walruses will soon be making "a desperate

last stand" north of Greenland, where he believes the final patch
of Arctic sea ice will linger before vanishing beneath the waves
about 2050. His prediction was supported by Professor Ola M.
Johannessen, director of the University of Bergen's Nansen
Environmental and Remote Sensing Center, who reported he
has discovered that hardcore year-round ice is shrinking twice as
fast as the overall winter perimeter. Noting that the coverage of
Arctic sea ice in winter has decreased since 1978 by the equivalent of an area the size of Texas, he said the receding and thin-
ning of the ice has in fact outstripped the theoretical effect of
global warming from greenhouse gases by a factor of three.
"The greenhouse is here, no doubt about it," he stated in the fall
issue of *Science Progress*, a British journal.

In the search for fingerprints or signals in the Arctic, scientists should, perhaps, have been looking at the business pages
too. While politicians dithered and stonewalled, businessmen in
the shipping industry were already taking advantage of climate
change. For shipping-company executives keeping an eye on the
melting ice in Hudson Bay, the issue isn't the survival of polar
bears. The issue is the bottom line. After a long history of ignoring Canada's northernmost port because of ice hazards, shippers
were finding by the summer of 2000 that the retreating ice cover
allowed deep-sea vessels that lacked reinforced hulls to reach the
grain elevators of Churchill as "early" as July 11, the earliest port
opening since international shipping started there in 1931. Total
tonnage hit 710,000, more than double the average annual shipments for the last five years. The Canadian Ice Service has measured ice extent on July 15, the benchmark date for the annual
start of shipping on Hudson Bay, every year since 1971. There is
some variation, but the trend is clear: over the last three decades
the expanse of ice on that date has decreased by about one-third.
A Denver-based company, Omnitrax Inc., which bought the port
and access rail in 1997, was reported to be lobbying Lloyd's of
London to drop a longstanding 15-percent insurance surcharge

on Churchill shipments and was seeking to expand the standard insured shipping season from three to five months, from July 1 until the end of November. Currently, the season is from July 21 to October 21. Said a spokesman for the company: "The fact is, the ice is gone from the port earlier and forms in the port later."

In July 2000, a group of ten scientists specializing in Arctic studies released the results of a review of nearly forty years of polar research, described as the largest focused survey yet of environmental change in the far north. According to the survey's lead author, Mark Serreze of the University of Colorado at Boulder, the team found a stunning range of effects, each one of which could be considered a climate-change footprint in itself:

- Since 1900, rain and snowfall have increased in a band running from latitude fifty-five degrees north to eighty-five degrees north. Northern Canada has seen a marked rise in precipitation during the past forty years.

- Since the late 1950s, changes in atmospheric circulation patterns have brought more storms to the region in winter, spring, and summer, and more intense storms during all seasons.

- Temperatures have risen since at least 1961. Tree-ring data suggests that Arctic warming in the mid-twentieth century is the most pronounced in four hundred years.

- Snow cover has dropped by about 10 percent since 1972, largely in the spring and summer, as residual snowfields have shrunk. Sea ice has been declining in thickness and extent, dropping to record lows in the western Arctic Ocean in 1998.

The shocking degree to which the change in the north is already being felt was captured in a dramatic *New York Times* dispatch from Anchor Point, Alaska, on June 16, 2002, by Timothy Eagan. What he describes is the transformation of an entire massive ecosystem after just a few degrees of heating:

> To live in Alaska when the average temperature has risen about seven degrees over the last 30 years means learning to cope with a landscape that can sink, catch fire or break apart in the turn of a season.
>
> In the village of Shishmaref, on the Chukchi Sea just south of the Arctic Circle, it means high water eating away so many houses and buildings that people will vote next month on moving the entire village inland.
>
> In Barrow, the northernmost city in North America, it means coping with mosquitoes in a place where they once were nonexistent, and rescuing hunters trapped on break-away ice at a time of year when such things once were unheard of.
>
> From Fairbanks to the north, where wildfires have been burning off and on since mid-May, it means living with hydraulic jacks to keep houses from slouching and buckling on foundations that used to be frozen all year. Permafrost, they say, is no longer permanent.
>
> Here on the Kenai Peninusula, a recreation wonder-land a few hours' drive from Anchorage, it means living in a four-million-acre spruce forest that has been killed by beetles, the largest loss of trees to insects ever recorded in North America, federal officials say. Government scientists tied the event to rising temperatures, which allow the beetles to reproduce at twice their normal rate.
>
> In Alaska, rising temperatures, whether caused by greenhouse gas emissions or nature in a prolonged mood swing, are not a topic of debate or an abstraction. Mean temperatures have risen by 5 degrees in summer and 10 degrees in winter since the 1970s, federal officials say.

It has been known since as early as 1990, when the IPCC was preparing its first report, that one potential feedback is the "plankton-multiplier" effect. In the event that North Atlantic Ocean circulation should turn off as a result of global warming, phytoplankton productivity would drop, which would result in a huge boost in atmospheric CO_2 levels, because a major system of soaking up and storing carbon — a carbon "sink" — would have been diminished.

One of the positive-feedback loops to have already emerged is the transformation in the region's carbon cycle. Writing in the August 2000 issue of *Nature,* Walter Oechel of San Diego State University notes that Arctic ecosystems have long been net "sinks" of CO_2, removing it from the atmosphere and sequestering it in the ground, mainly because of the wet, cold soil, which slows down the decomposition rates of organic matter. But in the 1960s there was a dramatic change in the carbon balance of Arctic ecosystems from sink to source. "To my great surprise, we found out that the Arctic has already flipped from a sink to a source. The source is actually very large: instead of a sink of 70–80 grams per square meter, we were seeing a source of up to 150 grams per square meter during the summer period. So that was our first indication that there had been a major change in the system."

In a private correspondence (February 13, 2001), a scientist with Canada's Department of Defence, who has spent considerable time studying conditions in the Arctic, responded to my question about what the melting of the ice cap would do to the planet's albedo, or reflective power, with this reply:

We know that the bulk albedo of open water is about 0.06, new snow is about 0.87, and bare ice about 0.52. Arctic ice is not uniformly flat and white throughout the year but is a complex changing landscape of jumbled ice blocks, drifted snow, ponds of melt water, and open ocean leads. There is not even a generally accepted "average" albedo for the entire Arctic Ocean (although 0.7−0.8 is commonly used). Suffice to say that, if the ice were to melt completely, there would be a dramatic change in the albedo of the Polar Regions. The albedo effect on climate may not be the largest component of any resulting climate change, because the Arctic Ocean represents only about 7 percent of the earth's surface. A much larger impact would (arguably) be the breakdown of the world's ocean circulation — surface fresh water in the Arctic and deep convection in the Greenland Sea are both important to ocean circulation and driven by sea ice.

In response to a further question — whether, if positive feedbacks are factored in, the rate of melting will accelerate — he answered:

> Quite likely, although the larger expanse of open water would create greater moisture fluxes into the atmosphere, likely increasing snowfall and causing a negative feedback. Again, scientific debate is rampant but generally scientists believe there will be more positive feedbacks than negative.

The first hard evidence that the Earth's albedo has *already* been affected was reported in *Newsday* in June 2001, when scientists acknowledged that the amount of "Earthshine" being reflected back onto the dark side of the moon is changing. The faint glow can be used to track long-term changes in the planetary atmosphere, such as increase in cloud cover, dust, and the planet's overall reflective properties. The new data suggested that a 2.5-percent decrease in the Earth's albedo had occurred over the previous five years.

Dr. William Gough of the University of Toronto, who has studied the impact of ice-melt on polar bears, told me in an interview that the material he has seen, based on computer simulations, show the seasonal ice cycle in Hudson Bay disappearing after "about 2040." This is "absolutely crucial" for the animals in the area, such as polar bears, "who go out onto the ice every year to feed on seal pups. They get big and fat, and then they basically starve for five or six months while they're on land, losing about 1.8 kilograms per day. Once the seasonal ice platform goes, probably well before 2040, there's no means for the polar bears to survive unless they can adopt a new eating style. The studies that have been done by biologists show that the average weight of polar bears is going down. In Churchill, Manitoba, the cycle used to be that food was sufficiently rich that mother bears could wean their pups within a year. Now it looks like they are going to a two-year weaning cycle, because of lack of food. The cubs just aren't big enough after one year to make it on their own, so that reduces the viability of the herd because it doesn't replace as quickly and it's more vulnerable. The ice extends from about November through to June or July in Hudson's Bay, depending on the location. The breakups are getting earlier and earlier and the weight loss in polar bears is correlated with that gradual breakup."

When I suggested to Dr. Gough that the computer models upon which the calculations of ice-melt were based are fairly conservative and don't really factor in positive-feedback loops, he responded: "Oh yes! If the land surface melts or the permafrost thaws and methane trapped there gets released, this would increase the amount of methane getting into the atmosphere and therefore accelerate the warming." He added ominously: "There don't seem to be feedbacks that work the other way."

I submit that the projected disappearance of the Arctic ice cap is both the greenhouse signal that scientists have been looking for, and also the likeliest single eco-trigger event to set in motion a domino effect, leading to Thermageddon.

In a private correspondence, dated May 2001, another Canadian Defence scientist who has spent considerable time in the Arctic, but who did not wish his name to be used, sent me the following reply:

> As to your polar ice pack questions, we're no experts here, but I can pass on what I've seen and heard from other places. The pack does seem to be melting, and forecasts for an ice-free Arctic vary anywhere from about twenty to fifty years. Some parts of it (e.g., the Northwest Passage) could well be ice-free before that. There's lots of debate over what will happen to the albedo. On one side of the argument are those who suggest that melting the ice cap will leave a dark ocean up there which will lower the albedo and, on the other, are those who predict even more cloud cover as a result (remember the fog when the ice opens up?), which will actually increase the albedo, leading to a sudden downshift in temperature and possibly even the onset of another Ice Age. So, in answer to your last question, yes, it would be a trigger for a major climate shift, but there are strong arguments for it shifting up or down. Don't know which side will win.

Either way, we can be sure the loss of ice will have implications for the entire global climate, because of its effects on what oceanographers call "thermohaline circulation," or, more popularly, the Atlantic "conveyor belt." Heat and salt change the density of water, which means that colder, saltier water tends to plummet to the bottom of the ocean while warmer, fresher water tends to rise. Any change in the conveyor belt has towering ramifications for Europeans.

Those areas of the oceans where cold, salty water predominates are called "sinks" (as distinct from a carbon sink), and those dominated by warm, less salty water are called "upwellings." The biggest ocean sinks are the North Atlantic and the Greenland and Labrador seas. In these regions, frigid polar air cools the surface of the ocean beyond freezing, which raises its density, forming ice. When ice forms, salt is squeezed out. This increases the salinity of the remaining cooled water, which sinks into the "abyssal ocean," as the depths are called. As polar water sinks, warmer water from the south flows in to take its place, creating a current that flows across the Atlantic from south to north. Driven in part by Caribbean tropical winds, this surface flow, known as the Gulf Stream, adds something like 20 percent more warmth to the air hovering over northern Europe in the winter. In the meantime, the dense, cold water locked into the abyssal ocean flows along the bed of the Atlantic, "carrying" the Gulf Stream on its shoulders, as it were, and sluicing on down to the Antarctic, where it merges with the "Southern Ocean Raceway," a complex of currents that circumnavigates the South Pole, taking in large flows from the basins of the Atlantic, Pacific, and Indian oceans.

In 1999, Jean Lynch-Stieglitz of the Lamont–Doherty Earth Observatory, Palisades, New York, was able to calculate the approximate temperature, and hence the flow, of the Gulf Stream some 12,000 years ago during the last ice age. By analyzing the thickness of foraminifera shells from the Caribbean and estimating the density of the water at the time the tiny sea creatures died, Lynch-Stieglitz's team uncovered a very different thermohaline circulation pattern from today's. There was far less cold, dense water in the current, so much so that it appears the sinking of dense water at the poles may have stopped entirely. As Jeremy Thompson wrote in the January 2001 edition of *Nature,*

> So there appear to be at least two stable patterns of circulation in the world's oceans, one associated with ice ages and the other similar to the present day. Unfortunately, it

is not yet clear what triggers the shift from one circulation
pattern to another. Changing from the current pattern to
the glacial circulation mode is one of the most potentially
worrying aspects of climate shifts: it could plunge the
planet into another ice age.

An even more depressing scientific discovery in relation to
the movement of these waters was reported by the Scott Polar
Research Institute's Dr. Wadhams back in 1994. Over a ten-year
period, he took several voyages to investigate a prominent tongue
on the edge of the Arctic ice cap, where the ice formation causes
dense, salty water to form, sinking downward and thus driving
thermohaline circulation. He found that, in the Greenland Sea
at least, convection has virtually stopped in the last decade.
Whereas the ice-related, density-driven convection pushed
down to 3,500 meters below the surface in 1984, five years later
it was only managing to get down as far as 2,000 meters. By
1993, it could descend only 1,000 meters. "It is a process that
has been going on for thousands of years," Dr. Wadhams said,
"and when you see it decline sharply over a decade it gets you
worried." This decrease was a side effect of less ice forming in
the region. What was most worrisome, the professor added, was
that the reduced convection would in turn reduce the amount
of carbon dioxide being absorbed into deep water. In "normal"
times — at least during an interglacial period — roughly 25
percent of the total global CO_2 load is "sequestered" this way,
meaning it is removed from the atmosphere. With less and less
of it being dragged down by convection into the abyssal ocean,
one more positive-feedback loop uncoils, and world temperatures are boosted still further.

A report published in *Nature* in the June 2001 issue, by
Professor Bogi Hansen of the Faroese Fisheries Laboratory, con-
firms that the flow of cold, dense water from the Arctic Ocean
and Norwegian Sea, racing through four deep channels near

Greenland, Iceland and the Faroe Islands, and Scotland, has declined by at least 20 percent since 1950. "If this reduction in deep flow from the Nordic seas is not compensated for by increased flow from other sources, it implies a weakened global thermohaline circulation." The decrease is due, Prof. Hansen argued, to the shrinking of the Arctic ice sheet and the ice-bound coastline of Siberia. "When you add fresh water, you reduce pumping efficiency," he said, explaining the lower flow through the channels. In the longer term, there could be a "cooling effect" on northwestern Europe, because the region will have less return flow from the Gulf Stream. "One can expect that northern parts of Europe, like the U.K. and Scandinavia, will be affected, and one can expect effects further south. You can also expect global consequences from this . . . if you look at the deep water of the world's oceans, they are fed by only two sources. One of them is the Antarctic and the other is up here, in this region. So if you reduce one of these sources, you reduce the whole circulation of one of the world's oceans."

Environment Canada's Dr. Henry Hengeveld cites a University of Quebec paper hypothesizing that the glaciation process at the end of an interglacial, such as the last one, ten thousand years ago, starts because of too much open Arctic water, resulting in more precipitation, while the tops of the Greenland ice caps remain below freezing. As the precipitation accumulates, you get snowier winters, which has a reverse albedo effect. With wider swaths of ice and snow, more heat is reflected, and temperatures drop. The increase in snowfall could actually start triggering accumulations of ice-mass on land.

The question of changes in albedo excites the juices of contrarians, as they are called, meaning skeptics, whether with vested interests or not, on both sides of the climate-change debate. We know that variations in reflectivity affect temperature. Anyone who has felt the cooling effect of a passing cloud on a hot summer day has experienced a negative-feedback loop.

Climatologists estimate that the clouds which cover half the planet at any given moment act like a giant umbrella, bouncing roughly 20 percent of the sun's light away. Snow and ice, of course, have a high albedo, whereas recently exposed mountaintops, naked glacial moraine, muskeg, tundra, and deep water absorb solar heat. Rising sea levels mean water spreading over a larger area. The fact that its temperature would be higher, since it is meltwater, means it would expand even more, and with each tidal surge upward and outward, it would absorb more heat. Whereas the melting of glaciers exposes rock to the sunlight an inch at a time, the collapse of the Arctic ice cap is a phenomenon that would have a dramatic, virtually overnight, impact. The decay of the ice packs, coming mainly from below, means that the surface will remain for all intents and purposes unchanged in terms of albedo until the final summer of dissolution. The heat from the sun is reflected just as blindingly from an inch of ice as a mile of the stuff. With the disappearance of that final scab on the surface of the deep black Arctic waters, a massive area on the far north will suddenly switch from heat shield to heat sink. Unlike most positive-feedback loops, whose impact is incremental, this event — the near-instant removal of the Arctic ice — will invite a blast of increased heat from space, virtually an explosion. The sudden heat-exchange transformation will be occurring in the very midst of the great ocean sinks of the Arctic, Greenland, and Labrador seas, the very source-waters of the mighty thermohaline circulation currents, with their power to alter climate everywhere, not just at the North Pole.

Dr. Hengeveld cautions: "It's not an obvious thing that an ice-free Arctic means we'll be locked into a long warm period in terms of century time-scales, although not necessarily millennial time-scales. One of the things you have to keep in mind is that the global system does have slow feedback processes that were probably factors in whole interglacial-glacial cycles [of melting ice] that passed. We don't understand these very well. The possibility is that the global system is a pretty delicate balance. We've only had interglacial-glacial cycles of melting and freezing ice for the last few million years. There have been enormously long periods in the earth's history when such cycles didn't exist at all. And there is the possibility that we could trigger a departure from this interglacial-glacial cycle."

The possibility that we could trigger a departure from this interglacial-glacial cycle . . .

What a phrase! In other words, plunge the whole world into a completely different kind of bio-geophysical reality, leaving what has proven to be an Eden for humanity far, far behind in the awful, awesome tumbling of climate from one epoch to another.

I asked Dr. Hengeveld whether he thought the date of 2050 for the Arctic meltdown could be substantially moved forward if positive-feedback loops such as methane being released from the permafrost were included in the models. Would such feedbacks accelerate the warming process? And if so, by how much? Rather than rejecting my premise, he acknowledged its validity. His answer was both astonishing and chilling.

"The climate models to date have not been factoring them in. They're merely beginning to. There's a new study that came out in the U.K., the Cox–Detz study, where they now for the first time have a fully interactive, biological model coupled with a climate model. What they show is that the terrestrial biosphere continues to absorb excess carbon for the next forty to fifty years, but then the shit hits the fan. The climate-change process begins to influence the biosphere quite significantly, particularly in the tropics, where drier conditions result in increased soil respiration and biomass loss. What happens is that by about 2050 the soils will have already become a source of carbon rather than a sink, and by 2070 the standing biosphere does as well. By 2100, the global biosphere is releasing all sorts of carbon into the atmosphere. When they add that into their normal business-as-usual scenario, which gives you about 580 parts per million of CO_2 concentration by 2100, it suddenly jumps to a little over 900 parts per million. So there's a very strong positive feedback that would accelerate the warming because of the increased release of carbon dioxide from the terrestrial biosphere."

The question of the rate of methane release is less easy to answer than it might seem because long-term monitoring of permafrost only began in earnest in the last few decades. But its importance is underlined by the fact that 25 percent of the land mass of the northern hemisphere is underlain by permafrost, including large regions of Canada, China, Russia, and Alaska, with smaller permafrost areas in mountain chains of other countries. Has it begun to melt? That part of the answer is clear enough: most definitely! There has been a general warming of the permafrost in the Alaskan Arctic of 2 to 4 degrees Celsius over the last century, according to the IPCC's calculations. "In North America, the southern boundary of the discontinuous permafrost zone has migrated northward. . . . In China both an increase in the lower altitudinal limit of mountain permafrost and a decrease in areal [*sic*] extent have been observed. . . . [P]ermafrost in many regions of the earth is currently warming [and] evidence of increasing thaw depths is starting to be reported."

It seems almost unbelievable that a major shift in climate could loom so near in the future, yet the IPCC is unsparingly blunt on this point:

> The central Greenland ice core record . . . reveals episodes
> of very rapid change. The return to the cold conditions
> from the incipient interglacial warming 13,000 years ago
> *took place within a few decades or less* [my italics]. The
> warming phase that took place about 11,500 years ago was
> also very abrupt and central Greenland temperatures

increased by 7 degrees C or more in a few decades. Most of the changes in climate indicators were accomplished in a few years. Broad regions of the earth experienced almost synchronous changes over periods of thirty years, and changes were even more abrupt in some areas, requiring as little as a single decade in Venezuela to change from one entire climate regime to another. A similar, correlated sequence of "abrupt deglacial events" also occurred in tropical and temperate North America, and in Western Europe. Almost synchronously, major vegetation changes occurred in Africa, where lake levels rose. Oxygen isotope measurements in Greenland ice cores demonstrate that a series of rapid warm and cold oscillations punctuated the last glaciation, with associated temperature changes that might have been as high as 16 degrees C.

In summary: "Current evidence indicates that very rapid and large temperature changes, generally associated with changes in oceanic and atmospheric circulation, occurred during the last glacial period and during the last deglaciation, particularly in the higher latitudes of the northern hemisphere."

So the possibility of a major climate flip within the next thirty years — difficult as it is to imagine — is not only real, it has plenty of precedents. And in these previous cases, none of the events involved the added atmospheric aggravation of a burst of man-made carbon emissions or a sudden convergence of positive-feedback loops.

Science writer Lydia Dotto writes in *Storm Warning*: "Climate change is like a ship that can't be quickly turned around. But perhaps a more important question is whether it can be turned around at all. Scientists are raising concerns that we may at some point unknowingly cross a threshold, a trip wire, that will suddenly throw the climate into a state that will be irreversible on human time scales." She quotes Wallace Broecker of Columbia University, who warns that it is wishful thinking to count on natural mechanisms to kick in to counteract sudden global warming. "I find absolutely no support for the self-regulation concept . . . the climate system has the bad habit of undergoing large and abrupt jumps from one mode of operation to another. The paleoclimate record shouts out to us that, far from being self-stabilizing, the earth's climate system is an ornery beast which overreacts to even small things." Broecker argues that, if thermohaline circulation shuts down, temperatures in the North Atlantic and surrounding land areas would drop by about 3 degrees Celsius — a bigger difference than between now and the last ice age — *within a single decade.*

Glacier-climbing along the Riviera, anyone?

CHAPTER   4

THE CARBON CLUB STRIKES BACK

THE DEBATE, IN SHORT, SHOULD have been laid to rest decades ago. It wasn't — and this is no accident.

Considering the advanced state of our science, the big question should be: why was there no serious call for political action on the global warming front *much* earlier than now? By rights, it should have got started back in 1957. That's when scientists at the respected Scripps Institute of Oceanography published a landmark paper noting that the oceans were not absorbing as much of the carbon dioxide being released into the environment as assumed, and this raised the disturbing question: where was all that "missing" CO_2 going? They warned that a "large-scale biophysical experiment" was being conducted on the Earth's climate.

No doubt the Scripps Institute fellows hoped their warning would be heeded, but they were to be disappointed. Monumentally, it was ignored. At a time when pesticide manufacturers in lab coats were still getting away with calling Rachel Carson a madwoman for her "scare stories" about the effects of chemicals on wildlife, humans, and ecosystems, it was too much of a leap for the media or even the intelligentsia, apparently, to grasp the meaning of a buildup of CO_2 in the atmosphere.

It wasn't until more than two full decades later, in 1979, that enough momentum had been engendered, almost entirely within scientific circles, for the First World Climate Conference to be held, which resulted in the setting-up of the UN World Climate Program. A panel of the U.S. National Academy of Sciences (NAS) weighed in at that point with its own warning, namely that a wait-and-see attitude might mean "waiting until it is too late." By 1983, NAS reported that a doubling of CO_2 would raise the world's temperature by between 1.4 and 4.5 degrees Celsius. (Which is remarkably close to the 2001 IPCC assessment of a rise between 1.4 and 5.8 degrees Celsius. In other words, while the scientific estimate hasn't changed much in those wasted years, virtually nothing has been done. We have been sitting here on the train tracks, as though mesmerized by the blinding light hurtling towards us.) Finally, in 1988, the IPCC was formed by the United Nations with a mandate to advise policy-makers on what is really happening to our atmosphere and climate.

At any point in history prior to the development of super-computers, the UN might as well have turned to witch doctors dancing around a fire, rattling bones. The art of predicting the future, however, has taken a quantum leap since the Second World War, and for the first time in history it is possible for scientists to deliver, if not absolute certainties, probabilities that are in the range of 95 percent or better. The most sophisticated tools of all are the three-dimensional General Circulation Models (GCMs), which use thousands of mathematical equations to represent the physical laws of nature that govern the inter-actions between the various components of the climate system, such as oceans, atmosphere, ice, snow, albedo, carbon sinks, seasonal temperature cycles, humidity, precipitation, cloud cover, wind speeds, geographical variations, etc. These models allow scientists to create a "virtual Earth," complete with all the major features of the current climate, which can then be run forward to see how climate evolves in a theoretically endless number of scenarios. And they are not untested, as critics like to claim. GCMs have proven their reliability by correctly predicting the cooling caused by the eruption of Mount Pinatubo, for instance. Models also anticipated the delayed response of plant life to warming and cooling episodes caused by El Niño. By way of testing their veracity, scientists have run the best of these models backwards and correctly replicated the climatic changes caused in the past by natural greenhouse-gas concentrations. In other words, the things have been test-driven. They *work* — although of course they remain limited by the amount of information we can put into them.

Here again, humanity lucked out. What the IPCC had going for it was a combination of calculating power and accumulated data that was unprecedented. And these were just the tools and the raw material. Some two thousand scientists were brought together for the first of dozens of conferences. Every word they wrote, every data-point they entered, every algorithm they used was peer-reviewed, meaning that each paper submitted for inclusion in the IPCC's work was picked at mercilessly by other scientists and experts before it saw print.

They were was also picked at, right from the beginning, by "observers" from the coal, oil, and chemical industries, who showed up in force to tamper with the drafting of the first Scientific Assessment Report at a Berkshire, England, country hotel in the spring of 1990. There some hundred scientists had gathered to put the finishing touches on what would arguably become the most important scientific document of all time.

In his invaluable record of that historic early meeting, *The Carbon War: Global Warming and the End of the Oil Era*, geologist and former Greenpeace activist Jeremy Leggett recalls that, after several days of meetings, as the executive summary was being written, a scientist on the payroll of Exxon took the microphone to argue that there were too many uncertainties about the behavior of carbon in the climate system to justify calling — as the scientists were indeed in the very process of doing — for a 60-percent cut in carbon-dioxide emissions to stabilize atmospheric concentrations of the gas. At that early, informal stage of the game, the company spokesmen — nobody thought to call them lobbyists yet — were allowed to make suggestions about the wording of the text. The Exxon man wanted the text altered to admit to "scientific uncertainty." Scientists from Germany, the United Kingdom, and the United States — the most eminent climatologists in the world — refuted this line of argument. Of course there were uncertainties, they said, but if the goal was to stabilize atmospheric concentrations of carbon dioxide, those uncertainties did not undermine the need for deep cuts in emissions. For the moment, the heavy hand of industrial self-interest had been stayed, and the objective scientists prevailed. But a pattern had been established. Wherever industry could find an opening to interfere, delay, obfuscate, or filibuster, it would.

When the chairman of the meeting, Dr. John Houghton, came to the critical sentence in the summary, he turned to his colleagues and asked: "Can we say we are *certain* that greenhouse-gas emissions at present rates will lead to warming?"

He was answered, Leggett reports, by a roomful of nodding heads.

There were certain points this first IPCC report made, right at the beginning of the debate, that have tended to get buried over the years as new information flooded in. In a section on the reliability of the report's own predictions, the authors were careful to acknowledge the existence of sources of natural greenhouse gases such as decaying vegetation and to note the absorptive powers of carbon sinks, areas of large biomass, like forests or tundra or algae blooms. Both sources and sinks were sensitive to changes in temperature, and any change in their equilibrium could substantially alter future concentrations of greenhouse gases. While this made predicting difficult, "it appears likely," the report stated, "that, as climate warms, these feedbacks will lead to an overall increase, rather than decrease, in natural greenhouse-gas abundances. For this reason, climate change is likely to be greater than the estimates we have given." The other main point doomed to be forgotten or ignored was the most shocking of all: if atmospheric concentrations of CO_2 were to be stabilized at present levels, which were already higher than at any time in the previous hundred and sixty thousand years, emissions would need to be cut by *60 percent or more*.

The Dutch contingent expressed deep unease when they submitted a written statement saying that they were worried that the "best guess" estimates being used by the IPCC, referring to trends over the next century and beyond, might blind the lay public to the fact that best guesses might prove to be underestimates. "Despite many uncertainties," they pleaded,

> we are concerned about our finding that future rates of climate change may exceed any rate of change ever experienced by humankind in the past. There are no reasons to expect that humankind itself, or the ecosystems on whose functioning humankind depends, will be able to adapt to such rates of change. A further point of great concern is that, although we have confidence in the results of our assessment, the complexity of the system may give rise to surprises.

But what was perhaps most significant about that final first draft was what was *not* in it.

Leggett relates in *The Carbon War* how he and a Greenpeace colleague arrived at the Berkshire meeting

with great hopes that the worst-case analysis would be
spelled out more starkly than it had been in the review
copy of the report sent to attendees ahead of the meeting.
We submitted papers to the IPCC, itemizing our concerns.
What worried us most were the feedbacks in the climate
system — the processes that can be triggered in a warming
world which either amplify the warming (positive feedbacks) or suppress it (negative feedbacks). Our concern
was that the former might end up swamping the latter.
We were far from alone in that fear.

Such concerns had been fairly well explored in the scientific
journals by then. A warming world could trigger, for example,
extra emissions of greenhouse gases from the vast repositories of
carbon in nature, such as warming oceans, drying soils, dying
forests, melting permafrost. These feedbacks were often impossible to quantify, and were mostly excluded from computer
climate models. But, Leggett wondered, shouldn't their role in
the climate threat assessment be more clearly flagged? Shouldn't
the worst-case analysis be clearly spelled out for policy-makers?

"I urged the scientists to mention specifically what in principle the very worst case might be for a world where emissions
were not cut deeply — a runaway, unstoppable greenhouse
effect." The suggestion was dismissed — not because of any
scientific consensus, but because of the political judgment of the
scientists themselves. A sea-level expert expressed concern that
the media would "sensationalize" any mention of anything like
that. The leading U.S. scientist at the meeting was Robert
Watson, who had headed the team that had proved the link
between CFCs and the ozone hole, and who was then still
working with NASA. "I have a problem with this," he said,
according to Leggett. "We mustn't give policy-makers the
impression that there's no point. We don't win that way." A
dubious strategy, at best: not telling the truth because it might be

too much to take? There was more than a whiff of scientific elitism at work here. In retrospect, the tactic of keeping the report within the bounds of solvability, of avoiding making it seem too dark or hopeless or pointless, can be seen as probably the most critical blunder in what became a long string of miscalculations by some of the smartest people on the planet. And it only happened when the scientists tried to get political, tried to start anticipating reactions, tried to aim for a certain effect.

There hadn't been any involvement in the IPCC process by the military, and while this would normally be something to applaud, there was one problem with purely "scientific" thinking: it apparently didn't include any requirement that a worst-case analysis be examined. In any situation involving military security, "threat assessment" *always* includes the worst-case scenario. The entire IPCC exercise could rightly be seen at a fundamental level as being nothing more or less than an elaborate, multi-disciplinary global-threat assessment. For its authors to leave out or airbrush the worst-case possibilities for fear that politicians and media might use scenarios that were too dark as some kind of excuse for inaction betrays a streak of intellectual arrogance that should not be forgiven. They got the debate off to a lame start, with smoother edges than a purely empirical approach warranted.

Still, blunted and conservative as its message was, the first IPCC report did trigger a debate. Indeed, it got off to a fairly spectacular start in the media, thanks in no small measure to British prime minister Margaret Thatcher, one of the first leaders to be briefed by the IPCC's John Houghton. Not famous as a "bunny hugger," the Iron Lady was nevertheless unequivocal in a press conference following the briefing.

Today, with the publication of the report of the Intergovernmental Panel on Climate Change, we have an authoritative early-warning system: an agreed assessment from some three hundred of the world's leading scientists on what is happening to the world's climate. They confirm that greenhouse gases are increasing substantially as a result of man's activities, that this will warm the Earth's surface with serious consequences for us all. . . . There would surely be a great migration of population away from areas of the world liable to flooding, and from areas of declining rainfall and therefore of spreading desert. Those people will be crying out not for oil wells but for water.

Shortly thereafter, in 1991, scientists who put their heads together at the Second World Climate Conference, sponsored by the UN Environment Program, unanimously called for immediate political action to ensure that "future generations will not be put at risk." That year, the United States National Academy of Sciences released another statement, this time signed by seven hundred scientists, including forty-nine Nobel Prize winners, which stated that "there is broad agreement within the scientific community that amplification of the Earth's natural greenhouse effect by the build-up of various gases introduced by human activity has the potential to produce dramatic changes in climate." A "prompt response" was needed to provide "insurance protection against the great uncertainties and the possibility of dramatic surprises." This was enough for the UN General Assembly to begin the international scientific consultation process that was to lead to the Framework Convention on Climate Change (FCCC) at the Earth Summit in Rio de Janeiro in June 1992.

It was also enough for the Carbon Club to start organizing its counterattack. "Carbon Club" is a term used by numerous writers to describe the cabal of oil, coal, auto, and utility interests, including Amoco, Arco, Shell, British Petroleum, Texaco, the American Petroleum Institute, DuPont, Dow Hydrocarbons, the Association of International Automobile Manufacturers, the American Electric Power Service Corporation, the

National Coal Association, and the Edison Electric Institute. One thing that has to be said about the executives in charge of those heavy-polluting industries is that they were manning the parapets, alert for any threat to their bottom lines. Indeed, they must have been scanning the horizon with binoculars, because climate was not yet a blip on the mass-media radar screen.

Yet as early as 1988, the $400-million-a-year coal giant Western Fuels Association had already decided it was "important to take a stand." According to its annual report that year, "scientists were found who are skeptical about much of what seemed generally accepted about the potential for climate change." A public-relations firm was hired, which stated that its tactic was to "reposition global warming as theory rather than fact," and to this end targeted "older, less-educated men," and "young, low-income women," especially in areas where energy came mainly from coal. Newspaper ads asked: "If the earth is getting warmer, why is Minneapolis getting colder?" (It wasn't.) Western Fuels also decided to finance and publish a magazine called *World Climate Review* as an organ for themselves and the skeptical scientists they would recruit. In the ultimate public-relations feint, they spent $250,000 on a video titled *The Greening of Planet Earth*. In the annals of propaganda flicks, going back to such classics as *Reefer Madness* and *Triumph of the Will*, there are few efforts to match this little masterpiece, which presents global warming as a godsend. Taking an evangelical tone, the video's narrator tells us in no uncertain terms that a golden age of agricultural abundance lies directly ahead so long as the doubling of glorious CO_2 concentrations is allowed to continue unabated. Yields of wheat, cotton, soybeans, for instance, *will* increase by 30 to 60 percent. Grasslands *will* replace deserts. The grasslands of today *will* become luxurious new bushlands, while a planet-wide infusion of CO_2 *will* cause the depleted forests of today to bloom. The video is Disneyesque in its sentiments, and it is bad science fiction. But it had the desired impact. The

White House became a favorite viewing venue, with George H. Bush–era chief of staff John Sununu showing it frequently.

The Carbon Club's antics have to be seen against the background of the times. Environmental history had recently been made, up in Canada. In September 1987, the Montreal Protocol on Substances that Deplete the Ozone Layer was signed by fifty-seven nations. It stands as "a unique example of scientists and industry working with governments to solve a global problem," as one text states — although, sadly, it should be noted that industry was only dragged to the table by political pressure. Before that, it had waged a concerted rearguard action against any bans or phase-outs from the very first day of publication of a paper by Mario Molina and Sherwood Rowland. These two chemists at the University of California, Irvine, theorized about the nature of a special molecule, acting as a catalyst, that *might* be causing ozone destruction. Indignant industrial squeals of protest had likewise followed the publication in 1985 of British scientist Joseph Farman's findings of a stunning 50-percent collapse of the Antarctic ozone layer, and his suspicion that chloro-fluorocarbons might be responsible. Even after NASA confirmed Farman's results on the basis of a reanalysis of data from a satellite ozone-mapping project that had been dismissed years before as a computer error, CFC-industry mouthpieces were still in full scientific denial mode. In the end, however, when commanded to by international treaty, they reluctantly obeyed the law. Indeed, to be fair, when new evidence showed that the layer was being destroyed even faster than calculated, a discovery which led a year later to a follow-up meeting in London to order even quicker, deeper cuts in CFC use, the industry notched its resistance down from a scorched-earth policy (in this case, literally) to mere foot-dragging. The original Montreal Protocol had called for a 50-percent reduction by 1998. In London, this time with ninety-three nations signing, the timetable changed: CFC production was to be totally phased out by the year 2000. What emerged out of the exercise was the most significant global environmental agreement to date.

It was against this optimistic background that the IPCC's first report was released in 1990, and it did trigger a minisurge of interest in a Montreal Protocol type of treaty. The attention of environmentalists had definitely been caught. Until then, the number of environmental organizations that had taken positions on the issue of global warming had been sparse indeed. This changed rapidly. The outline of the basic problem had emerged. A great dark cloud now lay across the event horizon, a cruel twist of fate, considering we had just emerged from under the shadow of the Cold War. Yet there it was: a bleak, oppressive, soul-crushing look at the future. Cautious as the wording sounded to a lay audience, among the two thousand scientists who had put their names on the original Assessment, the message was intended to be as somber, sober, and serious as it could be. What it meant, as Dr. Michael Oppenheimer of the U.S. Environmental Defense Fund observed, was: "We are sure that large and potentially disastrous changes are afoot. Let us be under no illusion. This is a consensus among scientists."

There was a parallel consensus among industrialists, although its conclusion was quite different. The dark cloud they saw was a loss of profits. In response, a number of new front organizations were formed, such as the World Climate Council, whose executive director, Don Pearlman, was destined to become the key go between for the eventual alliance of the worst polluting corporations, OPEC, and the oil-financed Middle Eastern, Asian, and African dictatorships. While Pearlman has earned the dubious distinction of becoming the environmental movement's *bête noire*, John Schlaes, executive director of the Global Climate Coalition, was to succeed in becoming only slightly less viscerally loathed. Both men started working closely behind the scenes with a group of utility and coal companies that banded together in 1991 to form the Information Council on the Environment

(ICE), which was, of course, a *dis*information agency. Behind the façade of ICE, they arranged for the so-called greenhouse skeptics — indeed, the very scientists Western Fuels had been looking for — to be set up for broadcast appearances, newspaper interviews, and op-ed pieces. For the record, prominent names among the hardcore greenhouse skeptics were: Pat Michaels, associate professor of meteorology at MIT; Robert Balling, associate professor of climatology at the University of Virginia; Sherwood Idso, narrator of *The Greening of Planet Earth*; Richard S. Lindzen, another MIT meteorologist; and the indefatigable S. Fred Singer, also from the University of Virginia, who morphed from stubborn academic contrarian into a frequent guest on the Rush Limbaugh show. A "star" global-warming denier, Singer has openly admitted getting huge amounts of funding from companies like Exxon, Shell, ARCO, Unocal, and Sun Oil, as well as the Reverend Sun Myung Moon. Robert Balling admitted under oath during administrative hearings in Minnesota in 1995 that he had received funding from such organizations as the German Coal Mining Association, the British Coal Corporation, and the Kuwait Institute for Scientific Research.

Although they formed only a small cadre, these "professional skeptics" proved extremely adept at "draining the issue of all sense of crisis," as Ross Gelbspan writes in *The Heat Is On*. "Their interviews, columns, and letters have appeared in newspapers ranging from local weeklies to the *Washington Post* and the *Wall Street Journal*. In the process they have helped create a broad public belief that the question of climate change is hopelessly mired in unknowns." Gelbspan states flatly: "Lindzen has been a paid consultant for major oil and coal interests. His 1991 trip to Washington to testify before Vice President Al Gore's committee was paid by Western Fuels. He addressed a meeting of OPEC delegates in Vienna in 1991 and an industry lobby group in New Zealand in 1995. Lindzen told me that he charges $2,500 a day to consult for fossil fuel interests." Some of Lindzen's backing, Gelbspan adds, was coming from a western mining company, Cyprus Minerals, which was at that time the largest single financial supporter of the rabidly anti-environmentalist Wise Use Movement. As publisher of *World Climate Report*, MIT's Pat Michaels took money from the same coal-industry donors who helped bankroll ICE. "By keeping the discussion focused on whether there really is a problem, these dozen or so dissidents — contradicting the consensus view held by 2,500 of the world's top climate scientists — have until now prevented discussion about how to address the problem," writes Gelbspan.

It seems incredible that a handful of academic contrarians and PR hustlers, backed by well-financed industrialists, could have a political effect that actually outweighed the combined opinion of thousands of the world's top scientists, but this is exactly what has happened. Of course, the scientists do not have the resources of gigantic political and commercial organizations behind them, and thus their opinions barely rise to the surface, or at least do so at the whim of an obstreperously indifferent media.

It was a very good thing, from the Carbon Club's point of view, that its cadres of mouthpieces and consultants were securely integrated into the media establishment to be available for slots as "experts" and representatives of something broadly referred to as "the interests of business," because the next wave of bad news about climate was coming in. On the eve of the United Nations 1992 Rio Summit, Oxford University reported that, in its scientists' view, contrary to statements in *The Greening of Planet Earth*, global warming would result in a decline of between 10 and 15 percent in grain yields in Africa, tropical Latin America, and much of Southeast Asia and India.

Within just fifty years, one in eight people could face irreversible famine. Another report released in April that year, this time by the World Health Organization, concluded that global warming would spread malaria far beyond areas where it currently thrives. Even a slight warming would result in insect-related crop losses, which would lead to a "significant disruption in the food supply."

Indeed, there was even a spasm of hopeful political activity in the American heartland of the oil beast. Democratic representative Henry Waxman devised the Global Climate Protection Act, and lined up an impressive bipartisan list of cosponsors in the House of Representatives. Waxman went so far as to complain that White House negotiators had jeopardized any hope of achieving an international agreement. Indeed, the George H. Bush administration had been doing everything it could to stall any action that might annoy its oil-money backers, and vigorously lobbied Congress not to support Waxman's bill, which was in due course defeated — although not before the Democratic front-runner, Bill Clinton, picked up the theme. "Our addiction to fossil fuels is wrapping the earth in a deadly shroud of greenhouse gases," he intoned. "Our air will be more dangerous because George Bush put [Vice President] Dan Quayle in charge of the Competitiveness Council, a group which lets major polluters in through the back door at the White House to kill environmental regulations they don't like." It seemed, for the first time, that there was a chance, at least, of a shift in the stubborn American position, which was to make sure anything *but* prompt action would occur.

At the last UN meeting in New York, prior to the Rio gathering, in a blatant attempt to derail the chances of a treaty going ahead, the U.S. State Department attempted to reword nothing less than the basic objectives of the proposed Framework Convention on Climate Change (FCCC). Instead of talking about stabilizing greenhouse-gas concentrations, as representatives from the European Community proposed, the U.S. delegates suggested governments should be talking about controlling the *rate of increase* in those concentrations. The attempted sidestep was obvious to everyone involved, and resulted in a string of denunciations from other countries, including even Japan. In the end, not even the Bush administration was willing to look like such a complete tool of the oil industry, at least not in front of the assembled world. And so, with just three weeks to go before the meeting in Rio, the FCCC was adopted. There were no commitments for reductions in emissions, but the convention at least established a process that would *require* governments to regularly review the progress of global-warming science and the impacts of climate change, and — somehow! — implement efforts to reduce greenhouse gases. This meant, in principle, the door was open to negotiate a protocol to the convention.

Thus, the world slouched towards Rio.

With ten thousand accredited media on the scene, the 1992 Earth Summit proved to be the largest media event in history, if nothing else. And it did, indeed, seem to offer a lot to report. By the end of the week, amidst bursts of self-congratulatory (even pious) hoopla, the Framework Convention on Climate Change was inked by the leaders of 154 countries, plus the European Union. What with the Dalai Lama climbing on board the Greenpeace flagship *Rainbow Warrior* in the harbor under the giant statue of Christ, it *did* seem like some mighty Rubicon was being crossed. Embodying the palpable sense that a breakthrough just might be coming, perhaps even the long-awaited paradigm shift, Senator Al Gore, journalist and author of the recently published *Earth in the Balance*, took the conference by storm, appearing everywhere. Gore did not hesitate to call climate change the number-one threat to the human future, eclipsing all the other threats that made up the planetary ecological crisis. Gore wanted to lead the charge to reorganize the human enterprise around a new principle, which would be the policy response to climate change. He actually proposed banning the internal-combustion engine within twenty-five years. A mood of revolution-in-waiting gripped the summit. The possibility of setting something tangible in motion hovered in the air.

Hovered. But that was about all.

As Tom Athanasiou wrote angrily in *Divided Planet: The Ecology of Rich and Poor:*

> No adequate response to the social-ecological crisis was ever on the agenda at Rio. . . . The Bush administration did lead the battle to contain the green agenda. It lobbied hard to strip the new climate treaty of emissions-reduction targets and target dates. . . . It was under Bush that "unprecedented and almost brutal" pressure was applied to force weaker countries to follow U.S. dictates. Bush was singled out for criticism at Rio because, choosing to play to his domestic anti-environmental constituency, he spoiled the mood.

And yet, the Bush administration was far from alone in having an anti-green agenda. Nearly every major nation played its part in trying to tie the Earth Summit up in knots. The British led the campaign to head off any serious European move towards carbon taxes, and was joined by poorer members of the European Community, plus, of course, the Organization of Petroleum Exporting Countries (OPEC). The EC proclaimed itself the world's leading bloc on the climate issue, and looked good compared to the Bush administration, but its emissions continued to rise.

"The Germans in particular came off as environmental good guys," Athanasiou writes. "Chancellor Kohl, the first Western head of state to agree to go to Rio, pledged a 25 to 30 percent reduction in Germany's carbon emissions by 2005, and for this he was celebrated around the world. Today it is clear that Germany will not meet this pledge, or even approach it, and this despite the carbon-abatement windfall it enjoyed with the collapse of the archaic factories of the former East Germany."

The Japanese came off even better, and were widely described in the press as "the first environmental superpower," a status Japan — a virtual environmental criminal state, especially in connection with whaling, tropical logging, mechanized fishing, and its role in the international plutonium trade — worked extremely hard to project. According to the *Financial Times*, "Japan approached Rio with a carefully planned diplomatic offensive, backed by the largest offer of new environmental aid made at the Summit" — some $500 million a year.

By the time the international consensus process had finished watering down the FCCC, it contained no timetables or binding commitments to reduce emissions. The way the deal was stick-handled through the labyrinth of conflicting interests, broke the nations down into different categories with different expectations. As the FCCC secretariat noted, developed countries "are responsible for over two-thirds of past emissions and 75 percent of current emissions." When the percentage of global CO_2 emissions produced by each country is measured against its percentage of the world population, an enormous disparity yawns. Emissions from the industrialized countries are between 4 and 5.5 times higher than our percentage of the total population. We are also, thanks to our wealth, better positioned to protect ourselves in the event of climate upheavals. Accordingly, the FCCC defined "developed countries" and countries with economies "in transition" as Annex I countries, which had now made oxymoronic "nonbinding commitments" to *try* (that was all!) to reduce their greenhouse-gas emissions to 1990 levels by the year 2000. Included as Annex I along with the alliance of Japan, the United States, Canada, Australia and New Zealand, and the

European Union, were the Russian Federation, Eastern Europe, and Scandinavia. The Annex II countries were concentrated in Africa, Asia, and South America. These included the two largest, India and China. The deal meant that Annex I countries promised to transfer funds and technology to Annex II countries to help them adapt to climate change. In signing the convention, the world's leaders were accepting, at least in theory, a principle of "differentiated responsibilities." The *realpolitik* of the situation was that the Annex II countries could not be asked to stop their march along the tried-and-true road of industrialization to politely watch while the tractor-trailer fleets of the developed world roared by along the highway, belching fumes.

Yet there was ultimately no incentive for the Annex I countries to clean up their act, only to see the developing nations replace them as the Great Satans of pollution. India's share of total emissions had climbed from 1 to 3 percent in the previous three decades, and China's emissions had jumped spectacularly from 2 to 11 percent, while the United States's relative contribution dropped from 45 to 22 percent. In Britain, where the spot on the planetary lung had first appeared, the share of global emissions shrank from 7 to 3 percent — a good sign that "healing" was possible. Yet, if China alone was to continue its headlong modernization, using coal and oil, all the gains made in the West would be wiped out within a couple of generations. The FCCC was asking the developed nations to "take the lead" in the fight against global warming. It also — and this was perhaps the core underlying principle — stated that "the Parties should take precautionary measures to anticipate, prevent or minimize the causes of climate change and mitigate its adverse effects. Where there are threats of serious or irreversible damage, lack of full scientific certainty should not be used as a reason for postponing such measures." This "precautionary principle" was to become both a rallying cry and a red herring in the political battles to come, as supporters of the treaty pushed for "responsible behavior" and opponents attempted to set the bar of scientific proof so high it could never be cleared.

The role of the South was in some ways no less sordid than the role of the Northern countries, which either openly protected their strategic interests or danced around the issue in such a way as to please domestic audiences, while avoiding any hard decisions. The Malaysian government, for instance, emerged as a leader of the South's opposition to the North's more obvious hypocritical initiatives, and yet Malaysia is a major culprit in the destruction of Southeast Asia's forests. And even though China wanted itself to be considered a "front-line" state in terms of its exposure to the risk of massive flooding by rising seas, it also made sure behind the scenes that no mention would be used in any of the treaties about ecological damage done by water channelization or dam construction — busy as the Chinese were with building the appallingly destructive Three Gorges Dam.

It was the Malaysian position that foreshadowed the disappointments to come, however. Malaysia is the base for rapacious logging companies that have gone from clear-cutting their home forests to competing with the Japanese and Thais for the rights to take down the remains of the forests of Cambodia and Papua New Guinea. According to then–prime minister Datuk Seri Mahathir Mohamad, any treaty that might attempt to protect the rainforests of the world would violate Malaysia's "national sovereignty." Furthermore, he asserted that the North "wants a say in management of our forests while we have no say on their carbon dioxide emissions." For a southern hemisphere politician this seemed like an altogether reasonable position to take, if it weren't for the fact that it was a cover for ongoing ecological pillage, and guaranteed a stalemate that might never be overcome.

At the end of it all, even serene Maurice Strong, the Canadian super-bureaucrat, UN fixer, and main organizer of the Summit, was left shaking his head. In his memoir, *Where on Earth Are We Going?*, he reflects:

> We had changed some minds at Rio, got some people, states and even alliances to shift ground, but we had, it appeared, failed to effect the fundamental change in political motivation that I know is called for — that I know the planet most critically demands. The doomsday clock is ticking toward a day of reckoning, if we fail to change our ways. The political will to stop it seems lacking. Late at night in the witching hours, or when I am weary, the questions intrude: Have we the collective political, moral and ethical will to do it? Do we have a chance? Someone asked me again recently: "Don't you ever get frustrated with this saving-the-world business?" Well, I said, the patient's still alive. In bad shape, yes, but still alive.

On the plus side, Jeremy Leggett recalls in *The Carbon War:*

> I took some solace in the manifest frustrations of [Carbon Club] lobbyists Pearlman, Schlaes, and company. They clearly thought they had lost important ground. But I knew that the toothless nature of the treaty meant that it could not provide the stimulus to instigate the fundamental changes needed in energy markets: the beginning of the end for the oil era, and the end of the beginning for the solar era. Legally binding targets and timetables for reducing emissions, no matter how small, would have had a chance of doing that. But not the convention as it stood.

Little as the summit had accomplished in terms of altering "fundamentals," there was at least a mechanism in place establishing follow-up steps, which included biannual negotiating sessions to see if the convention could somehow be given some teeth. This was called the Berlin Mandate. Falling under the auspices of the United Nations, it was an agreement to spend two years working on a protocol to establish binding — yes, this was the actual word used, "binding" — post-2000 targets and timetables for reducing emissions in the industrialized countries. The first such preliminary meeting to set up the Berlin session was held in New York in March 1993, and the American delegation, this time, was composed of appointees selected by the new team of Bill Clinton and ecostar Al Gore. Environmentalists licked their lips in nervous anticipation. If ever the moment had come for a serious push to reduce emissions, this was it.

The main instrument being considered, logically, was a carbon tax. At a single legislative stroke, the United States and other industrialized countries could lure people and industries away from oil and gas and into the embrace of renewable energy sources by upping taxes on fossil fuels and eliminating them for solar, wind, and other renewable forms of energy supply. It was the essence of simplicity. In the wake of Rio, most European countries had come around to accepting the idea, although there were foot-draggers, notably Britain. President Clinton had already made encouraging noises, saying: "The idea of a tax shift to discourage polluting is right in line with the principle of making polluters pay." It sounded good, but when Madeleine Albright, the new U.S. Permanent Representative at the UN, rose to speak to the massed diplomats, all she was authorized to promise on behalf of the new president and the ecostar was that America would "review all its options" to reduce greenhouse gases and report back later — scarcely a recognition of emergency. No timetables. No targets.

And this became the pattern. As the world leaders returned home, they found themselves caught in the undertow of national strategic interests. As the new battle lines formed, divisions appeared even between nations within the same Annexes. Among the Annex II countries, for instance, the Alliance of

Small Island States (AOSIS), fearing nothing less than a forced exodus, as their territories disappeared under the waves, pushed for strong and swift implementation of the precautionary principle. They were joined by Annex I countries like the Netherlands, which also fears the sea, and which soon found itself opposing the consortium of rich industrialized countries whose naked self-interest, masked in politically correct sustainable-development rhetoric, only became apparent as powerful internal oil lobbies in places like Texas, Alaska, and Alberta consolidated their grip on their national governments. They were also opposed, of course, by the OPEC countries, which feared the impact of reduced international demand for petroleum products on their one-note oil economies. Among the otherwise sane, cutting-edge greening Scandinavian countries, only oil-rich Norway sided with the petrotyrants and the Carbon Club boyos, who had formed up into an identifiable and predictable cabal known derisively among environmentalists as the "Juice Cans," meaning Japan, the U.S., Canada, Australia, and New Zealand.

The year 1994 saw Europe hit by a string of billion-dollar windstorms, a widespread visceral factor that found political expression in a push by the European nations to strengthen the Annex I commitments. Environmental groups were lobbying for fast action on emissions, as expected, but this time they were joined by an ally from the capitalist side, in the form of several major European insurance companies, alarmed by their mounting losses to weather-related disasters.

Indeed, the following year set new records. It was the hottest summer in 136 years. The hottest eight years on record had all occurred in the last decade. But for the insurance industry, what stood out was another set of records, in this case those documenting property-catastrophe losses. Total losses to insurers were $180 billion, and this would have been a record, even without the Kobe earthquake. One of the biggest insurers,

Munich Re, counted 577 natural catastrophes around the world, including flooding in northwest Europe that had forced a quarter of a million people from their homes in the Netherlands alone. On the other side of the Atlantic, American weather researchers logged nineteen cyclones; eleven of them attained hurricane status, which was the highest number in one season in well over a century.

By the fall some sixty, mostly European, insurance companies had signed a "statement of environmental commitment" that required them to make "every realistic effort" to incorporate environmental concerns into their business practices. The group issued a paper stating their belief that industrialization had already had a huge impact on climate, and that the projected human-caused changes would lead to more extreme weather, with serious consequences for insurers. The paper was strongly in favor of governments adopting the "precautionary principle," and insisting — strong language, indeed! — that negotiators pull together a treaty that would achieve "early, substantial reductions" in emissions.

For the first time, the "business community" was divided. Until then, the Carbon Club had been able to present itself as the united face of Big Business. Not so any longer. The global energy industry suddenly found itself on a different side of the ring from the global insurance industry. (North American insurers, it should be noted, did not sign on for fear that legal liability might result from signing the statement. European insurers were advised otherwise.)

In September, an early draft of the IPCC's second report was leaked on the Internet. It stated that the observed planet-wide warming "is unlikely to be entirely due to natural causes and that the pattern of climatic response to human activities is identifiable in the climatological record." Environmentalists and a handful of journalists were quick to identify this as a categorical scientific statement that the "fingerprint" had been found.

In just the way the discovery of the ozone hole had kicked the debate about CFCs up to a new level, the "discovery" that industrial processes were indeed heating the planet up should have triggered the loudest international alarm bells imaginable. Instead, when the second IPCC conference was held in Madrid, Spain, in December 1995, the wording of the draft came under fierce fire. This meeting, it should be noted, was the first in which the 150-plus scientist-delegates found themselves joined by new players. Two officials from their oil ministries, for instance, had replaced the scientists who formerly represented Saudi Arabia and Kuwait. These gentlemen, in turn, were observed to be working closely — indeed, accepting direction from — none other than the ubiquitous Don Pearlman of the Global Climate Coalition, with backup from Mobil Oil's Leonard Bernstein. At one point, the Saudi and Kuwaiti delegates stonewalled for eight hours, bringing proceedings to a complete halt, until they finally got their way.

By the time the final draft of the *Summary for Policymakers* was approved and published, the language had changed remarkably. Instead of saying "a pattern of climatic response to human activities *is identifiable*," the official version had been hammered down into what became the famous line that "the balance of evidence . . . *suggests* a discernible human influence." There is a huge difference, especially in the language of science, between something being identified and being suggested. It was ironic that the World Energy Council (WEC), representing energy companies and utilities in over a hundred countries, immediately attacked the IPCC report over even the *suggestion* of a discernible effect, complaining bitterly that the document had been "politically influenced." Indeed, it had been. But not in the direction of saying more than the science warranted. Rather, it had been influenced in the direction of saying *less*.

Jeremy Leggett, who was attending the meeting as a Greenpeace NGO, offers us an insight into the way in which science was beaten into shape to fit political needs. In *The Carbon War*, he writes:

> This watering-down was achieved entirely by the Carbon Club, the Saudis and the Kuwaitis, who knew the scientists would have to exercise compromise while at the same time racing against the clock. True, they did not achieve their complete objective, or anything like it. At one point [Mohamed] Al-Sabban, the [Saudi] oil ministry official, proposed to 100-plus of the world's best climate scientists the following: "Preliminary evidence which is subject to large uncertainty points toward a human influence." He did not get his way with this. But this was not the point. The point was to wear the scientists down with diplomatic gutter tactics, if possible to derail the meeting procedurally, but certainly to reduce the impact of the product. This, to a significant extent, they succeeded in doing. The final product was not 40 pages as it started, but a mere 11, with the rest as a technical appendix. Vital sections of text, and crucial diagrams of the kind that had been so important in the first IPCC scientific assessment, had been denied the official blessing of an IPCC plenary.

It is interesting to speculate what difference it might have made if the IPCC's original declaration had survived to the final draft. Faced with an identifiable anthropogenic effect, would legislators have found more courage? Would environmentalists have been able to muster more support? Would the Carbon Club's minions have lost some of their clout with the media? Would the academic contrarians have been forced to eat their own words? It certainly did not help that the watered-down phrase is the one that became the political baseline.

Still, by the time the Second Assessment was released in Rome, plenty of scary material remained in the scientific sections — if anyone cared to look. A mid-range estimate of a warming of about 2 degrees Celsius was predicted by the year 2100, with a high estimate of 3.5 degrees Celsius. The mid-range estimate for sea-level rise was fifty centimeters (19½ inches) by 2100, with a possible high of ninety-five centimeters (37 inches). In all sectors — agriculture, forestry, fisheries, water resources —"potentially serious changes have been identified." Specifically, "entire forest types may disappear . . . large amounts of carbon could be released into the atmosphere . . . desertification is more likely to become irreversible . . . between one-third and one-half of existing mountain glacier mass could disappear over the next hundred years . . ." etc.

It added: "When rapidly forced, non-linear systems (like climate) are especially subject to unexpected behavior. . . . Further unexpected, large and rapid climate system changes are by their nature difficult to predict. This implies that future climate changes may also involve 'surprises.'"

The new report went further than the first in offering possible policy responses. "Significant reductions in net greenhouse-gas emissions are technically possible and can be economically feasible using an array of technologies. . . . [E]arlier mitigation may increase flexibility in moving toward stabilization of atmospheric concentrations . . . significant 'no regrets' opportunities are available in most countries."

It was not entirely a coincidence, therefore, that when the Second Conference of Parties (COP) was convened in Geneva in July 1996, the position of the Council of European Union Environment Ministers had hardened into a specific historic stance. In their communiqué prior to the gathering, they declared: "Given the serious risk . . . and particularly the high rate of change, the Council believes that global average temperatures should not exceed 2 degrees above preindustrial level and that therefore concentration levels lower than 550 ppm CO_2 should guide global limitation and reduction efforts." This would allow a doubling of preindustrial levels, but it would still mean the reduction of global emissions to less than one-half the current level. To achieve a target like this, the ministers agreed, the process of reductions would have to start immediately. It wouldn't be enough, they said, merely to limit the growth of emissions.

In fact, the Dutch introduced a new analysis of how to go about avoiding "dangerous" levels of climate change. A maximum allowable threshold of 2 degrees Celsius was all that should be permitted, the Dutch argued. They called this the "safe-landing corridor" concept. It meant, in practical terms, that industrialized countries would have to cut emissions between 19 and 46 percent from 1990 levels, depending on the country, by 2010.

In *The Carbon War*, Leggett reports:

> Corporate America was also setting out its stall, but rather differently. On July 8th, the day on which a week-long pre-COP2 session began in Geneva, the White House received a "Dear Mr. President" letter signed by 119 chief executives and chairmen, including those of Amoco, ARCO, Chevron, Chrysler, Exxon, Ford, General Motors, Mobil, Occidental, Shell, Texaco and a host of coal companies. The only interesting absentee was BP. The bottom line cannot have been encouraging to anyone on Clinton's staff thinking of the U.S.A. making a bold move at Geneva. "The U.S. should not agree to any of the three proposed protocols presently on the negotiating table. Your leadership on this issue is critical to assuring a continuing strong U.S. economy."

This was a foreshadowing of the American posture to come. . . .

At the Geneva session's opening, the British secretary of state for environment, John Gummer, warned: "It's simply not good enough for major producers of fossil fuels, both oil and coal, to

claim that their financial interests should stand in the way of
progress in making significant reductions in greenhouse-gas
emissions. The alarm bells ought to be ringing in every capital
throughout the world." His blast was aimed mainly at Australia,
which had gone from being an early advocate of emissions
reductions to making an enormous fuss about how much its
economy depended on coal. Indeed, it was now the world's
number-one coal exporter, putting it firmly in the Juice Cans'
camp, along with Japan, the United States, Canada, and New
Zealand, the cabal of pro-petroleum-and-coal countries, which
had taken to coordinating their negotiation strategies openly.

The Canadian delegates were working so closely with the
Aussies to block any progress that there could no longer be any
doubt that Canada had decided to rebuild its climate-change
position entirely around the wants and needs of the oil-rich
province of Alberta — the promises of Rio notwithstanding. It
is likely that the Juice Cans would have succeeded had the
Americans not broken ranks. Instead of bowing to the domestic
business lobby, as the Canucks and Aussies had so obviously done,
the head of the U.S. delegation, Undersecretary of State Tim
Wirth, boldly denounced "the naysayers and special interests
bent on belittling, attacking and obfuscating climate-change
science. So let's take a false issue off the table: there can be no
question but that the findings meet the highest standards of
scientific integrity. The science calls us to take urgent action."
The United States, Wirth proclaimed, was ready to set legally
binding targets to reduce greenhouse-gas emissions. Not only
that, but the newly enlightened Americans were willing to let the
potentially divisive issue of joint implementation and involvement by developing countries be set aside until somewhere down
the road. The main thing was to get the process in motion.

This was astonishing! The American shift unleashed energies
that had been bottled up virtually since negotiations had begun.
In one spectacular late-night session, a draft ministerial declara-

tion was hammered out, instructing diplomats "to accelerate the negotiations on the text of a legally binding protocol" by the time of the next meeting, to be held in Kyoto. They actually used the words "quantified legally binding objectives for emissions limitations and significant overall reductions within specific time frames." Finally, some sign that the U.S. administration really had changed from the Bush era! Whereas, at every previous session, the American delegates had been on a very short, pro-business leash, for the first time the hand of Al Gore could be seen at work behind the scenes. While this was jubilantly welcomed by eco-hawks, the sullen Aussies turned their backs on the whole process, refusing to sign. But in their rush to satisfy their domestic coal industry, they had isolated themselves. Only New Zealand, acting like the regional lapdog that it was, went along with them — as did Russia and the usual gaggle of OPEC states.

The IPCC Second Assessment was overwhelmingly endorsed. A statement released by the negotiators at the end of the Geneva conference described it as "the most comprehensive and authoritative assessment of the science of climate change, its impacts and response options now available." Agreeing that the substance of the report called for "urgently strengthening action," the participants urged Annex I countries to lead the charge by cutting greenhouse emissions, starting in the year 2000. The final statement of the conference became known as the "Geneva Declaration." There were still no specifics about targets, but the evolutionary step from the nonbinding FCCC to the verge of a legally binding protocol had been taken, despite the advertising and lobbying efforts of the Carbon Club. The only black cloud on the horizon that day was the fact that, while the rhetoric had improved, a review of Annex I countries' CO_2 emissions revealed that most of them were rising steadily, not falling. The industrialized world, for the most part, had not only failed to live up to its promises of voluntary reductions, but the statistics were all heading for the ceiling. Canadian and American emissions were up 8 percent over 1990 levels and were projected to reach 13 percent by 2000. Most other developed countries were at about the same level. Japan's emissions had risen slightly more, although Britain and Germany, for different reasons, had come close to meeting their Rio targets. In the United Kingdom's case, the former Conservative government had privatized the power and coal industries, precipitating a shift from coal to cleaner fossil fuels like oil and natural gas, while Germany, of course, had benefited from the collapse of inefficient East German polluting industries. Those factors were one-time wonders, however, and both countries, along with their EU partners, were on track to exceed 1990 levels by 8 percent by 2000, not as bad as the North Americans, but not that much better.

Still, the political climate had improved marginally. Britain's newly minted prime minister, Tony Blair, was saying pointedly to the Juice Cans: "The biggest responsibility falls on those with the biggest emissions. We in Europe have put our cards on the table. It is time for the special pleading to stop and for others to follow suit." He added, just in case the point could possibly have been missed: "Our targets will not be taken seriously by the poorer countries until the rich countries are meeting them." But in Washington, facing an election, the Clinton administration was taking a pounding from outraged Republicans, echoing the line of the Carbon Club: "We deplore ceding U.S. sovereignty on environmental issues to international bureaucrats and our foreign economic competitors." A Republican Party statement also deplored "the arbitrary and premature abandonment of the previous policy of voluntary reductions in greenhouse-gas emissions." The fact that the policy had *not been working* did not deter the Republicans or their industry allies in the least.

For their part, the OPEC nations continued to peddle to the developing giants of India, China, Brazil, and Mexico the line that the "climate scare" was based on flawed science, and more perversely was basically a plot by the rich countries to keep them in relative poverty forever. Accept no restrictions that do not fall equally, or more heavily, upon the industrialized countries, OPEC argued. Anything else, of course, would be unfair to fossil-fuel producers. The OPEC strategy had the desired effect, which was to prevent any possible agreement between North and South.

As fate would have it, 1996 turned out to be the worst year for CO_2 emissions, with levels rising to 6.35 billion metric tons. It was also noteworthy for producing the biggest one-year leap — some 2.4 percent — since 1988.

By March 1997, when the Ad Hoc Group on the Berlin Mandate (AGBM), comprising all the governments involved in the negotiations, sat down to hammer out final positions before moving on to the crunch session in Kyoto, fifteen European Union environmental ministers met in Brussels and declared that henceforth they would adopt a Union-wide stance. They called for industrialized countries to agree to a flat-rate reduction of 15 percent in CO_2, methane, and nitrous oxide by 2010. They described this as the minimal first step toward limiting average global temperatures to 2 degrees Celsius above pre-industrial levels. Minimal indeed! The Alliance of Small Island States and environmentalists had been lobbying hard for action by 2005, but even the relatively ecohip European ministers saw that as politically impossible — the 2010 date, like everything else, was a compromise. Even then, the United States, Japan, and Australia immediately opposed the 15-percent figure. It was, to be sure, a "composite" number. Within the EU, big cuts would be made by some members, like Denmark and Germany, while others like Spain, Sweden, Ireland, Greece, and Portugal would be allowed increases of up to 40 percent. This scheme was to become known as the European "bubble" proposal. The Juice Cans replied that a differentiation of targets within the EU was "unacceptable."

The talks adjourned in chaos.

In the United States, the Carbon Club juggernaut rolled out three full-page ads in the *Washington Post*, disingenuously tossing around code words like "a balanced approach," while basically claiming that, if the likes of China and India didn't undertake immediate emissions-reduction targets, jobs and industries would be sucked out of America (and other developed countries). This was patent nonsense, since two-thirds of U.S. emissions come from the building and transportation sectors, which weren't going anywhere. As for the remaining sector, industry, the competitiveness issue applied only to a few energy-intensive activities, representing a few percentage points of manufacturing jobs and shipments. But that didn't matter. The thrust of the ads was that Clinton and Gore "must not rush to policy commitments until the environmental benefits and economic consequences of the treaty proposals have been thoroughly analyzed." Every industrialized country had its share of skeptical corporations, but in the United States, as Jeremy Leggett observed, "the scale of the collective denial was unique. There was something primitive, even frightening about it." It has to be noted that, at this vital stage, rather than fighting back against the Carbon Club's propaganda, the White House treaded water, leaving the field to the greenhouse deniers. In June that summer, when members of the G7 countries met in Denver, rather than making *any* specific commitments to reduction targets, President Clinton sat on the climate file. Worse, his officials insisted on excising urgent language about the need for a protocol from the gathering's final communiqué. Frustrated environmentalists started warning then and there that, if the administration weren't going "to stand up to special interests," green voters would abandon Al Gore, a warning that the Democrats failed utterly to heed.

Immediately after the dismal Denver meeting came "Rio Plus 5"—a special session of the UN General Assembly intended to assess progress since the Earth Summit five years before. The secretary-general of the UN, Kofi Annan, tried to set an urgent tone: "At stake this week is the capacity of the international system of states to act decisively in the global interest. Failure to act now could damage our planet irreversibly." Alas, not only were there few signs of decisiveness, just about everyone's emissions were up and on track to continue rising. From the start — in dispiriting contrast to the high hopes of 1992 — the conference was full of a litany of *mea culpa*s, admissions of failure, recrimination, and pessimism. Despite the fact that the Berlin Mandate required them to announce their negotiating positions for Kyoto, none of the developing countries had any binding targets or timetables in hand. Only the Europeans were ready on that score. The Juice Cans resisted the EU's efforts to pin them down, although President Clinton did promise a billion dollars to help developing countries reduce *their* gases, and even pledged to put solar panels on a million American rooftops by 2010.

The small island states begged for a 20-percent cut below 1990 levels by 2005, but without even the Europeans on board, there was no chance. The attitude of the industrialized countries seemed to be summed up in one cynical observer's phrase: "Too bad, Tuvalu." Tuvalu was a South Pacific archipelago that was at its highest point only five meters (sixteen feet) above sea level, and would be an early victim of any rise in sea level. The other divisive issue concerned — surprise! — funding. At Rio, developed countries had promised to increase their aid to developing countries by .33 percent of their own gross national product, which would have brought funding to a total of .7 percent. Instead, by 1997, aid had actually stumbled, dropping to about .27 percent. Razali Ismail, president of the General Assembly, sternly pronounced the achievements since Rio as "paltry," and warned that humanity was "teetering on the edge, living unsustainably and perpetuating inequity, and may soon pass the point of no return." In the end, all the conference managed to produce was a statement expressing concern that "overall trends for sustainable development are worse today than they were in 1992." About the best that could be said was that while there had been virtually no progress, at least no ground had actually been lost. The only thing that had come to pass was the failure to act that Kofi Annan had worried about.

Nevertheless, the Kyoto endgame had begun. Objections to the exemption of developing countries from the treaty's timetable mounted, especially in the United States, where automakers lined up beside consumer organizations and labor groups and conservative politicians. In early September, the new front organization for the various anti-treaty interest groups, the Global Climate Information Project, launched a $13 million television and print advertising campaign. The ads were blatant: the treaty would smash the American economy, allowing China and India to leapfrog ahead to some kind of vaguely defined world dominance, while gasoline and grocery prices soared at home. It was almost as though the economic consequences *had* been thoroughly analyzed — which, of course, was not the case. The ads were briefly pulled by CNN, after pressure from environmentalists, then rebroadcasted after more pressure from the ads' sponsors. J. R. Eaton, chairman of Chrysler Corporation, wrote an op-ed piece in the *Washington Post*, saying that the climate-change debate had become an economic, foreign aid, and trade issue "disguised as environmentalism." If developed countries were to stabilize their emissions while allowing up-and-coming economies to increase theirs, the result would be "a massive transfer of American wealth" that would not stop the melting of the ice caps but would "severely undermine" U.S. competitiveness. Climate negotiations were promoting a "punish-the-U.S.-first" agenda. Farm and labor groups were equally skeptical. The AFL-CIO weighed in with the view that exempting developing countries was a fundamental error. It would only give the multinationals an excuse to shift capital, jobs, *and* pollution to the Third World, while not achieving the goal of stabilizing emissions.

On Kiribati that year, two huge tidal surges rolled across Tarawa Atoll in January and February. They came without warning: unrelenting tides rising ever higher, all the more sinister for the lack of rain or storm as they swallowed up homes. Nobody on the atoll had seen such a thing before.

By the end of July, despite powerful opposition at home, there were signs that Clinton was ready to give the issue high priority. At a press conference at the White House, backed up by a phalanx of scientists, he declared: "There is ample evidence that human action is already disrupting the climate. We can see the train coming, but most ordinary Americans, in their day-to-day lives, can't hear the whistle blowing." He promised a "sustained effort" to win public support for action going into Kyoto. Alas, the U.S. Senate promptly voted an incredible ninety-five to zero to reject the Berlin Mandate. The administration was plainly told to avoid signing any agreement, at Kyoto or anywhere else, that did not entail emissions reductions by developing countries.

Against this sad background, the seventh session of post-Berlin negotiations was held in Bonn. A grim procession of delegates haggled and maneuvered, as usual, but the acrimony had spread. In addition to the North-South split, the Americans and Japanese were attacking the EU bubble. Carbon Club lobbyist Don Pearlman was quoted in the nongovernmental organization (NGO) newspaper *Eco* as telling a Nigerian delegate: "We can kill this thing." It was during the Bonn session that the Americans, backed by Japan, started pushing the ideas of emissions trading and joint implementation. (Trading emissions would allow those who cut more than their target to sell unused quotas to somebody who wasn't meeting theirs. Joint implementation means that a country investing in emissions-reduction programs overseas would be able to claim credits at home.) This wasn't rejected out of hand. The EU gave a cautious nod of approval, providing the overall target in the protocol was "adequate." Brazil, surprisingly, conceded that developing countries might have to commit to some emission targets, after all. But the other developing nations were unwilling to give away their exemptions. The hard position of the South collided with the U.S. Senate's tough demands, and whatever rabbit the White House or anybody else had planned to pull out of the hat, no "meaningful" breakthroughs occurred. The results were a complete deadlock.

Thus the world slouched, growling, toward Kyoto.

CLIFFHANGER AT KYOTO

I WAS AMONG THE HORDE OF reporters who arrived in the ancient Japanese capital in December 1997, hoping to witness some sort of a deal to save the world.

From the outside, Kyoto's futuristic International Conference Center had the look of a starship that had retained its metallic gleam even though a small forest of cherry trees had grown up around the hull. It had landed among the little hills and lakes in the northern sector of the city only a few miles from the world's oldest Zen Buddhist monastery. Inside the center, there was little doubt that the architects were offering a homage to *Star Trek*'s set designers. As for the script, well, there were as many scripts as there were reporters, activists, politicians, bureaucrats, lobbyists, sheiks, and executives. The media contingent numbered 3,500. There were 1,500 government delegates, and 3,000 representatives of nongovernmental organizations — meaning the warriors on both sides of the carbon war. Since the main hall had only 400 seats, giant TV screens had been mounted all over the place, bringing to mind another, more disturbing, science-fiction scenario: Orwell's *1984*. The flickering screen loomed over the huge media holding compound, with its rows of tables littered with computers and camera gear. Every single member of the media — the reporters, camera-people, techies, and producers — had a cellphone, and so did most of the observers, which ensured a background cacophony of chimes, buzzes, and beeps.

There was more than a hint of apocalypse in the air. Outside, the "unusually warm" late autumn had extended into what would normally have been early winter. Ice sculptures set up outside the center's main entrance pod, where everyone was X-rayed and screened before gaining entry, were melting in full view of the cameras. A no less conservative personage than Japan's own former director-general of the Japanese Environment Agency, Saburo Kato, warned arriving delegates and media: "It seems clear that environmental problems have the potential to irreversibly destroy the conditions necessary to support not only human life but all life on earth in the twenty-first century." The headline writers and field producers had something to work with right off the top.

It was along the fringes of the media area that the propaganda battles were being waged. Inside the Conference Center, behind sealed doors, in the relative calm of a diplomatic setting, the delegates were nearly evenly split between those in favor of action and those who perceived their interests to lie in the CO_2 status quo. But a survey of the booths and tables and kiosks set up at strategic locations where delegates and media would pass revealed that, on the lobbying side, the petroleum lobbyists outnumbered the ecofreaks by a wide margin. The Global Climate Coalition, representing such corporate worthies as the U.S. National Coal Association, the American Automobile Manufacturers Association, and the American Petroleum Institute, had fielded sixty-three elite arm-twisters. Don Pearlman, the *éminence grise* of the Carbon Club hit men, led his usual merry band from the Climate Council, who were still unrepentantly flogging their video, *The Greening of Planet Earth*. The International Chamber of Commerce had dispatched over a hundred foot soldiers, headed by Clem Mallin, chief flack for Texaco; they had instructions to do everything they could to wreck any chances of a protocol being achieved. The World Wildlife Fund and Friends of the Earth had smaller teams, by far. Only Greenpeace could muster a sizable international contingent of forty-five, who fanned out each morning to tap their various countries' delegates on the shoulders and try to drum some sense into them, or else meet in back rooms to strategize with voting members from island nations. A weird nightly ritual developed, wherein a hundred or so industry representatives would be ushered into a cavernous room and briefed by members of the negotiating team. Then they'd be led out, and the smaller contingent of environmental NGOs would be escorted in and given the same briefing. Armed with identical nuggets of information, the antagonists would sweep towards the media bearing strikingly different sound bites. The United Mine Workers, for instance, said: "We think our government negotiators need to be prepared to walk away from Kyoto without a treaty in hand." On the other hand the Natural Resources Defense Council said: "The U.S. must not evade its own responsibilities by making unrealistic demands of poor countries."

The real action, however, was to be observed in the luxurious space-station–like lounge, where delegates, journalists, and lobbyists sought relief from the frustrations of a ten-day sentence to the mother of all negotiation hells. It was here that Don Pearlman would casually stroll into the circle of Arab princes and potentates who were holding court through the afternoons and evenings, exchanging nods, smiles, and whispers. In a nonstop procession, delegates from one country after another made their way obsequiously into the inner Arab circle, mainly, it seemed, to bow, nod a lot, and then leave, looking precisely like minions receiving their orders. The circle, it should be noted, was exclusively a male preserve until Lois Corbett, a long-time environmental activist and member of the Canadian delegation, pushed her way past the outer perimeter of goons and plunked herself in an empty chair in the midst of the men with the large rings and dazzling gold jewelry. This caused considerable dismay, but what could they do in a foreign democracy where women have the vote? The discussion, although somewhat strained, went fairly well, until one of the senior Arabs patronizingly told her that the price of oil had to be kept low so that "poor people in my country can drive to work." When Ms. Corbett suggested that perhaps a "redistribution of wealth" might be a more appropriate solution, she was promptly escorted from the circle.

Most of the Carbon Club lobbyists' work had been done, of course, before the conference began. They had succeeded, in part through a $13-million U.S.-wide advertising blitz, with not-so-subtle xenophobic undertones, in derailing the momentum so laboriously built up since Rio. They'd done this in two ways. First, by claiming that emission reductions would ruin the economy, throwing workers out on the street by the millions. Television viewers had been warned that the price of gasoline would shoot up by fifty cents or more, heating and electricity bills would soar, and — in a preview of what would become the rallying cry of the George W. Bush administration — the "American lifestyle itself" would be endangered. Secondly, the Carbon Club strategists fished out the issue of equity, which had been basically deep-sixed at Rio as a way of allowing negotiations to progress. The idea of Kyoto had been for developed countries to make a "good-faith showing" that they were serious about keeping the promises *they'd* made, and this would pave the way, morally and politically, for the developing countries to start getting serious about tamping down their own emissions. The agreement in Berlin specifically set aside the question of participation by developing countries until *after* Kyoto. But industry pressure had succeeded in stirring up an American hue and cry against letting China and India, in particular, off the hook. Even Al Gore was forced to glower that the

United States was "perfectly prepared to walk away from an agreement that we don't think will work."

The success of the industry offensive was evident in the disingenuousness of the American position, as laid out on the first day of the conference by Melinda Kimble, an acting assistant secretary of state left over from the disastrous era of Bush senior, the Clinton administration not having gotten around to making its own appointment. Kimble insisted all six greenhouse gases, plus sinks, be included in the Protocol, along with trading and joint implementation for credit. The United States was aiming for a decrease in emissions of roughly 30 percent below the "expected" levels for 2010. Alas, none of this amounted to real emission reductions. The Americans were playing a numbers game, talking about reductions in Department of Energy *projections* of emission increases based on the assumption of an absence of a protocol. Among the loopholes this left wide open was the possibility that American emissions might actually have risen more than was projected, thanks to slick trading of credits and the offsetting of emissions against reforestation projects. For a moment, it seemed that the Americans might be willing to consider differentiation of country targets, but this openness soon disappeared. In pre-meeting press conferences, U.S. negotiators had promised "flexibility," but as the ambassador for Luxembourg, Pierre Gramegna, speaking as president of the European Union, said immediately after Ms. Kimble's speech, the flexibility was heading in the wrong direction. "We get the impression that the game is to find ever more loopholes in these negotiations, and that is a bad omen. We need credible targets." Credibility of any kind, however, was in short supply.

Nowhere was this more the case than with the Canadian delegation, representing just .5 percent of the world's population, yet responsible for 2.1 percent of humanity's CO_2 emissions. Out of 169 countries attending the conference, only the Americans had sent a larger delegation. There were at least sixty and probably eighty Canuck delegates. (When pressed, government spokes-persons were skittish about the exact number.) Rather than making me proud that my government cared so much about the issue, I, for one, was left with the suspicion that Kyoto was a choice travel destination. Spouses were in full attendance.

It was not to be a moment of True North ecoglory. The *realpolitik* of the Canadian government's subservience to the Carbon Club's Alberta Oil Patch branch was finally to be flushed into the open on the world stage. Until then, Canada had been dragging its heels and fudging behind the scenes, but it was still basking in the public image of one of the good-guy nations that had signed on the dotted line at Rio, on both diversity and climate change. This had been the work of Brian Mulroney, the same former prime minister on whose watch the Montreal Protocol had been inked. It was ironic indeed that Mulroney was so thor-oughly loathed by environmentalists in Canada, mainly because of the North American Free Trade Agreement; by the eve of Kyoto, the dithering over greenhouse-gas controls by his Liberal successor was making the old Yankee-loving Conservative arch-fiend look like a pillar of greenness.

Prime Minister Jean Chrétien had not given any sign that he had ever *heard* of climate change until, suddenly, in November 1997, a month before Kyoto, during a junket through Europe, he finally had some sense knocked into him during private ses-sions with German chancellor Helmut Kohl and Britain's new leader, Tony Blair, both of whom were pushing for some kind of "no regrets" action — in other words, let's do something just in case the danger is real — to reduce emissions. Back in the House of Commons in Ottawa, Chrétien blurted out a new policy: henceforth Canada would seek to do *more* than whatever it was the Americans were going to do. (It was as though some sort of competition for Europe's affection was going on, as opposed to a penultimate issue of state!) Nobody could possibly know what this meant, but Chrétien swore it meant a "serious commitment" would be made at Kyoto. As clarified later, this amounted to Canada standing nobly ready (aye ready!) to start cutting emissions as early as 2015 — *eighteen years in the future!* Since someone else would be in charge by then, the problem had nicely been shelved. An eighteen-year delay might as well be a thousand years in politics, as cunning old Chrétien, a survivor, knew better than just about anybody. Carbon tax? *Excuse-moi?* End subsidies for oil and gas development? *Pardon?*

The Canadian position, overall, was a mirror of the American position. Canada and the United States were particularly tight in support of an emissions-trading mechanism, which would allow both countries to meet 50 percent of their targets by buying emissions rights elsewhere. Likewise, they were both insistent on joint implementation, meaning that everybody would have to take a step forward at the same time. Of course, the bloc of developing countries calling themselves the G77 and China would have none of this. The Tanzanian G77 chair, Mark Mwandosya, said categorically: no. "We need to see leadership from [developed countries] who have been historically responsible for the majority of emissions." So far, all the developed countries had to offer was their failure to live up to the pledges they had made in Rio, let alone take a single step forward. Their promises had turned literally into hot air, with nearly every Western industrialized nation's emissions having gone *up* in the meantime. The exceptions were the former Soviet-sphere countries, where the decaying infrastructure had largely been allowed to collapse, and the newly united German state, which could now subtract East Germany's decrease in emissions from its own total. Indeed, the Annex I countries could point to an overall reduction of 4.6 percent from 1990 levels precisely because of the Eastern European economic debacle. If anything seemed apparent in all the murky intrigue, it was that the Juice Cans were positioning themselves for something like a 3-percent cut, which — given the East European depression — would actually permit Annex I countries' totals to *rise*, while still remaining technically within the scope of a treaty. No moral high ground there. No leadership. Only a search for loopholes.

Within days, the momentum — such as it was — had stalled. Led by the European Union, many developing countries were asking for reductions of 15 percent or more below 1990 levels by the year 2010, but the Americans were dug in around the idea of stabilization at 1990 levels, period. Under plenty of pressure from its own industrial sector, Japan's boldest vision amounted to a willingness to consider a 5-percent reduction, providing it could be phased in over the next twelve years. The Canadians had muddled themselves into agreeing, more or less, that they might go as far as a 3-percent cut. The Arabs and the Aussies were fighting a fierce rearguard action against the very *idea* of binding targets. Depending on economic circumstances, some countries wanted to set different emission targets than others. Some demanded a one-size-fits-all approach. The Europeans didn't like the notion of different targets, but wanted to apply the rather similar concept of a "bubble," which would represent the averaged-out emissions among its members. This was viewed by those outside Europe as pure sleaze. There was even a bitter debate over whether to include only the three main greenhouse gases (CO_2, methane, nitrous oxide) or add other gases, which, while small in quantity, were major "magnifiers" of the warming effect. Also, *if*, God forbid, actual targets should be set, how would they be monitored, and what kind of sanctions would be involved?

There was a certain air of unreality to reports of the debates among the delegates. It was as though most of the players were *trying* to lose. While there seemed to be moments when the political will to act was almost palpable, as when Britain's environment minister, Michael Meacher, upped the ante by urging a *20-percent* reduction below 1990 levels, he somewhat negated any chance of being inspired by acknowledging in the same speech that the most advanced computer models were now projecting that emissions would have to be cut by *at least* 70 percent — up 10 percent from earlier estimates — in order to offset the warming.

There was, however, some pressure on the Americans from behind. The *New York Times* ran the results of a poll that showed 65 percent of Americans wanted to do something about global warming, regardless of whether anyone else did or not. The margin of error in the poll was just 3 percent. "The American people are far more willing than their government to take early, unilateral steps" to reduce emissions, the *Times* noted. Americans were also "unimpressed," it turned out, by coal- and oil-industry arguments that reductions would lead to economic ruin — an encouraging sign that even $13 million in advertising wasn't enough to manufacture sufficient consent in the United States any longer. The paper also ran a "Medical Warning" signed by four hundred doctors from thirty countries, calling for immediate action. More amazingly, an ad appeared in the *Wall Street Journal* on the second day of the conference, signed by sixty business leaders, calling for the Clinton administration to "provide incentives to act quickly." The Carbon Club could definitely no longer claim to speak for the "business community" as a whole, no matter what the Chamber of Commerce said.

Late on the third day, there was a buzz through the entire convention: *something might be happening!* Mysteriously picking up on the vibe, the media throng had expanded to about six thousand journalists, a critical mass. With proceedings moving at a slower-than-glacial pace behind closed doors, and one cluster of newshounds or another always on a deadline, the scene teetered on the edge of some kind of meltdown. Stressed reporters and floor directors jabbered into cellphones, fending off distant editors and producers. It was always *The Evening News* or *The Late* or *The Early Edition, The Night Show, The Noon Show,* or *The Morning Show* in some time zone or another.

Desperate to justify their exorbitant expense reports (a more expensive place than Kyoto could scarcely have been found), reporters were reduced to actually interviewing the ecofreaks and industry lobbyists. So hungry were they for real news that, when one poor, distracted female delegate blundered by mistake into the media holding-tank, she was swarmed. The giant TV screens came alive with raw footage of the chaos around her as she made a sweep of the entire area, surrounded by a herd of reporters with cameras and huge fuzzy boom mikes poking above their heads, lights blinding her, questions being shouted in a dozen languages. As it turned out, she was looking for the ladies' room.

Behind the scenes, the frustration levels were certainly no less intense. Some delegates had already begun drafting a statement to cover their tracks in the event of a complete failure. The cumulative fog of hypocrisy had become almost impenetrable. After listening to the Americans lecturing China, Brazil, India, and Mexico about the need for *them* to start cutting emissions immediately, one observer commented icily: "A nation of sports utility vehicles lecturing nations of bicycles?" The problem of just how and when the developing countries were to be brought on board was a critical issue, certainly. But to insist that the bicycle riders start cutting their emissions at the same time as the SUV operators was patently unfair — indeed, it was exactly the kind of unfairness the developing and underdeveloped "South" had come to expect from the overdeveloped "North." If anybody wanted to throw a monkey wrench in the works, this was the most effective way to do it.

Clearly, the tactic of the Juice Cans was to sabotage the proceedings by aggravating the North–South split. In the background, the invisible guiding hand of the Carbon Club could be glimpsed at work, as when New Zealand suddenly demanded that the developing countries agree to freeze any increase in emissions after 2015, something that would shunt the G77 countries off onto dead-end developmental tracks, slamming the door on further industrialization. This was something that might have been fervently hoped for by Deep Greens, but it was as politically unspeakable as the idea of messing with the Sacred American Lifestyle. Just whose ends were being served became apparent when the U.S. delegation let it be known that the Kiwi proposal had "conditional" American support. What this guaranteed was that the developing countries would be in a large huff. The North-South rift would widen. The negotiations would grind deeper into deadlock. And it wasn't just a geopolitical accident that things were working out this way. It was all quite deliberately orchestrated, as Jeremy Leggett recounts in *The Carbon War:*

> Ten minutes before New Zealand made this intervention, which was of course was bound to inflame many of the developing countries, Don Pearlman was overheard by an environmental NGO asking a delegate whether "the bomb had dropped yet."
>
> Could his influence even extend to stooges in countries like New Zealand? Who could know? Pearlman was constantly to be seen hovering outside the closed sessions of the negotiations, cigarette in hand. He conducted earnest conversations with many diplomats, some of whom clearly came out to brief him — or receive instructions — and who then went straight back in again. Without observing the secretive man around the clock, it was impossible to work out whom he might be working with, apart from the obvious players in the Saudi and Kuwaiti delegations.

I remember having Pearlman pointed out to me in one of the vast, tubular hallways linking the conference hall and the press arena. There he was, a kind of near-mythic Bad Guy in the eyes of the world ecocommunity, more powerful than entire coalitions of small nations, and certainly more able to influence and manipulate events than any number of elected prime ministers or presidents. Such was the power of Western petro-money coupled with Middle Eastern despotism. As far as we were concerned, if ever there was a man working for the Dark Side, here he was, suntanned, white-haired, impeccably pin-striped, with a tie that was too tight, and polished shoes, chain-smoking, brash-yet-furtive. He looked *exactly* as I would have expected an upscale corporate backroom fixer to look, not like the grand architect of a multimillion-dollar antienvironmental, antibiospheric, ecocidal gameplan. I thought of the thousands of scientists whose meticulous feats of measurement and calculation had led to the mighty compilations of the IPCC reports, with their terrible warning for our species, and it seemed even *more* terrifying that a single political operative, backed up by a trillion-dollar-a-year industrial alliance, could monkeywrench humanity's best hope for avoiding a global ecodisaster.

An awful thing to say, but that was precisely what was going on.

The *New York Times* muttered that a "near-miracle" was required for the meeting to produce anything useful, and by the fifth day, there was a widespread feeling that the talks were on the verge of collapse. The word, however, was that Al Gore would be riding to the rescue. In retrospect, this moment seems almost quaint. Even hardened campaign veterans like myself felt a rush of excitement. I had just emerged from the subway and was starting to walk across the park to the conference hall when the heavy *thud-thud-thudding* of a massive presidential chopper flanked by three military choppers broke over the scene. One had to admit they sure knew how to stage an entrance. Ta-rah! Ta-rah! The vice president of the United States of America had arrived in cacophonous *Apocalypse Now* style. So maybe there was a game plan, after all. If ever the world needed saving, it was now. If ever there was a moment when it *could* be saved, this was it. And, amazingly, onto this monumental stage came riding a man who had written *the* book on ecology, now arguably the second most powerful man in the world, and if anybody could do the saving, it was him. The script seemed almost too incredible. *Who writes this stuff?* I wondered, not for the first or last time. Try as I might, I couldn't entirely resist the tempting thought of a Hollywood ending. Then we could all go home and live happily ever after. Like I say, quaint. Yet so compelling.

Greenpeace had erected a two-meter-high "Carbonosaurus," made of mashed-together car parts and fuel drums, in the parking lot outside the center, had set up a solar-powered kitchen to distribute free renewable-energy-heated coffee and tea, and had beamed laser messages onto downtown skyscraper walls.

There had been a feeling of "having the bastards surrounded" for a few days, but it was abundantly clear that, while the conference could be placed under siege, it couldn't be taken from outside. The battle was within the walls, and here, surprisingly, the eco-troops were making some headway — at least on the PR front. The first week of the gathering had provided enough time and material for the ensconced media army to get the basic picture of what was going on behind the scenes. And, just in case anybody missed it, Friends of the Earth set up a balloting process to determine the winner of the Scorched Earth Award among the companies and front organizations actively lobbying against a treaty, eventually conferring the distinction upon the Global Climate Coalition. At one press conference after another, eco-spokespersons denounced the industry lobbyists for "obstructionist roles," and for "unabashedly playing games" with science. Accustomed to working with smooth dignity behind the scenes along the corridors of power, it was obvious many of the professional lobbyists were unhappy with being flushed into the open, made part of the story, with hippies, for God's sake, baying at their heels. Who let the riffraff in here, anyway?

When Vice President Gore's face appeared on the giant TV screens and he began talking, he was watched by the thousands of journalists, lobbyists, and planet-savers like a man on a high wire, and it had to be admitted he was smooth and forceful. What he was saying *seemed* to cut through the diplomatic fog. On President Clinton's order, he had instructed the U.S. delegation "to show increased negotiating flexibility" in the hope that "a comprehensive plan can be put in place, with realistic targets and timetables, market mechanisms and the meaningful participation of key developing countries." He managed to express himself in such a way that it was hard not to be convinced that he was sincere, yet the content of his little speech was less than revolutionary. The American bottom line was still that developing countries needed to accept emissions trading in order to help the developed countries do the right thing.

In a significant juxtaposition, the man who had introduced Gore was the leader of the small island state of Nauru, an elderly gentleman named Kinza Clodumar, whom nobody had heard of before. His soft but passionate words were the ones that got played over and over again on the giant screens and, I gathered, on the networks themselves, partially because they contrasted so dramatically with Gore's technocratic exhortation. After poignantly describing how most of his country's interior had been destroyed by colonial mining interests, Clodumar had paused, composed himself, and said:

> My people have been confined to the narrow coastal fringe that separates this wasteland from our mother the sea. The coastal fringe where my people live is but two meters above the sea surface. We are trapped, a wasteland at our back, and at our front, a terrifying, rising flood of biblical proportions. *We submit respectfully that the willful destruction of entire countries and cultures, with foreknowledge, would represent an unspeakable crime against humanity. No nation has the right to place its own misconstrued national interest before the physical and cultural survival of whole countries* [my italics].

Unless, of course — I could not help but think — it is a very big nation with lots of helicopters and SUVs and nobody else with enough power to tell it otherwise.

Despite my cynicism, however, Gore left me with a flicker of hope.

The final night of the Kyoto conference, December 10–11, was endless. The media arena looked like a refugee camp. I managed to get on CNN by falling asleep on top of the World Wildlife Fund's larger-than-life-size stuffed panda. Industry lobbyists and ecofreaks alike were slumped at their desks, and in some cases on the floor under tables, having exhausted themselves cajoling, pushing, pestering, goading, and poking delegates, until now it had all come down to the wire. Among the greens, there was a feeling of dazed amazement that the talks actually had not collapsed. In the industry encampments, the mood was much the same, but for the opposite reason. For a deal to still be a possibility, after all the money they'd spent, all the political arm-twisting they'd done, was a disaster in itself. A last-minute press release had gone out from the Global Climate Coalition, saying: "This is a terrible deal. The United States should not walk away. It should run." But a sea change in media consciousness, at least, had occurred, because when Greenpeace, the World Wildlife Fund, and Friends of the Earth called an early-evening press conference, the room was jammed to the walls with reporters, while cameramen climbed on tables to get their shots. Across the empty media arena, only a handful of financial-page stiffs bothered to ask the industry lobbyists what *they* were thinking. "The next few hours are the most important in the history of this planet," said one greenie spokeswoman. And no one laughed.

What a thought! As the hours crawled by with no word from behind the sealed doors of the main hall, rumors spread like sparks from an almost-burned-out campfire that this country or that was about to walk out, and the whole deal was finished. The only two people left outside the hall who had any real idea of what was happening were Don Pearlman, the arch-fixer, and Bill Hare, the policy director for Greenpeace, whose agents among the delegates were probably more numerous than Pearlman's, but as a rule far less influential. Both men hovered outside the doors, whispering urgently to their operatives as they came and went. For what it was worth, Pearlman's body language had become furtive and edgy, while Hare, sensing the chance of victory, was in constant, straining motion.

The final do-or-die meeting had been scheduled to start at 1 p.m., but the deadline came and went. A notice appeared, stating it had been rescheduled for 6 p.m. to give delegates more time to cut some kind of deal. An inner circle of eleven countries, representing all the blocs — the United States, Japan, the United Kingdom, the Netherlands, Luxembourg, India, China, Brazil, Samoa, Tanzania, and Colombia — had got together in a hotel downtown for a last-ditch secret arm-wrestling session. By the time the conference of the whole was finally called to order at half past six, gossip had it that the G77 bloc itself was being torn apart, with India and China holding out against the others over a compromise on emissions trading and joint implementation. The sense of gloom deepened when ambassador Paul Estrada, the conference chair, announced that the final draft text would not be available until 11 p.m., so there was no point in even starting until then. "If we can reach agreement," he said hopefully, "this day will be remembered as The Day of the Atmosphere." If not, of course, it would be remembered as The Night They Drove the Atmosphere Down.

By this time, everyone was virtually sleepwalking. The giant video screens had gone blank. Even the buzz of cellphones seemed to have ebbed to an unprecedented lull. It was strange, I mused, but in all the science-fiction stories I had read about the End of the Earth, none had conjured an image such as this: a desperate, last-chance meeting of all the nations in the world in which they *failed* to agree on a draft treaty to save the planet. Surely, it couldn't end like this! With all these resources at our disposal — supercomputers, satellites, incredibly sensitive instruments, fantastic data, an instantaneous global communications system, more scientists than ever existed in all of history, diplomatic skills acquired over millennia, a planetary political network, plus the space-age technology to bring all these people and information together — how could we possibly blow it? Yet we were on a knife-edge.

Of all the speeches and lectures I had heard in the previous nine days, the words that stood out the clearest were those of Dr. Robert Watson, now the chief IPCC spokesman, who told me in an interview: "Even if the tiny compromise steps that were being proposed here at this possibly most historic of all moments were to be adopted, they were probably doomed to be seen in retrospect as having been far too little, far too late." On the other hand, this *could* be the beginning of the great turnaround. This *could* be the moment when humanity came collectively to its senses and applied the brakes. We would begin to skid, for sure, but at least we'd have a fighting chance of not going over the cliff. There was very little talk as we waited. This might very well be the moment when we humans proved ourselves to be dysfunctional as a species in the face of disaster. After all those thousands, hundreds of thousands, if not millions of years of fighting each other's clans and tribes, maybe we just did not have the right instincts for the kind of supratribal action that the emergency called for.

As the hours wore on, like most of the remaining journalists slumped in chairs in front of the blank TVs, I drifted into an extremely detached state. It was an excellent technique for avoiding giving in to emotions. Not far beneath the cool, objective surface, my feelings were in turmoil. I felt flashes of rage and dizzying plunges into despair. Why should it have to be so hard? Agreeing to limit emissions into a finite atmosphere should be a no-brainer. But I could see how an evolution spent learning how to successfully compete against its own kind would leave a species at a distinct disadvantage in the face of a threat to *all*. There might not be an "all" to respond appropriately. Thus, divided, we would fall to the one enemy bigger than any of us — the human collectivity. It was *this* we were up against, it seemed. This was about the most crushing thought I had ever had. And then there were other moments when I saw through this as delusional, defeatist thinking. Stay real! This was about strategic interests, corruption, propaganda, power, and petro-wealth. There was nothing deterministic about it at all. Politically, it was the Great Game of our time. And while it would take a Solzhenitsyn to begin to track the subplots at play, one did not have to struggle too hard to see the main outline of the story, an age-old tale repeating itself on a colossal scale: powerful vested interests trying everything they can to prevent a revolution. And now they were within a hair's-breadth of succeeding.

It was 1 a.m. before the final session began. There were now just seven hours left before the UN's team of utterly exhausted translators were all scheduled to leave Kyoto. Their flights could *not* be rescheduled. Come morning, if a deal wasn't reached, the Convention Center would dissolve into a Tower of Babel, and any hope of agreement would be lost — maybe for good. Nothing quickened the adrenaline like the realization that we now had a deadline. And it was closing fast.

There were twenty-eight articles and two annexes to be ratified. Chairman Estrada ran through them as fast as he could, banging his gavel resolutely, getting as far as the issue of emissions trading before China brought everything to a standstill by objecting to "new language," meaning any change in wording. India objected too. Saudi Arabia jumped to their side. Then the split went the other way. Brazil and Russia were in favor of trading. Others weren't. The first hour disappeared. Delegates inside the hall reported later that the crunch came when U.S. undersecretary Eizenstat rose to state, "This discussion is the most important in the history of the global climate-change issue." He noted that the American position had moved from being in favor of a freeze by 2010 to "very deep cuts," but that "innovative options" were needed in order for it to be possible to meet the targets — a trading mechanism being the key. Canada and Japan were on board immediately with that, and there things might have stalled, except that the delegate from Samoa stood up slowly, on behalf of the Association of Small Island States, and spoke in favor of the Juice Cans' position. *Anything*, the AOSIS had decided, to get a deal. Still, China balked. Compromise language deferring rule-making and guidelines until later was deemed unacceptable, and India stood firmly beside its sometimes arch-enemy, China, on this issue, namely their fundamental right to pursue the industrialized developmental path as long as they wanted.

With 4 a.m. approaching, Chairman Estrada called for a five-minute recess that turned into half an hour of backroom haranguing. As the minutes ticked by, I could see the faces of the greens hardening to control their despair. At the twenty-five-minute point, I couldn't take it any longer and got up to pace around in a nearby empty cubicle, and thus I missed the moment when Estrada returned to the podium with a final compromise. Trading would be *included* in the protocol, but it would be subject to a fresh article with special diplomatic powers to be detailed *later*. When his gavel came down, most of the delegates applauded, and I could hear the ecofreaks cheering. A few minutes later, an obviously pumped Estrada brushed aside a Kuwaiti stalling tactic, and declared the trading article passed.

As though a dam had been broken, floods of articles were now passed. The triumphant beat of Estrada's gavel soon had my own heart pounding. The digital clocks were closing on 5:00, but the man had his shoulder to the protocol, and was shoving it through. He got as far as Article 9, which set out the terms for involvement by developing countries, before Saudi Arabia stepped in to ask for its deletion, with China and India in agreement that it had to go. The Americans, Russians, and island states rose to denounce the deletion. By then, it was 6:00. There was no chance of consensus. Estrada's shoulders sagged. "We will delete this article," he rasped, fully expecting these to be the final words of the conference. If ever the U.S. were going to walk, it would be now, when China and India could be blamed for the failure.

Everyone held his or her breath.

It was as though an invisible hand had reached down. And, of course, one had: Al Gore's. The VP's order for flexibility finally kicked in. The U.S. delegates did not look happy. They squirmed and slouched, in fact. But they stayed in their seats. A relieved chairman Estrada moved swiftly forward, seizing the opening. Still, there were snags. Argentina tried to bring the article on developing-country participation back for debate. But China said, "Drop it." Finally, at 9 a.m., the interpreters stood up as one, disconnected themselves from their earpieces, and walked out. I remember nodding off, missing the moment when Annex B, the final draft, was sent off to be typed. It took an hour to come back, and by then the media arena was two-thirds empty. Entire television networks had decamped, leaving a shambles of Styrofoam cups and plates, plastic utensils, cut wires, buttons, badges, recyclable bags, and sheaves of documents.

Because of the daylight flooding into the arena, and thanks to the fact that the building's staff had all gone home and there was no one to pull the blinds, the picture on the big video screens was pale, but the sound came through loud and clear as Estrada tapped his gavel for the last time, and said: "I will now forward this protocol for adoption by the plenary." He was radiant. The roar of sustained applause from inside the main hall could be heard as the doors swung open. Seasoned diplomats were said to be weeping.

What the bleary-eyed negotiators had achieved was a tangible deal whereby thirty-eight developed countries actually agreed to cut their collective emissions by an average of 5.2 percent between 2008 and 2012. Three extra halocarbon gases would be included in the list of gases to be reduced. Different countries would have different targets. The European Union, Switzerland, and many Central and Eastern European countries agreed to reduce their emissions by 8 percent below 1990 levels by the same time. In the end, the United States had pledged a 7-percent reduction. Canada (casually ditching prime minister Chrétien's solemn vow to do *more* than the Americans) promised to go along instead with Japan, Poland, and Hungary with a piddling 6-percent cut. Russia, the Ukraine, and New Zealand grudgingly promised to stabilize at 1990 levels, nothing more. Coming in under the umbrella of the developed countries, Norway got away with a 1-percent increase, Australia was allowed up to 8 percent, and Iceland 10 percent, each citing special needs and problems. A "clean development mechanism" was set in place to allow the industrial countries to obtain credits against their own targets by funding emission-reduction programs in developing countries. Emission trading among industrialized nations was *still* in the document, but subject to special side-agreements. Carbon emissions from deforestation and the capture of carbon by reforestation would both be considered part of a developed country's emission total, and, in exchange, developing countries would be exempt from making any reductions at all until some point in the future. And, finally — deep pause — none of this would come into effect until at least fifty-five countries, representing 55 percent of global greenhouse-gas emissions, had ratified the treaty at home — a prospect that looked, particularly in the United States and Canada, extremely unlikely.

It was not much. But it was *something!*

Scattered among the thousand journalists and NGOs still glued to the big screens, the Carbon Club lobbyists sat in uncharacteristic, almost stunned, silence. Their body language said it all: their jaws had tightened and the veins stood out on their necks. They did not look at each other, or at anyone else, as they stared into the blackness. The eyes of some of the eco-freaks had, meanwhile, widened. They couldn't quite believe what was happening — although some of them narrowed their eyes in suspicion. Was this good? Was it bad? For the Carbon Club boys, *any* protocol was bad news. For the environmental groups, it wasn't so easy. The spectrum of opinion ran from the Washington-based National Environmental Trust's description of the agreement as "an immensely important turning point," to Greenpeace's Bill Hare holding up a copy of the draft with a dozen holes cut in it, saying it was "made out of Swiss cheese."

It was also possibly destructive in the long run, because it would allow the public at large to believe that something was being done, while in real terms nothing tangible would *begin* to happen for over a decade. The Kyoto deal risked lulling the public back to sleep with promises of action, whereas, in fact, all that happened was that the Juice Cans got loopholes, the petrotyrants got a reprieve, the developing countries got let off the hook, and the small island nations got ignored. Yet — and this was the buzz-phrase standing between many a despairing activist and too many *sakis* — "the process had been kept alive." That much was true. Otherwise, the plan of action amounted to chipping away with spoons at the foot of a cliff. That didn't stop William O'Keefe of the Global Climate Coalition from thundering: "We gave the store away. We conceded everything. We got nothing. There is no way, if the President signs this, the vote in the United States Senate will not be close. We will kill this bill!"

Coming back from Kyoto a few days later, I found myself on a 747 that felt more like a long, nearly abandoned theater. There were two women I knew from Toronto on the same flight, but they were seated together a couple of rows over, across an aisle, keeping their distance. We were all burned out and depressed. What was amazing was that there was nobody between us. Nobody! Unused seatbelts dangled in the aisles. Inflight magazines waited, perfume ads untapped, in their pouches. I pushed the armrests up on four adjacent seats and stretched myself out on half a dozen cushions collected from the empty seats around me. God, such luxury! Especially after the confines of Japan. Having psyched myself to endure ten hours of elbow-to-elbow, knees-to-bum, astronaut-like encapsulation as we crossed the Pacific, I could hardly believe my good fortune. On this level, at least, there were barely two dozen passengers, instead of nearly three hundred. I wondered if it was possible for one of these monster-planes to be flying *too light*. The noise of the engines seemed louder without the sound being cushioned by tightly packed bodies. Empty luggage bins rattled. It was nighttime. Except for the vibration in the deck that passed through the seat cushions into my bones, and the occasional clunky bump out of nowhere as we punched through an air pocket, I had no way of knowing I wasn't sprawled out in a basement auditorium somewhere, and those drawn curtains, instead of leading to first class, led to some sort of stage. And what was the name of the play? I was trying to figure out what had happened. The human race had come within a whisker of failing to take any action at all to save itself. The oil cabal might not have won the total victory it wanted, but this emasculated treaty was a close second. And I was flying across the Pacific — being *allowed* to fly across the Pacific — in a nearly empty jetliner, blowing off thousands of gallons of greenhouse-enhancing gases per hour.

The world, I sensed, was not quite saved.

CHAPTER 6

LARGE-SCALE IRREVERSIBLE CHANGES

İNDEED, IN THE WAKE OF Kyoto, humanity floundered. At the follow-up meeting in The Hague, in November 2000, an unfortunate new alignment of nations solidified, pitting science and ecology against oil and politics, with the steadily greening democracies of Europe, in league with the beleaguered island states, lined up against the pro-petroleum forces. These included every tyrant, dictator, despot, and coup leader in the world, along with their allies of convenience, the Juice Cans cabal of highly industrialized countries. Between them, they had managed to stall negotiations completely. Personifying the mean new spirit, the Canadian government sidelined its scientists and instead sent a team of negotiators led by two assistant deputies from the trade department, adopting the cynical position that the climate crisis could be exploited by setting up a system of "carbon credits," whereby a country, like Canada, blessed with vast forests, could earn points by planting more trees — thus sequestering carbon — and use these credits to justify carrying on with heavy-duty industrial pollution as usual. The scheme was transparently self-serving, and earned Canada the designation as the worst offender on the climate front — that is, until George W. Bush's cowboy heel came down. A few months into the process the United States announced it was pulling out of the Kyoto Protocol.

Within barely a year of its birth, the Protocol looked like roadkill. It was against this background of political paralysis and environmental despair, on February 13, 2001, that the IPCC's long-awaited Third Assessment, *Impacts, Adaptation, and Vulnerability,* was released in Geneva.

This should have turned the whole debate around, for buried in its detailed references and graphs (the likes of which the world has never seen before) is enough verification of global warming to settle the political debate once and for all. Since 1860, the earliest date for which globally significant data is available, temperatures have risen nearly a full degree Celsius. Indeed, rather than allow policy-makers the luxury of dismissing the findings, as previous Assessments had been dismissed, by wrangling endlessly over the issue of anthropogenic effects, the scientists took the step (which should have been taken a decade ago) of breaking the "global warming" debate into two components. First is the question of whether or not it is happening. Second is the question of human culpability.

In Footnote 1 of the *Summary for Policymakers,* the IPCC's scientists make it clear that *climate change* refers to any change in climate over a period of time, whether caused by natural variability or as a result of human activity. This language is significantly different from that used in the Framework Convention on Climate Change, where *climate change* referred to a change of climate that is attributed directly or indirectly to human activity, that alters the composition of the atmosphere, and that comes on top of natural climate variability observed over comparable time periods. In other words, while the issue of the impact of human activities is inherently political and has massive economic and social implications, the fact is that the biospheric stage upon which the human drama is being enacted is tilting. Scientists are now able to state that the global average surface air temperature has increased since the mid-nineteenth century, temperatures have risen during the past four decades in the lowest few miles of the atmosphere, snow cover and ice extent have decreased, global average sea level has risen, and ocean heat content has increased. These findings aren't the work of computer models, incidentally. They are the result of scientific research, using an array of techniques from tree-ring measurements to ice-core boring and calibrating salt content in water from the thickness of shells and fossils. Among the details thus compiled:

- On average, nighttime daily minimum temperatures over land have increased at about twice the rate of daytime daily maximum temperatures since about 1950 (approximately .2 degrees C compared to .1 degrees C per decade). This has lengthened the freeze-free season in many mid- to high-latitude regions.

- Since the start of the satellite record in 1979, both satellite and weather-balloon measurements show that the global average temperature of the lower atmosphere has increased by about .05 degrees C per decade.

- There have been decreases of about 10 percent in the extent of the snow cover since the late 1960s and a reduction of about two weeks in the annual duration of lake- and river-ice cover in the mid- to high latitudes of the northern hemisphere over the twentieth century.

- There has been a widespread retreat of mountain glaciers in non-polar regions during the twentieth century.

- Northern hemisphere spring and summer sea-ice extent has decreased by about 10 to 15 percent since the 1950s.

- Tide-gauge data show that the global average sea level rose between .1 and .2 meters (4 to 8 inches) during the twentieth century. It is "very likely" (meaning there is a 90- to 99-percent chance) that this is due to thermal expansion of seawater and widespread loss of land ice associated with the twentieth-century warming. (While this may sound insignificant, the rate of sea-level rise in the twentieth century was about *ten times* larger than the average rate over the last 3,000 years.)

- Precipitation has increased by .5 to 1 percent per decade in the twentieth century over most mid- to high latitudes of the northern hemisphere continents, while rainfall has decreased over much of the subtropical land areas at the rate of minus .3 percent per decade.

The significance of these figures, which to an untrained eye may seem rather low, if not marginal, can only be grasped when they are viewed in context. The IPCC's scientists, who released a vivid graph prepared by the University of Massachusetts showing the average global temperatures over the last thousand years, provided just such a context. Called the "Hockey Stick," the graph shows that average global temperatures fluctuated over the last millennium only by about half a degree Celsius, but in the twentieth century a spike appears that looks ominously like the beginning of an exponential curve.

What is particularly frightening about this spike is the fact that it has happened although greenhouse-gas emissions have risen to "only" 7 billion metric tons annually. Without population controls and a major switch to renewable energy, the IPCC's computer models show emissions increasing throughout the twenty-first century by as much as *two and a half to five times*, which is not likely to bring the curve down, by any stretch of the variables. And here is the real soul-breaker: even if carbon-dioxide levels were to flatten and start to go down by 2025, the concentrations in the atmosphere will continue to grow through the twenty-first century and only begin to flatten — in theory — afterwards. They might also continue to surge for centuries. Humanity, it appears, is not just being challenged to take responsibility for conditions a few generations from now, we are being required to take responsibility for *all* of the future. It is clear now that the kind of planet this is going to be depends on what course of action we take, or don't take, immediately. Every year that emission levels keep rising worsens conditions appreciably, and makes the eventual costs of a stabilization program or recovery program greater, assuming such a thing is even possible.

The first question is answered, so it is to the second question — whether the warming has been caused by human activities — that the IPCC's Third Assessment turns its attention, and finds:

- Since 1750, the atmospheric concentration of carbon dioxide has increased by one-third. The present CO_2 concentration has not been exceeded during the past 420,000 years and likely not during the past 20 million years. The rate of increase is unprecedented in the past 20,000 years.

- Over two-thirds of the increase in atmospheric CO_2 during the past twenty years is due to fossil-fuel burning. The rest is due to land-use change, especially deforestation, and cement production.

- The rate of increase of atmospheric CO_2 concentrations has been about .4 percent per year over the past two decades.

- Atmospheric methane (CH_4) concentrations have increased by a factor of 2.5 since 1750, and continue to rise.

- The atmospheric concentrations of nitrous oxide (N_2O) have increased by 16 percent since 1750.

In its initial report, the IPCC concluded, famously, that "the balance of evidence suggests a discernible human influence on global climate." It also noted that the "anthropogenic signal" — evidence of human activity at the root of changes — was still emerging from the background of natural variability. Now, however, the authors state that new estimates of climate response to natural and anthropogenic forcing are available, and new detection techniques have been applied. These studies "consistently find evidence for an anthropogenic signal in the climate record of the last 35 [to] 50 years." Model estimates of the rate of anthropogenic warming are consistent with observations in the majority of cases. Simulations of the response to natural "forcings" alone, including the response to solar variability and volcanic eruptions, indicate that natural pressures may play a role in the observed warming in the first half of the twentieth century, but fail to explain the warming in the latter half of the century. "*The effect of anthropogenic greenhouse gases over the last 50 years can be identified despite uncertainties in other forcings*" [my italics]. The scientists conclude that the twentieth century's climate was unusual. The observed warming in the latter half of the century is "inconsistent" with models of natural internal climate variability. Thus, anthropogenic factors do provide an explanation for the twentieth-century temperature change.

There is still a handful of people getting their funding or salaries from the oil, coal, and chemical industries who continue to try to argue that it is purely a coincidence that greenhouse-gas concentrations, particularly CO_2, are at their highest levels in millions of years, just as global temperatures begin to soar. It is to be expected that such people would deliberately distort or ignore the IPCC's findings. Their behavior, under the circumstances, is merely repugnant.

What is truly terrifying is the fact that the IPCC's Third Assessment, with its awesome message, was published *with no discernible political effect!* Here we finally have in hand the accumulated wisdom from seventeen years of sustained effort by teams of scientists around the world, using the most highly sophisticated instruments, techniques, and models, drawing in some cases on recently declassified data gathered by nuclear submarines and spy satellites, and as far as having any effect, it might as well not have been written. Not a single nation's political position shifted. Yet, arguably (this is the truly maddening part) the IPCC Third Assessment represents humanity's greatest interdisciplinary scientific achievement, to say nothing of it possibly being the most important document of all time. No fewer than 183 lead authors and coordinating lead authors, and 243 contributing authors, were involved in the project, and their material was in turn reviewed by 440 government and expert reviewers.

For George W. Bush to say, as he did shortly after taking office as president of the United States, that he doesn't "buy" the science, is amazing. Surely he must tell us what he *does* buy then. There is no alternative to the science, except non-science.

For any objective observer, as of February 2001, the century-long scientific debate over the physical fact of global warming itself, going back to Svante Arrhenius's 1896 theoretical paper on the enhanced greenhouse effect, was essentially *over.* Warming signals are being picked up everywhere, the report shows. It contains forty-four regional studies of over four hundred plants and animals, which varied in length between twenty and fifty years, mostly from Europe, North America, and Antarctica. There are sixteen other regional studies of about a hundred physical processes, covering most areas of the world, varying in length from twenty to a hundred and fifty years.

It can safely — that is to say, rationally — be said now that, just as the debate over whether the Earth was at the center of the universe ended, except among the lunatic fringe, after the telescope was deployed, so has the debate over global warming been basically ended by a combination of computer modeling and observation that now match up.

If, indeed, there were any lingering doubts after the publication of the Third Assessment, they should have been erased for good in mid-March 2001, when National Aeronautics and Space Administration (NASA) satellite measurements of greenhouse gases taken in 1970, which had been lost, were found and compared to current readings, giving us solid proof of a "significant" effect on the radiative forcing of the climate. This means that the change is already upon us. Until then, researchers had depended on ground-based measurements and theoretical models to gauge the change in greenhouse gases. New sets of data taken twenty-seven years apart from two satellites now orbiting the Earth allowed scientists to measure long-wave radiation and compare it to emissions increases, especially of methane, which were completely consistent with ground-based measurements, "conclusive" signs that the buildup of greenhouse gases has disrupted the Earth's natural thermostat, according to Richard Bantages, head of the research team at Imperial College in London, who analyzed the data. The findings, he said, "show definitely" that the greenhouse effect is taking place in the atmosphere and that it is linked directly to increases in greenhouse gases. All of this was perfectly consistent with the IPCC's advanced General Circulation Model (GCM) calculations.

In its *Impacts, Adaptation, and Vulnerability* report, the IPCC stated: "The globally averaged surface temperature is projected by models to warm 1.4 to 5.8 degrees Celsius by 2100 relative to 1990." The significance of this should now be clear. If temperatures reach the higher figure, we are in deep trouble. Anything above a change of 2 degrees Celsius takes us into what climatologists describe as "climatic realms that reach beyond the current experience of science and scientists." Keep in mind that a difference of only 3.5 degrees Celsius separates our time from the depths of the last ice age — a period when Canada and the northern United States, for instance, lay crushed under mile-high blocks of ice.

But it wasn't just future impacts that the IPCC addressed. Global surface temperatures have already increased between .4 and .8 degrees Celsius since the late nineteenth century, the report states. Most of this increase has occurred in two distinct periods, from 1910 to 1945, and since 1976 (suggesting a Depression-era drop in industrial and automotive emissions, taking fifteen years to effect a cooling). The rate of temperature increase since 1976 has been almost .2 degrees per decade. "Our confidence in the rate of warming," the scientists write, "has increased since IPCC (1996) due to new analyses including . . . new studies of the effect of urbanization on global temperature trends, new evidence for mass ablation of glaciers, continued reductions in snow cover extent, and a significant reduction of Arctic sea ice extent in spring and summer and in thickness." Seasonally, the greatest warming has occurred during the northern hemisphere winter and spring. Larger rates of warming continue to be found in the middle- and high-altitude continental regions. Examples of observed changes include shrinkage of glaciers, thawing of permafrost, later freezing and earlier breakup of ice on rivers and lakes, lengthening of mid- to high-latitude growing seasons by twelve days, poleward and altitudinal shifts of plant and animal ranges, declines of some plant and animal populations, and earlier flowering of trees, emergence of insects, and egg-laying in birds.

As the report says:

> We conclude that in the twentieth century we have seen
> a consistent large-scale warming of the land and ocean
> surface. . . . Independent estimates of hemispheric and

global ground temperature trends over the past five centuries from sub-surface information contained in borehole data confirm the conclusion that the late 20th century warmth is anomalous in the long-term context.

Anomalous!

"The probability that the observed changes in the expected direction ... could occur by chance alone is negligible" [my italics].

As Prof. Barry Smit of the University of Guelph, one of the coordinating lead authors of the report, put it in an interview: "The scientific and political debate is no longer, 'Is climate change real?' That's been accepted in the IPCC reports and by the political process. So the debate now turns to, 'Does it matter, how much of a change, and what does it mean to ecosystems and people, economies and societies?'"

The short answer, the IPCC report makes painfully clear, is: it does. A lot.

Human systems that are sensitive to climate change include mainly water resources, agriculture (especially food security) and forestry, coastal zones and marine systems (fisheries); human settlements, energy, and industry, insurance and other financial services; and human health. . . .

That pretty much covers it *all*, doesn't it?

The most widespread direct risk to human settlements from climate change is flooding and landslides, driven by projected increases in rainfall intensity and, in coastal areas, sea level rise. There is *high confidence* (between 67 and 95 percent probability) that river and coastal settlements are particularly at risk, but urban flooding could be a problem anywhere that storm drains, water supply, and waste management systems have inadequate capacity. In such areas, squatter and other informal urban settlements with high population density, poor shelter, little or no access to resources such as safe water and public health services, and low adaptive capacity are highly vulnerable. ... Model-based projections of the mean annual number of people who would be flooded by coastal storm surges increase several fold (by 75 million to 200 million) for mid-range scenarios of 40 cm sea level rise by 2080s.

That's *every year!* How much unrelenting punishment can human beings be expected to take?

Moreover,

Many coastal areas will experience increased levels of flooding, accelerated erosion, loss of wetlands and mangroves, and seawater intrusion into fresh water sources as a result of climate change. The extent and severity of storm impacts, including storm-surge floods and shore erosion, will increase as a result of climate changing including sea-level rise. High latitude coasts will experience added impacts related to higher wave energy and permafrost degradation.

We are in for a pounding. And while hundreds of millions flee the rising seas, a vastly greater number face the threat of slowly dying of thirst.

There are currently 1.7 billion people, a third of the world's population, living in countries that are already water-stressed, which is to say they use more than 20 percent of their renewable water supply. "Population growth and increased water withdrawals are projected to increase this number to around five billion by 2025, depending on the rate of population growth."

Five billion people without enough water! Surely a vision of a living hell on Earth. The full horror of this situation is not that five billion people are going to be suffering horribly twenty-five years from now, not only from thirst but from hunger brought on by the failure of crops and the collapse of fish stocks and herds. No, awful as that picture is, it is just a snapshot of a moment in the near future. What about after *that?* How long will the suffering go on? Are we talking decades? Or are we possibly talking centuries? Could we in fact be talking about millennia or a state of affairs that goes on forever?

Is such a scenario possible? According to the IPCC, absolutely!

"Projected climate changes during the 21st century have the potential to lead to future *large-scale and possibly irreversible changes in Earth systems* [my italics], resulting in impacts on continental scales." The examples include significant slowing of the ocean circulation that transports warm water to the North Atlantic, large reductions in the Greenland and West Antarctic ice sheets, accelerated global warming due to carbon-cycle feedbacks in the terrestrial biosphere, and release of terrestrial carbon from permafrost regions and methane from hydrates in the coastal sediments.

> If these changes in Earth systems were to occur, their impacts would be *widespread and sustained.* For example, significant slowing of the oceanic thermohaline circulation would impact deep-water oxygen levels, carbon uptake by oceans and marine ecosystems, and would reduce warming over parts of Europe. Disintegration of the West Antarctic Ice Sheet or melting of the Greenland Ice Sheet could raise global sea level up to 3 meters each over the next 1,000 years, submerge many islands, and inundate extensive coastal areas. Depending on the rate of ice loss, the rate and magnitude of sea-level rise *could greatly exceed the capacity of human and natural systems to*

adapt without substantial impacts. Releases of terrestrial carbon from permafrost regions and methane from hydrates in the coastal sediments, induced by warming, *would further increase greenhouse gas concentrations in the atmosphere and amplify climate change* [my italics].

When activist/author Jeremy Leggett polled four hundred climate scientists who had been involved in the IPCC process, asking them if a runaway greenhouse effect was a serious possibility, 15 said that it was *probable*, 36 said that it was possible, and 53 *probably* not, which meant that 51 out of 113 believed it was at least a *possibility*. Those are odds you don't want to face in an operation, let alone when it comes to your entire planetary biosphere.

Consider the implications of the ecological declines, degradations, collapses, shrinkages, and die-offs that are taking place *already*, before anything more than the first few ripples of climate-change effects have been felt. On virtually every front, scarcities of renewable resources are expected to exacerbate or trigger civil strife. At a glance, the graphs assembled by Thomas Homer-Dixon of the Peace and Conflict Studies Program at the University of Toronto reveal the retreat of croplands around the world as a result of population growth and the degradation of fertile land. The amount of cropland per person can plainly be seen to be plunging everywhere. In Africa, by 2025, only a third as much land is expected to be useable. In Oceania, barely half as much will be left by that date. Asian losses are expected to amount to one-third of existing available land, while the Americas will lose at least a quarter.

Yet an April 2001 study, published in *Science* by a team of leading ecologists and biologists, estimated that an area of land larger than the United States would have to be opened up to cultivation in the next fifty years in order to feed the world's burgeoning population. After that, there will be no more land that could possibly be converted. Of the 12 billion hectares (46 million square miles) available, 5 billion (19 million square miles) have been cleared and plowed. As a result, drinking water from Kenya to Kentucky has been fouled by agricultural runoff. Fertilizers and manure washing into the Gulf of Mexico are turning it into a dead zone. David Tilman of the University of Minnesota writes in the same report: "We have doubled the nitrogen economy in nature." Right now we are releasing an amount equal to all the combined natural processes. Because nitrogen has always been scarce, over the course of evolution it has served as a "limiting" nutrient; adding even a small amount of nitrogen can alter the pattern of which species will survive and which will disappear. The study documented dramatic changes in grasslands, and noted that the same could be true of forests, as more nitrogen falls with the rain and more calcium is leached from soil. If current trends continue, farmers will *double* their use of fertilizers made from nitrogen and phosphorus within the next five decades. By then, the authors warn, "massive, irreversible environmental impacts" will be under way. The Green Revolution has massively increased food production over the last generation, of course, but there has been a major, so far unaccounted for "dark side": the effect on the environment of pesticides and herbicides and fertilizers. With current chemical-based techniques, in order to feed the 9 billion people expected on the planet by 2050, the use of pesticides would have to triple. Coupling that with the extra nitrogen load, the result will be a combination of oxygen-starved waters, destroyed habitat, species extinction, and loss of clean drinking water, posing "an environmental challenge that may rival, and significantly interact with, climatic changes."

In fact, the impacts of climate change will be coming *on top* of all the other ecological disruptions already in the works.

The kind of suffering caused by a hopeless mess like this is not something anyone wants to contemplate. But contemplate it we must, because the kinds of economic and political stress induced by population pressure on cropland alone fall under the category of events that would take place in the very lower end of the projected range of global warming. The IPCC states that the available literature has not yet investigated climate-change impacts, adaptation, or vulnerability associated with the upper end of the projections. And that's because, so far, no one wants to even consider the worst-case scenarios. They are just too appalling. The reality is that as the heat rises, the impacts across the board will magnify and exacerbate the existing population-driven problems by creating more erosion, changing evaporation patterns, lowering lakes, rivers, and water tables, reducing not just cropland but also the amount of fresh water available. Any acceleration of climate change would bring the years — eons? — of drought and famine nearer.

NO PLACE TO RUN

THE WORLD OF *MY* CHILDHOOD, which I have described briefly in these pages, will be as remote to you, Dexter, as ancient Egypt is to me. There is no way for me, your grandfather, to anticipate the technological advances your generation and your father's will have made, at least not without straying into science fiction. And there is no way to predict the unexpected, like an invasion from space or another dimension or parallel universe, a too-big-to-blow-up asteroid or comet, a nearby supernova, or the passage of our solar system into an interstellar cloud. A disaster caused by genetic engineering might very likely have occurred, with God-knows-what effect on you. The accumulated load of pesticides, fertilizers, carcinogens, radioactive material, hormone disrupters, and heavy metals in your environment must be so intense the chances of you having reproduced naturally are probably very slim. You are possibly the last in the long line of Hunters, barring reproduction-technology breakthroughs, which suggests, in any event, a descendant who would be more of a clone or at least a partially tooled mutant.

In truth, the question of whether you'll even still be alive, apart from the chances of ordinary accidents, is less answerable now than at any time in our species's recent history. Never before was there a real chance of a catastrophe brought on by strange new potential menaces to our survival, like nanotechnology or computers, biotechnology, chemical or biological terrorism, or superbug pandemics. Of course, an old-fashioned nuclear war or a nuclear terrorist attack may indeed have come to pass, although a full-out exchange such as we envisioned at the peak of the Cold War, leading to a life-eradicating nuclear winter, does not seem likely from this vantage point. Smaller exchanges, yes. It is almost impossible to dare to hope that India and Pakistan, or the antagonists in the Middle East, with all their competing cabals of religious zealots and dictators, might have got through the first half of the twenty-first century without nuking each other. Especially with the aquifers of Arabia gone dry and the Bay of Bengal having surged over the lowlands of Bangladesh. It is equally difficult at this moment to see a way for China, in the throes of ever-worsening drought and facing the inundation of its major cities, to get through two generations of a vast surplus of males without throwing them into battle.

What I *can* be sure of is that the impacts foreseen in the IPCC material will be the stuff of your life. There is no need for me to qualify the prediction that your fate will be shaped overwhelmingly by a changed biosphere, a horribly debased, stripped, bleached, leached world. I don't know which term will become the chosen phrase to describe the overall effect, but if Thermageddon doesn't take, I suspect it will sound something like industrial weather, climate decay, climate rot, climate cancer, climate tumor, climate crash, climate collapse, climate breakdown, climate disintegration, slob climate, junk climate, mutant climate, something that denotes humanity's arrival in a hostile post-natural world. Climate desynchronization is the phrase that says it best, in my mind, but that is surely too esoteric. The phenomenon — whatever it ends up being called — will have continued to come in like a tide, like the ripple from a slow-motion asteroid strike, throughout your lifetime, forcing you to back away, step-by-step, and sooner or later to simply run for it — if there is any place to run to that isn't already stressed. The chances, I must never forget, are *negligible* that the geophysical changes already documented are anything other than the *beginnings* of a planetary fever that we can no longer hope to inoculate ourselves against. It seems all rather hopeless.

But this feeling is familiar.

Back in the middle of the last century, it was almost impossible to imagine surviving the clash between nuke-armed communists and capitalists. The wail of the air-raid sirens I listened to in high school was terrifying, but at least it gave us *warning* that our world was in jeopardy. Had we not been shocked into the realization that it could all be blown to plasma at any time, a generation of antiwar activists might not have risen. Had we not read the sci-fi and comic books about radioactive monsters and decaying subhuman survivors struggling to survive in a ruined world, we would probably have remained on course for self-indulgent lives as happy consumers, or unhappy lives as self-indulgent artists, as the case might have been, indifferent to remote and "abstract" political matters.

The sirens did not begin to wail over climate change in time, Dexter. And I think I understand why, apart from the machinations of the hard-eyed men in the Carbon Club, the even more hard-eyed dictators, and the ayatollahs and mullahs. It was a failure of imagination.

The threat of nuclear destruction, you have to understand, had fantastic press! It was ubiquitous. There wasn't a single living person of sound mind who didn't know that The Bomb existed and that it hung over the destiny of the world like a Damoclean sword. All you had to do was draw a crude outline of a mushroom cloud, and the whole message was conveyed. The fact that everybody in the world knew what a mushroom cloud represented made the anti-nuke activist's job simple beyond belief. Of course, prior to 1945, nobody had ever heard of a "mushroom cloud." Hiroshima and Nagasaki changed this forever, and then came the well-documented tests in Nevada and the Bikini atolls. The soundtracks alone were awesome. Someone remarked, "The survivors will envy the dead." How that sentence resonated! Science-fiction writers fed upon that concept from the late forties all through after the fall of the Berlin Wall.

It was not just intellectually fashionable to be a pessimist, it was nearly unavoidable unless you were willing to screen out the mounting evidence that nuclear doom was inching closer with every new computerized hair-trigger missile-response innovation. The media — mainly newspapers and radio, of course — were quick to report on nuclear military matters. They knew it mattered, even if they were mostly hawks. So there was no lack of coverage. Nuclear arms (forgive me) were a story with legs. And they were reported against a background of expanding cultural awareness. Nukes weren't just news and political reality; they were part of the entertainment package. How many movies were there about nuclear war? More than I can count. Most of them slotted into the dreadful sci-fi mutant-monster genre, like *Them*, a bad early special-effects attempt from the fifties that featured giant ants, transformed by nearby nuclear tests, emerging from caves to shred the garments of the beautiful damsel. Far more profound, and moving, was the impact of *On the Beach*, based on Neville Shute's grim tale of an American submarine captain who decides to return to the northern hemisphere after it has been contaminated by a radioactive death-cloud and surfaces outside a lifeless, abandoned San Francisco, where one of his crew, knowing they are all going to die soon, escapes ashore. Set to the poignant music of a dozen different versions of "Waltzing Matilda," the film left my generation all but traumatized by the inevitability of our doom.

The positive side of all this was that by the time we set out to demonize the makers of nuclear weapons, the main objective had already been achieved. Everybody knew *exactly* what we were talking about. It was possible to build a mass antinuke movement because the image was already there in everyone's mind. It helped enormously, of course, that the mass media had metamorphosed into an instantaneous global visual grid, eager to transmit the most potent images it could find. The Bomb lent itself admirably to the cause. The media didn't have to "sensationalize" when it came to The Bomb. It was *inherently* sensational. And so were bomb tests, which was the media "opening" we needed back in the seventies to get the anti-nuke message across.

At its early stages, the barbecuing of the planet came without an apocalyptic boom, without a blinding flash, without a mushroom cloud, without a visible fallout zone or crater. It was the very opposite of an atomic explosion. And this made it almost unsaleable, at least so far as television was concerned. I remember once growing frustrated with my own TV station in Toronto. Normally, CITY-TV was the most progressive station in the world when it came to environmental coverage. Its founder, Moses Znaimer, had hired me as an "Ecology Specialist" in 1988, and, while there were the usual differences in judgment between the reporter and his producers in the newsroom, I was never turned away from a story strictly because of commercial considerations or fear of offending officials other than lawyers. But, as the saga of the collapse of the ozone layer unfolded, I found myself having a hard time selling the story to guys whose job it was to string moving pictures together in time for the *Six O'Clock News,* our dinnertime news broadcast. It wasn't that they didn't believe what I was telling them, it was just —*no viz!* Driven at dizzying speed by time-sensitivity and the need for visuals, television proved itself to be nearly useless in the battle to phase out CFCs. Indeed, it fell almost entirely to scientists to make the case for the Montreal Protocol. In *Beyond the Limits,* Donella H. Meadows, Dennis L. Meadows, and Jørgen Randers point out that a large factor in the signing of the Protocol was the announcement by NASA that the ozone hole over the Antarctic had been discovered. This information arrived late in the game. It had a huge psychological effect on the international negotiations towards a CFC phase-out, which had been in the works for years but were sputtering along, languishing in diplomatic backrooms. I found it a frustrating time to be an "Ecology Specialist," aware of the importance of the ozone drama but unable to meet the visual imperative that ruled my medium — until I finally went to the graphics editor and asked her to design a globe with an ozone "bubble" around it, and then to have it disintegrate dramatically, allowing beams of searing cosmic rays down onto the surface. We intercut that with close-ups of aerosols and chimneys and tailpipes, and added a bit of eerie industrial music. It was not *scientific*, but it was a damn good approximation of what was actually going on, and it was fantastic eye candy. For a while, until another producer got bored with the graphic, it was easy for me to get ozone-layer stories on air. Their news value jumped astronomically once I could portray the event.

With climate change, the pictures may soon come, but as of the time of this writing, the "face" of climate change has not shifted into focus. In the search for fingerprints, we seem to have overlooked the fact that there is a bigger picture that needs to be articulated or rendered perceivable, let's say, and which has so far not emerged from the background tumult. The Bomb arrived upon the stage of history in a burst of sun-like heat and a tremendous thunderclap. But a change in ocean convection currents? What does that mean? Variations in size-fractionated phytoplankton biomass? Beg pardon? Vegetation changes? Really! Changes in abiotic variables? Uh-huh. Early spring blooming of indicator species? Sure. It would have been better by far in the long run if climate change had entered our lives in such a way that it shook our souls. Instead, it is even now only inching down from the tops of the mountains, the tips of rock furthest from any human habitation, or climbing barely more than a molecule at a time silently up the sides of the sea rocks and across the beaches.

The decay of the atmosphere began in the stratosphere, as far from our reach as it would seem possible. The jungles that burn are still mainly in places where no towns have been built, so there are few witnesses. Most of the oil that is spilled is at sea or underground or on tundra or deserts — out of sight, out of mass mind. Only through our instruments can we hear, detect, measure, and quantify the disintegration of the natural world. The IPCC's Third Assessment stands as a monument to our capacity for gathering and correlating data on climate change. But all this has the emotional and psychological sex appeal of facing a final term exam in physics. Nobody wants to examine the mountain of accumulated evidence. The threat we faced during the Cold War was right in our faces. It was stark, simple, visceral, life-or-death, heaven-or-hell, and the end of the world. *This* creeps, crawls, inches, percolates, simmers, coagulates. It is an underground fire coming at us from all directions. Our instincts say something is wrong, but our senses are not yet picking up anything that would trigger the flight response.

A failure of imagination! How disappointing! You would think our specialty, as a species, was imagination. Think of Leonardo da Vinci's drawings of helicopters, so far ahead of their moment of technical achievement. Surely, with all the visual aids at our disposal, you'd think we would be able to haul the monstrous eventuality of climate ruination up out of the depths of the supercomputers and make it as real as the famous mushroom cloud. So far, we have failed abysmally.

It has been, perhaps most poignantly, a failure of art. With the most powerful tools for visualization and manipulation of emotions that have ever been devised at their disposal, it seems almost perverse that our artists — the antennae of the human race, as Marshall McLuhan called them — have for the most part kept their heads buried in the sand, concentrating on the creation of spectacular but trivial entertainments. As yet, no modern climate-change cinematic or video equivalent of *On the Beach* has been produced, or, for that matter, written. No "Carbon Bomb" war stories are in the works. If comics or video games touch on climate change, it is only occasionally and purely as a background. I do not see TV shows about it. Indeed, nobody knows what "it" will look like when it goes off. There is no single iconic image of destruction. It will come in stages of ecological regression, die-offs and extinctions, critical biological thresholds being crossed, systems giving way, diversity collapsing at every level from the micro to the macro. The "face" will be that of a gaunt, maddened, dysfunctional ecosystem, almost psychedelically fluid: ice storms one moment, a deluge the next; high tides, dried-out creek beds; dust clouds and monsoons; wild swings, like the mood of a crazed creature; a hungry, thirsty world racked by great storms, with disaster a constant.

The catastrophe is occurring on such a scale that it seems totally, cumulatively out of control. Yet this is too fatalistic a thought for me to bear. And having admitted to you, Dexter, that I saw it coming, how could I look you in the eye if I didn't try to do *something* to change the way things are going to work out? I feel like an ant struggling in an avalanche. If we were going to play this strictly by numbers, the actions of an individual are virtually meaningless. One chance in 6 billion of changing the balance. Why squirm? Why wiggle? Why dig your heels in? Why claw for a foothold? It's futile!

Faced with a problem as overwhelming, as *huge,* as crushing as climate change and ecological devastation, there is only one starting point. And that, at least in the case of those of us living in the industrialized countries, at the very top of the food chain, is *within ourselves.* At this stage, with the planetary cancer as advanced as it is, there is no way any of us can project enough force out there into the super-mass cauldron of 6 billion destinies to substantially alter anything — not with humanity segregated into gigantic economic/mental/emotional/spiritual blocs with contradictory mindsets, each of which is fixed on its own survival, and so entrenched by now that its overthrow does not lie reasonably within sight. Perhaps it is time to reverse the impetus. Rather than putting the emphasis on attempting any longer to project power outward, locked as we are into a closed and finite system that is rapidly overloading, we might try reversing the primary thrust of our intervention.

All things being relative, it is a trivial (that is, undemanding) matter for me to worry about the rainforests of Papua New Guinea, since they do not directly impinge on my daily existence at all — at least in any way that I am liable to notice, unless I set out to study the matter. On the other hand, it is a major (demanding) matter for me to consider whether or not to leave a light switch on in my basement, just in case anyone wanders down there in the middle of the night. When I say "major," I mean something that recurs, that is central to my lifestyle, which has become so commonplace that I hardly think about it. Moreover, this is something completely within my personal sphere. The truth is that the simple act of switching off or *not turning on* a light bulb is the equivalent of lifting a small but razor-sharp sword against the oppressor.

It is the banality of the way we destroy the world that stops us in large measure from rising up in rebellion. How do you throw yourself upon your own light-switch finger? How seriously can you take the struggle against the toaster in your kitchen? Is there any romantic image to give emotional resonance to your solitary decision to wait until the dishwasher is full before turning it on? Can you see your thermostat as one of the trigger mechanisms in a doomsday scenario? If you disconnect the electronic garage door-opener and resort to using your muscles to pull it up and down, have you really done something like clashing shields against the would-be slayer of your descendants? Well, yes.

To *not* act at this stage is to line oneself up squarely on the side of the planet-eaters. It might have sounded — indeed it *did* sound — like the hippest advice ever when Timothy Leary, the LSD guru, urged my generation to turn on, tune in, and drop out. Turn your back on it — that was the idea! The trouble with dropping out, alas, was that it meant passing up on any chance of ever managing to grasp, for however short a period of time, the levers of power. Just how dropping out differed in its social effect from apathy or fatalism was unclear. Fortunately, instead of curling up around their hookahs, many of the dropouts landed on the streets waving picket signs, and a lot of that drop-back-in activism had to do with the dawning mass awareness that The System was part of the ecosystem, and that, as of our era, the fate of the two systems were forever inextricably bound. Unlike The System, the ecosystem could not be dropped out of, which meant, basically, that we were *trapped*.

Even though, from the beginning, Rachel Carson had warned of worldwide chemical fallout patterns, the individuals who were most sensitive to her message believed (some still do) it must be possible to find a haven or refuge outside The System, *somewhere* beyond the reach of the thrashing tails of the dying urban dinosaurs. The back-to-the-land movement, with its flurry of communes being set up as close to the end of the road as possible, in remote valleys or on the shores of isolated bays, was a reenactment of the North American pioneer stage, embodying the same spirit of independence and naive faith in Utopia. A fantasy existed that even a nuclear war was survivable if you lived far enough away from any big cities and you had a supply of seeds, some solar panels, iodine pills, a gun, and a copy of *The Whole Earth Catalogue*. And it was true, should the nuclear exchange be limited, that it was just possible there would be survivors out in the bush and the countryside, somewhat unscathed. In the face of a truly drastic climate flip of the ecosystem, unfortunately, there ultimately will be no safe, remote places left anywhere. The Pacific Northwest's coniferous forests are expected to last longer than boreal forests, as rising temperatures turn the glacial moraine into a frying pan, but with climate itself affected, everything — everywhere — is affected. The skies and air and water of even Walden Pond are already degraded and slipping further. If the sudden global heating we have triggered does indeed activate an ice age, there will be no place in the entire northern hemisphere to hide. In the worst-case situation, a runaway greenhouse effect, there would be no place on Earth, period. The fantasy of escaping to an organic farm is no longer a reasonable, let alone viable, option. A better, more realistic hope, by the time my grandson is my age, will be to head out into space. Good luck making the final crew list, Dexter.

No place to run. That sums up the human dilemma in the face of major climate crunch. The IPCC notes that the suffering will fall mainly upon the poor in countries least able to afford the costs of constructing dikes, reclaiming deserts, reforesting, rebuilding storm-smashed infrastructure. But that's really in the short term — that is, for the duration of this century. Once the big, millennial climate change starts rolling, everybody gets hit, including, and probably especially, the Northern industrialized countries. The Southern lands, which suffered the most through the twenty-first century from drought and flooding as a result of the self-indulgence and irresponsibility of the unrepentant, industrialized West, are unlikely to welcome refugees from an ice age willingly, especially the descendants of North American energy pigs.

Environmentally, as a species, we have *already* run out of places to run to, because there is no place left where the air and temperature and seasons and water levels have not been tweaked, however slightly, but with gathering momentum. And, in all too many places, it is not a matter of subtle variations in annual precipitation, it is a matter of major heat waves, drought, collapsing water tables, of wetlands gone bone-dry, of the Gobi and the Sahara being lifted on winds and spread across oceans and continents.

In the summer of the year 2002, it was no longer possible for any literate person to pretend ignorance of the climate/eco disaster. In fact, literacy is not a requirement. Eyes for television or ears for radio will do just fine. And in the event you live in such a remote corner of the world you possess neither TV nor radio, the likelihood is that your local environment is being cut down or set aflame or dug up or contaminated and you don't need media to tell you that the world is being destroyed. In Western jurisprudence, ignorance of the law is no excuse. In the harsh judgment of history, ignorance of ecological laws will prove to be no defense either.

By *any* rational measure — legal, ethical, and survivalist — it should be clear by now that serious action is required. Indeed, a revolution of some sort is required. Since it has become useless (worse, a waste of precious time) to think of escaping, standing one's ground might seem to be the next logical defensive position to adopt. But that's not any use, either, if all it means is maintaining the status quo. What has to change, above all, is the North American fossil-fuel habit. And it has to be a systems-wide change. Since Bush and Cheney have turned the United States — actually, all of NAFTA— into a pollution-level maintenance and enhancement zone, there is, objectively, no hope of avoiding the worst-case course of events until at least the middle of the first decade of the millennium, when Bush might be replaced by a reincarnated green Al Gore, or at least by somebody with advisors capable of understanding science, who aren't pawns of the Carbon Club. In the meantime, we cannot afford to sit idly by, watching the final, dwindling opportunities for some kind of decent future slip away.

We need to get on with nothing less than a revolution, which is easy to *say*. Where it gets complicated is when you consider how to go about it. A revolution obviously has to occur at the global level, where hundreds of squabbling sovereign nation-states have so far shown themselves to be spectacularly dys-functional when it comes to avoiding ecocollapse. We'll get to that, the geopolitical level. But, to begin with, it most definitely has to be a revolution from within. That is, from within the belly of the beast, from within the heart and mind of the beast. The beast, in this case, refers to George W. Bush's America, including Canada's look-alike, pollute-alike, imported-car culture, which is almost fully integrated into the U.S. economy. That's the big picture, the macro-political reality that we somehow have to engage. Tackling it physically is the most direct approach, as waves of tear-gassed anti-globalization activists in places like Seattle and Quebec City have demonstrated. And that's some-thing that those of us dwelling inside the American fossil-fuel fortress can do at any moment on a dozen different fronts. We can actually come to grips with the Carbon Club, grapple with the Juice Cans, and pit ourselves against the petrotyrants.

First, it involves a realization that, in an ecological sense, the Big Picture and the Small Picture are *literally* one. Modern ecology teaches that there is no actual separation between events, effects, and environment. Ecology is flow. Macrocosm and microcosm are in synch. The use of ordinary light-switches and extraordinary thunder over the tundra are directly, causally linked. All you have to do is dig deep enough to find the thread weaving its way through the ecosystem. There is much good news attached to this discovery that we are integral, linked parts of a super-system. While few of us, as individuals, have the per-ceptible power to reach much beyond our workplace, home, or immediate neighborhood, each of us does have the power of the Butterfly Effect at our disposal. That's a term used in ecology to describe the rippling chain of impacts in the atmosphere that begin at some insignificant starting-point, like the fluttering of a butterfly's tiny wings, and build up centuries later into a hur-ricane on the other side of the world. Like it or not, conscious of it or not, simply at the physical level, every person's actions ripple through the biosphere and *never stop rippling*. That is the basic eco-insight. We human beings, like butterflies, are dynamic, physically manifested functions of the ecosystem. We *are* the ecosystem. Physically, we are sand and water and air and mud that coagulated over the billions of years into an amazing but terrifyingly clumsy mutated creature that is poisoning and overheating the planet, a creature that can be opposed at this stage by no one but ourselves. Unless, of course, Gaia steps in and makes a necessary adjustment — like hitting us with an uncontrollable pandemic as a way of ridding the biosphere of the human parasite that is eating it alive. In my view, technically neat as this solution may be from a Deep Ecology perspective, to wait for Gaia to save the world by cutting the humans down to size is surely the intellectual equivalent of "finding Jesus," which is to say, it is an abandonment of rationality. It is like waiting for a wrathful Jehovah to smite the sinners. The meek may indeed inherit the Earth, but will there be anything left by then? Not likely. It is an act of despair, I think, to leave the fate of our descendants in the hands of an invisible, unproven, very silent divine or quasi-divine entity. Of course, humanity's descent into ecological hell may very well be part of some Cosmic Cycle, as Hinduism tells us, with this millennium being the time of the world-destroying Dance of Shiva. The Hopi prophecies see a Great Cleansing coming, and, as we know, the Bible and Nostradamus predict the worst. Any of these mystical world views could be true. But somehow, Dexter, I don't think you'd be happy to read here that I decided to abrogate any responsibility for the stricken biosphere you are stuck with by blaming God, Shiva, or the Great Spirit. Sure, I was bad. I burned incredible amounts of fossil fuels and consumed mountains of natural resources, but *they* — the gods — made me do it! And now you, my grandson, must pay for my sins.

I have to do better than that. We can't escape. I can't find a sanctuary for us. Dropping out isn't an option. Closing my eyes and praying is too long a shot to countenance. Carrying on with the North American petroleum-based lifestyle is nothing less than commission of an ongoing ecocrime. Ergo, I guess we have to fight.

C H A P T E R   8

DON'T WEEP FOR MOTHER EARTH

I HAVE IN FRONT OF ME A COPY
of *Ecodefense: A Field Guide to Monkeywrenching*, edited by Dave
Foreman and Bill Haywood, first published in 1985. Based on
the ecoguerrilla concept introduced by Edward Abbey in his
novel *The Monkey Wrench Gang*, it is *the* how-to manual of
ecotage. It tells you how to destroy or wreck heavy equipment,
fences, aircraft, billboards, and snowmobiles; spike trees and
roads; take down power lines. The manual doesn't suggest
targets, but it shows in pictures and drawings exactly how to sabotage computers and plug waste-discharge pipes. The disclaimer
at the beginning says it is intended only for "entertainment."
The authors would never "encourage anyone to do any of the
stupid illegal things contained therein." By coincidence, people,
especially in the United States, have turned to destroying property in defense of the planet over the last two decades. Estimates
vary as to the amount of property damage done by monkeywrenchers or contemporary ecotage groups like the Earth
Liberation Front (ELF), which in one case torched a car lot where
thirty-seven new SUVs were parked; but it is in the billions, for
sure. *Ecodefense* has had a fairly long run at it, as these things go.
When the FBI busted Dave Foreman and locked away Ron

Coronado, two of the most serious monkeywrenchers of all, the steam seemed to go out of the radical Earth First! movement. At least one of the cofounders showed up recently, having taken a job with nonviolent Greenpeace, even though Greenpeace doesn't tolerate destruction of property. Other radical ecoguerrillas have been reincarnated as somberly dressed employees of mainstream environmental groups. If not a trend, this is surely a sign that something has not worked.

There is little evidence that the culture of economic growth and development has changed in any substantial way in the United States. If a backwoods ecoguerrilla war had been raging for perhaps three decades, surely by now it should have achieved *some* of its objectives. It would appear, instead, that the anti-growth forces have been severely body-checked. Will they recover? As things get worse — as Bush comes to shove, so to speak — we may guess that the ecoguerrillas will strike back harder. But it may also be that they are exhausted, clobbered basically by American federal forces, and that a certain avenue of ecological politics has reached a cul-de-sac.

In Canada, we had a similar phenomenon back in the late seventies and early eighties, when the so-called Squamish Five blew up a few power lines and a hydro building in British Columbia and later attacked an American subsidiary plant that was helping to build missile components in Toronto, seriously injuring a guard. Among the Five were a couple who had been involved in Greenpeace activities on the West Coast before deciding that sending peaceful ships out to protest nuclear tests or save whales wasn't enough. Planting explosives was so much more *direct*.

Some months before the police eventually captured them, I was approached by a friend of mine, who happened to know these people, and warned that they were thinking of blowing up the Greenpeace office in Vancouver. The reason? Greenpeace wasn't "radical enough." It was diverting The People's attention from the real revolution. I was, of course, enraged — and for the first time, knew the chill of learning there is a paramilitary death squad out there with you and your group in their sights. A *green* one, at that!

Until that point, I confess to having had doubts about a purely peaceful approach to change. Historically, the record is grim. Any shift in hegemony has traditionally been resisted with force and only overcome in the end by force. If an environmental revolution was necessary — and even before climate change hove into view this was the view of many, including myself — how could it possibly achieve its goals when confronted by overwhelmingly superior firepower and technology? Quasi-mystical Maoist doctrines of mass uprising in the countryside, with the cities being surrounded and taken, are as quaint today as tales of ancient siege machines and nearly impregnable cities. Cities are now the places to which the vast mass of humanity has fled or been driven, and unless we address the crisis of the cities or tap their tremendous human potential for exercising a measure of control over all our fates, there will be no ecorevolution, merely an eco*reaction,* which will be reactionary rather than enlightened.

As Ross Gelbspan writes in *The Heat Is On*: "In our . . . fast-forward world, institutions respond to events only when they reach emergency proportions." With regional emergencies, there is always room for displacement. There is somewhere to go to survive: a place of higher ground, food, and medical aid. The political barriers are porous. Even along the U.S.–Mexico border, where a virtual anti-immigrant Maginot Line has grown up, the movement of refugees grows like an avalanche that cannot be checked without resorting to Berlin Wall–type atrocities. How long, if everything continues the way it is going, before there are hundreds of millions of environmental refugees wandering the globe? Many of them will have legitimate grievances, for the droughts and floods they are fleeing will have been caused by industrialized countries, which now owe them, at the very least, shelter. The political repercussions include resorting to military measures on the part of one state after another. Gelbspan makes this chilling observation:

> . . . it is the poor, precarious, nations of the developing world that would face the threat of totalitarianism first. In many of these countries, where democratic traditions are as fragile as the ecosystem, a reversion to dictatorship will require only a few ecological states of emergency. Their governments will quickly find democracy to be too cumbersome for responding to disruptions in food supplies, water sources, and human health — as well as to a floodtide of environmental refugees from homelands that have become incapable of feeding and supporting them.

Guerrilla doctrines, in any event, have little useful application at the international level, where power is diffused, and coalitions are the name of the game. The unilateralism of an old-style uprising bumps quickly up against the need for global cooperation to preserve and maintain a common biosphere. Climate change, because of its global nature, *forces* humanity to either make an evolutionary jump to a wholly new level of cooperation, or wipe out. We have to break out of the gridlock of sovereignty as an end in itself. If this means letting go of some of our national autonomy in order to join forces, so be it. We gain far more than we lose.

Yet even minor reforms take decades, in some cases many decades, to get pushed through, moving at a glacial political pace. And, tough as it is to effect change in the democracies, there are huge sections of humanity locked in functioning Dark Ages who have no say in our collective destiny, which means that the power to effect change in time to deal with a planetary crisis is basically limited to a minority of the human race —

those of us who have been lucky enough to have been born free, and who have a reasonable scope of activities open to us before we are locked away or shot. I think the disparate political situations increase the degree of responsibility for those who *can* act, as well as those who could, but don't.

Here is the dilemma, as I have seen it for some time: as the disaster intensifies, the resistance to government intervention in the form of rescue and relief will lessen, leading to a diminishment of freedoms. If we do not start applying the rule of law to ecological sustainability now, the situation will deteriorate to the point where, when enforceable regulation is finally introduced, it will have to be commensurate with the extremity of the situation, which is to say, draconian. Anybody interested in preserving liberty as well as the biosphere should ponder the price of delay and inaction.

The sooner we start getting tough on planet-despoilers, the better — which means laws that can be enforced. At the moment, in lieu of a global environmental protection agency, individuals and small bands of ecoguerrillas have found themselves trying to plug the gaps, and I have no end of admiration for these people. But there are two problems with environmental vigilantism. First, it is by nature a local reaction. We need universal solutions. Secondly, I don't trust people with guns and bombs and no rulebook.

In the end, the state is going to have to step in. If some kind of organized force — or at least the threat of organized force — is going to have to be brought to bear to push through the changes that have to be made to avoid unacceptable ecological and human damage, then let's get on with it. The guerrilla approach, I submit, has not made much of a dent. Given this pace, in the time it would take to overthrow global capitalism, the biosphere would have long since been reduced to a smoldering ruin. It is pure romanticism, at this stage, to think that the joint powers of the state, sometimes combined with private armies, can be defeated under the conditions of advanced industrialism, which include mass manipulation on a scale never before possible and surveillance and detecting methods that were science fiction barely yesterday.

I don't want to see "Green Brigades" deciding to take matters into their own hands, even in the face of near-certain catastrophe, because they will abuse their power, of this much I am sure. And, worse, since they will have to start up indigenously, they will have virtually no chance of effecting systems-wide change as long as they remain wedded to an armed path, surrounded by hundreds of countries equipped with as much sophisticated weaponry as they can afford.

Even if they do win their battle for national control, they are barely at the gate opening onto the larger — and far more urgent — battle for *global* control. It is ironic that, while we vilify the generations of power elites who have struggled so bloodily for "control of the world," in our time we find, no matter how ultra-liberal we might be, that control of the world (meaning the fate of the biosphere) has become the thing we *must* attain — for the good of everyone and everything.

For me, the struggle came into focus on July 1, 1976, after I had nonviolently interfered with a Soviet whaling operation in the Pacific Ocean, just off California's Mendocino Peninsula. A group of us, trying to apply a new formula for change, triumphantly sailed our chartered fishing boat, the *Phyllis Cormack*, renamed *Greenpeace V*, under the Golden Gate Bridge to the haunting sound of Tibetan horns. A horde of media was waiting at the dock in San Francisco's Fort Mason — and we were ready as well, with scores of dupes of our 35 mm film, to be distributed free on a pool basis. The film showed a Czechoslovakian named George (Jiří) Korotva and myself in our Zodiac, with a two-hundred-fifty-pound harpoon being fired over our heads and exploding in the flank of a sperm whale we were trying to shield with our bodies.

This is old history now, but the sound of that harpoon became the "shot heard around the world" of ecoactivists. It gave Greenpeace — then not much more than a little group in an office in Vancouver's Kitsilano hippie-ghetto — a boost to true international fame, while at the same time drawing a good portion of the human race's attention to the issue of whaling, which had been evolving completely out of sight and out of mind since Herman Melville's *Moby Dick* dropped off the best-seller lists in the late 1800s. Indeed, our film, showing gigantic ships and tiny whales, plus the black-and-white photos we got of a dead juvenile whale in the water, were so mediagenic that it caused even the seemingly invincible Soviets to back down. The next year, when we went out again to confront them, the whalers covered the harpoon with a tarpaulin to hide it from the cameras, and called off the hunt. Indeed, at one point we had a six-hundred-foot factory ship and a fleet of seven big steel chaser boats fleeing across the water ahead of us, while we pursued them with nothing more lethal than a camera. In a time of near-instantaneous global communications, a billion television sets, and an uncountable number of newspapers, all hungry for dramatic images, the camera had become mightier than the harpoon, for sure. But there was more to it than that.

There was a geopolitical hegemony issue involved, which never became part of the story. The fact was, whales were only being hunted along the west coast of North America because the Soviets were using their whaling fleet as a cover for espionage operations focused on American missile sites and military bases in California. At this point, the superpowers were locked into a habit of set-piece moves and countermoves, and the whales were being slaughtered partially to create a smokescreen of blood.

The first time we approached the factory ship *Dal'nyi Vostok,* we were astonished to see an array of electronics gear, including satellite dishes, that went far beyond any requirements of whaling. Later, I was told the dishes were mainly scanning U.S.

missile silos, and relaying everything back to Moscow. I also learned later that, when the Russians on board the whaling ships first saw *us*, they automatically assumed we were the CIA. The crews must have known perfectly well what their real purpose was, even if it was some kind of official secret. Certainly they could see for themselves that the whales were almost gone. The amount of time — and, more to the point, the amount of fuel — they had to expend to find anything to hunt was absurd. Over the days in which we chased the whalers and kept trying to interfere — *always* nonviolently — it became obvious that there simply weren't enough whales left to justify (even under communism) an eight-ship flotilla at sea for months on end so far from home. And at that time there was another entire nine-ship Soviet whaling fleet at work. Only the remnants of the great pods were left to be hunted down.

On top of all this horror were two additional chilling details: the Soviets, as it was revealed many years later, had been lying about how many whales they were really killing, so it would look as if they were sticking to a quota. The International Whaling Commission, without a blink, had accepted their faked reports. The other detail was that that sperm-whale oil was being used, because it was the best oil around, in the Soviet Union's intercontinental ballistic missiles. The Americans also had a stockpile of sperm oil. The tragedy of the sperm whales was that they not only provided a cover in a covert operation just as their species was dying out in the latter half of the twentieth century, but their oil had become a lubricant in the greatest engines of destruction ever devised. It was therefore a real hunt, but steadfastly for a pretend official reason. It was not to "harvest whales," as the Soviet delegates kept droning at the IWC meetings, it was to eavesdrop on a mortal political enemy. The enemy knew perfectly well what was going on — even if our small band of whale-lovers and media theorists didn't have a clue until we were out in the middle of it.

At that time, it was perfectly legal, according to the Law of the Sea, for ships from any nation to fish right up to the edge of the three-mile limit. The scene, for anyone going out in those waters for the first time, was a shock. The number of draggers, mainly of East European and Asian origins, was astounding. They were rusting, nearly derelict boats, their cables squeaking as they hauled in their massive nets, devastating the Continental Shelf. American fishermen loathed the foreign trawlers, of course, because, while the Americans had to obey fairly strict conservation quotas, just beyond the three-mile limit the Poles, Taiwanese, Japanese, Soviets, Spaniards, and Czechs, most of them flying Panamanian or Liberian flags of convenience, gouged the bottom with their dragnets, like strip mining or clear-cutting, and netted virtually everything that moved in the waters, casually shoveling the "by-catch" overboard. The rust-bucket Soviet whaling fleet crept along the coast, losing itself as much as possible among the armadas of other dilapidated hulks. The U.S. administration was eager to extend the three-mile limit as far as it could, but not primarily for conservation reasons. That was just the cover, and a good one, because there was an element of truth to it. But the real concern was military. At that time, America was braced for a nuclear attack by ICBMs over Canada. The B-52s were on twenty-four-hour patrol. But the specter of Soviet subs launching from just offshore was something for which there was little real defense other than retaliation.

When we had begun our anti-whaling campaign in April 1975, none of us had any idea that we were sailing directly into the middle of a great secret underwater chess game being played by the Americans and the Soviet Empire. For us, it was to be a lesson in how inextricably environmental issues are interwoven with strategic political interests. The bad luck of the whales, to be caught in the middle of the Cold War, was a foreshadowing of the climate crisis that was foreseen by virtually no one back then. Now, the parallel between the plight of the whales and the plight of the biosphere is clear. In both case, we are caught up in a nexus of ultra-Byzantine geopolitical machinations, with so many vested interests, military interests, commercial interests, state interests, regional, ethnic, religious interests, and above all so much *personal* self-interest involved that the knot may be truly, impenetrably Gordian.

The whale campaign had been a new thing. Up until then, Greenpeace had been fiercely anti-nuclear, anti-military, and had even, in its earliest incarnation as a Canadian West Coast phenomenon, flirted with anti-Americanism. Of course, to the security agencies in the West, the fact that the West Coast radicals had gone from protesting American tests to protesting French tests was all the evidence they needed to lump us with every other leftist conspiracy ever hatched. For us to go chasing after whalers suddenly — *Soviet* whalers — was quite a leap. Where did that fit on the chessboard? There was nothing inherently left-wing about whales. Why were these guys out here? If we weren't on the Commies' side on this one, whose side were we on? And, above all, how could our presence on the playing field be put to advantage?

Doubtlessly, the American authorities that watch over such things pondered the pluses and minuses of tying us up in red tape and confining us to port, as they might easily have done. They had done it before, in 1971, when we sailed the very same *Phyllis Cormack* into the waters of the Aleutian Islands. The minute we were in American waters, we were allowed free movement only so long as the Pentagon gave the nod. There were files in Washington, D.C., on most of our crew, many of whom had been arrested at various times over the years in one political protest or another. As it later came out, my own phone line had been tapped for a couple of years by then. In fact, the Royal Canadian Mounted Police had more wiretaps going in British Columbia, spying on suspected ecoterrorists, than in all of Quebec. We were, of course, self-confessed agitators, and one can hardly blame the security people for doing their jobs. The RCMP, as per mutual security agreements, had handed over copies of those files to the Central Intelligence Agency, so we were sure that the Coast Guard and the U.S. Navy had been briefed, in case they should have to arrest us.

It was flattering to be spied upon by the state, although it could also be disconcerting. One day at sea, when we were in hot pursuit of the *Vostok* fleet, we found our electronic equipment oscillating wildly. We were being scanned by unbelievably powerful surveillance beams, which could only be coming from a submarine. Since we were a thousand miles out at the time, the sub had to be nuclear. It was only when someone in the wheelhouse caught a glimpse of an enormous conning tower surfacing briefly a mile away that we were able to confirm that we were, indeed, being shadowed by *somebody's* nuke, but whose we didn't know. If it was American, did that mean they were exposing themselves to let us know they were on our side, and presumably to tell the Soviets to keep their mitts off us? Or, if it was a Soviet craft, riding shotgun on the "whaling" fleet (i.e. protecting their espionage cover), were they reminding us, none too subtly, that they could sink us like snapping a finger?

For a golden moment in San Francisco, however, with all that tension behind us and our footage of the confrontation going out around the world, I felt we had gained new, wider support, albeit some of it pretty weird. Our office in Vancouver got a call from a fellow in Texas wanting to "saddle up and ride with you boys after the Ruskies." But whatever new-found cachet we had with the folks on the right, it wasn't going to take up much room in the police files, because we had no sooner made our quantum media leap than we were back to being treated as potential terrorists.

It was guilt by association, but there was nothing we could do about it. The day after its front-page coverage of our encounter with the Russians, the *San Francisco Chronicle*'s news-room got a call from an anonymous woman who read the following statement:

> The International People's Court of Retribution is a new justice movement for the balance of the earth. All state, federal and private money interests are now warned. Stop whaling.
>
> We consider all wildlife to be part of ourselves. Anyone caught killing wildlife, polluting or cutting down trees will be maimed, poisoned, or chopped in a similar manner. A whaler without arms cannot swim.

It was a message from a love child on an eco-bummer, and it would have been a joke except for the savagery. The *Chronicle* was too responsible to print it. It was only after September 12 that year that an editor remembered it, and they pulled the file. "Squeaky" Fromme had just launched her clumsy attack on President Gerald Ford. Squeaky was linked in the press to the Manson family, and to . . . the International People's Court of Retribution.

Just like that, anti-whaling activists everywhere were back on the blacklist. Again, I didn't blame the authorities. There was, in fact, a dark vortex stirring in the wake of our peaceful, media-hip "direct action." Probably unwisely, I had started using that term as a way of describing what we did, not realizing (in my backwater Canadian state of blissful ignorance) that certain armed terrorist groups in Europe, and even one in British Columbia, had been using exactly the same term to designate *their* idea of the right thing to do. I could see how the RCMP and the CIA, and, indeed, the FBI could get edgy over the language.

We at Greenpeace professed to be believers in the Gandhian concept of *satyagraha*, according to which there should be no word in your mind for *enemy*. It was a step further, in some ways, than turning your cheek. This was a very good thing to profess. It struck the right note of piousness. Whether anybody in the employment of a state surveillance agency believed it for a moment was the question. Probably not.

By 1980, three whaling ships had been sunk by limpet mines as they sat tied up at their docks in various ports. The outlaw whaler *Sierra*, which had been rammed by Sea Shepherd Conservation Society founder Paul Watson on his first solo run, was finally blown up in Lisbon harbor. The Spanish chaser boats *Ibsa I* and *Ibsa II* were sunk in the same manner.

So what was going on here? A lost tribe of the People's Court of Retribution? Berserk Greenpeacers or Sea Shepherds? *Or*— and this was why the wiretaps continued, I guess — was it some hard-nosed, steel-nerved conservationists who saw no other road than the ancient and cursed path of violence?

I had been a believer in the political power of *satyagraha*, more or less certain it had some kind of strange spiritual power, even if I was certain that real, deadly enemies existed. One had to look no further than the sight of a pod of whales being pursued by harpoon ships to see what sure as hell must have *looked* like an enemy as it charged across the waves towards them. What good did it do the whales not to have a word for enemy? In any event, it was clear by 1980 that some of the whales' defenders had shed the *satyagraha* thing.

Noting the trend, I wrote an article that year in *New Age* magazine entitled "Should We Fight to Save the Earth?" This was a publication in which the ads were for herbal medicines and the travel section featured ashrams; it was not the logical forum for the advocacy of violence. Indeed, after the article appeared, a storm of letters from shocked pacifists landed on the editor's desk. I was accused of encouraging terrorism, betraying the Buddha, giving in to evil. My reply was that I was just posing a philosophical question, examining an ethical dilemma that is becoming central to our time as species after species disappears.

The question went like this: if there are two blue whales left in the world, and they are about to be killed by ten human beings who refuse to stop unless you kill *them*, what is your ultimate moral responsibility — to kill a few of your fellow humans or stand aside and let an entire species be eliminated? Obviously, an excellent compromise is to blow the ships out from under the whalers, ideally hurting no one.

The dilemma for conservationists is comparable to the one faced by American Quakers just before the Civil War began. Their pacifist ideals, on the one hand, precluded any direct involvement in an armed struggle to overthrow the institution of slavery, yet those same ideals cried out for the liberation of the slaves. Prominent Quaker thinkers came up with an eminently practical compromise: they decided that, while they themselves could not take part in a violent effort to end slavery, they had "no argument" with others who felt bound to take up arms. Slavery itself was an ongoing form of institutionalized violence, they reasoned, and as such deserved what it got.

There were critics who saw a moral ambiguity here, perhaps a huge one, but in the harsh light of the reality of life in a semibarbaric society trying to civilize itself, brute force was seen as the only mechanism available to bring about change.

In the case of violence being brought to bear to end slavery, it is perhaps arguable that, without the Civil War, there could still be real slaves in America, even though technology might have eventually rendered the institution obsolete — without bloodshed. Here, the parallel with the modern whaling issue and the moral position of environmentalists ends, because in this situation, when the dust of debate has settled, there may not be any whales left. Extinction is irreversible.

Even if we could not see a coevolutionary imperative to protect species like the whale, we can certainly see the objective need to protect the interests of our own direct descendants, and these interests, it should be clear, include the right to be able to admire a living whale, to study the mystery of its existence, and, through it, perhaps, to learn more about existence itself.

The genius of nonviolence, as it emerges from the teachings of Christ and Gandhi, is that it breaks out of the remorseless spiral of violence begetting violence ad infinitum. No eye is taken in return for the one that is lost, and so an alternative opens up to the dead end of eternal attack and counterattack. No one can seriously question the moral purity of such a strategy. But so far history has not shown much evidence that the strategy is inevitably going to triumph.

My 1980 *New Age* article ended:

> In North American Plains Indian society, there is a class of medicine men who lead by example, but when "medicine" fails to solve a problem, the warrior class steps in and goes to war — as the Oglala Sioux did against Custer in a bid to save the buffalo from extinction at the hands of the White Man. In terms of the survival of the whales, have we reached a juncture as desperate as that? It may be a coincidence, in this year when whaling ships are coming under guerrilla attack, but at a recent Survival Gathering in the Sacred Black Hills, the motto was: "Don't weep for Mother Earth, fight to save her!"

When I'd gone on my first Greenpeace trip in 1971, I was a full-time employee of the *Vancouver Sun*, writing a column, which meant that I was allowed to express opinions, instead of merely passing along factoids. Which was good, because I quickly got sucked into the vortex of ecopolitics, and turned my column into a platform for green advocacy. Eventually, that wasn't enough, and I quit the newspaper business to take on the job of Greenpeace's first president and chairman of the board. I was the guy who stitched the Cree mythology of the Warrior of the Rainbow to the intellectual material of ecology. It was my

idea to use Zodiacs in the first place, vessels that have become signature protest icons. I test-drove them, in fact. I stood with Paul
Watson in front of an icebreaker off the Labrador coast one fine
spring day a year later to try to save harp-seal pups. Eventually I
got so carried away in the frenzy of trying to save the world that
I alienated many of my brothers and sisters, as we so optimisti-
cally called each other. I won reelection by only one vote. I
resigned a few months later, thoroughly disillusioned, but stayed
on the board of directors long enough to push my old comrade
Watson out on his own, whereupon he formed the now-famous
Sea Shepherd Conservation Society. I stayed involved with the
local Greenpeace scene long enough to help with the difficult
(and messy) political transition from Vancouver-based "environmental action group" to one of the world's biggest international
eco-outfits, with headquarters in Amsterdam. By then, my *com-
pañera*/wife, Bobbi, and I had retreated to a farm to raise animals
and children.

From our perch on the edge of British Columbia's rainforest,
we watched Greenpeace's fortunes rise and slump and rise again,
like a distant empire seen through glimpses on the *Six O'Clock
News*. The battles were far away — in places like Mururoa and
the Antarctic. And while people we had known who stayed in
the movement kept in touch, we mostly slipped out of the ever-
expanding loop, although a number of times over the years
I stuck my nose back in to help out with anti-whaling actions. I
was at Brighton, for instance, in 1986, when the moratorium on
the killing of the great whales was passed. I was involved in the
brainstorming around the ozone issue. I convinced Greenpeace
at the time of the Falklands War to deploy the *Rainbow Warrior* to
New Brunswick, to try to blockade a shipment of Canadian
CANDU nuclear fuel rods to Argentina. But more often, I rode
off, dutifully performing the functions of reporter, with my old
colleague Watson, the two of us having reconciled in the wake of
the early power struggles — in one case ramming some driftnet

ships, and in another case *failing* to ram any of the replicas of the
Niña, Pinta, and *Santa María,* being sent by Spain across the ocean
blue to mark the five-hundredth anniversary of the voyage of
Christopher Columbus, a story documented in my book *Red
Blood.* So, philosophically, I had always been of two minds: in the
main, nonviolence must be the rule, but there are extreme situations where violence may be the way to go. When it involves the
defense of an endangered species, for instance, and it only
involves the destruction of property, I have been known to buy
into it. But that's a job for somebody like Watson, who is willing
to plunge precariously along the edge of terrorism, not
Greenpeace, which derives much of its broad-based political
influence from its strict adherence to Gandhi-style pacifist tactics.

Other times, I traveled with Greenpeace, either by myself or
accompanied by a camera operator from CITY-TV: once we went
out into the spring storms off Labrador to cover the Turbot War;
once we journeyed into the heart of the Amazon rainforest,
where you dared not urinate in the river for fear of parasites that
could swim upstream. I missed the manifestations of the darker
side. I was not present, for instance, when two Norwegian
whalers were sunk and Watson's operatives scuttled the entire
Icelandic whaling fleet, and neither did I know anything about
these actions beforehand. I was not along when a Norwegian
Coast Guard cutter rammed Watson's ship in 1996, slicing off the
entire bow, and Norwegian commandos tried to sink him with
depth charges. I wasn't on board the *Rainbow Warrior* when she
was sunk in Auckland harbor, nor was I aboard in the Antarctic
Ocean in 1999 when a Japanese whaler turned and rammed the
Arctic Sunrise. So my experience of violence in the course of ecological crusading has been limited, consisting mainly of bracing
myself against the bulwark, rolling videotape as the *Sea Shepherd*
smashed into the hulls of two Japanese drift netters, enraging
the fishermen so much that a couple of flensing knives were
thrown at us. In the Îles de la Madeleine, after Watson had

been pummeled and kicked and dragged away by the mob, my cameraman, Todd Southgate, and I joined a half-dozen other reporters, fleeing our hotel rooms to avoid being captured and, we presumed, beaten.

The violence, in my experience (except for some large dents in a couple of drift netters) was coming mainly from the other side in its extreme, state-sponsored form. Nigerian author, poet, scriptwriter, and columnist Ken Saro-Wiwa was hanged in 1995 for his crusade against oil drilling, although that was not the official charge. Chico Mendes was fatally shot in Brazil in 1988, and of course a French limpet mine killed Fernando Pereira in 1985 during the sinking of the *Rainbow Warrior*. Karen Silkwood was assassinated in 1982, Diane Fossey in 1985. Estimates vary, but the often-cited figure of one thousand individuals murdered in the last two decades for their attempts to head off specific ecological disasters will probably turn out to be as much a lowball estimate as the old Soviet whale-catch numbers.

If this is indeed a *fight* to save Mother Earth, we are losing badly.

And, of course, now there is the added visible menace of terrorists obtaining nuclear weapons, either slipped to them from highly placed supporters in Pakistan or stolen from a half-abandoned Russian weapons cache. Look at the persistence of modern Japan and Norway when it comes to the whale hunt, despite international agreements and censure. Look at Newfoundland's continued scapegoating of seals as the cause of the collapse of the fisheries. Look at the Faroe Islanders with their "sport" butchery of trapped pilot whales. Look at Canada's Assembly of First Nations demanding the right to kill endangered species, if so required by tradition. And look at the Makah Indians *reviving* a long-abandoned hunt on traditional grounds. It would seem that atavistic mindsets were acting as a drag on any progress. As we came up on the turn of the twenty-first century, the vision of conservation pioneer John Muir was shriveling under the deluge of acid rain, extra ultraviolet radiation, clear-cutting, erosion, fires, and an inexorable heating of the ground, air, and water. We seemed to be skidding toward a Dark Age, rather than toward any kind of green soft-energy-path future.

It is against this desperate background that Watson launched his latest project in November of 2000, having struck a deal with the Ecuadorean government to provide a ship to patrol the Galapagos Islands, where poachers had been steadily decimating the famously diverse population of mutated creatures who inspired Charles Darwin. It was not just poachers that were active, either. In recent years, fishermen from mainland South America have surged in flotillas across eastern Pacific waters to invade the Galapagos, at one point holding the world's oldest tortoise hostage. The Ecuadorean government, beset by social problems, has virtually no budget for something as exotic as the rescue of an offshore natural paradise, or even its protection. So Watson undertook to provide a ship and crew, and to underwrite their costs, in order to carry armed Ecuadorean sailors to the Galapagos archipelago to maintain a permanent anti-poaching patrol. Like all cops, the Ecuadorean sailors have the power to make arrests and license to shoot, if necessary.

In effect, *Sea Shepherd* has acquired arms. This doesn't turn Watson into a terrorist, because he is simply assisting a legitimate governmental authority, in this case, the Ecuadorean navy, in the enforcement of its regulations.

I think this is one of the new formulae we need. It's time to get serious, to start demanding environmental-protection laws that specifically defend us from special corporate interests operating both within and without national boundaries. It should be apparent that the only solution to transboundary ecological threats is the implementation of international laws. It is not enough to declare moratoriums or designate sanctuaries if there is no enforcement mechanism.

I would like to see the Watson formula applied on a much larger scale. A good starting point would be for someone to convince the CIA that global warming represents "a clear and present danger to the Republic." There is no reason why the CIA couldn't be put to effective use in defense of America's "climate security," which is essential to everything else, from the security of the food supply to freedom from flooding, fire, and superstorms. The intelligence-gatherers with their "high-leverage" technology simply have to be directed by the president and the National Security Council to shift their "environmental" operations from spying on bunny huggers to protecting America's biodiversity. Give the spooks a serious ecological mandate!

Similarly, the sleuthing skills of Britain's MI-5, Israel's Mossad, France's Direction générale de la sécurité extérieure (DGSE), Russia's FSB, and the Canadian Security Intelligence Service (CSIS), to mention a few, could be redirected from the pursuit of ecoterrorists, as currently defined, to the pursuit of the actual perpetrators of crimes against the environment.

The biggest application of the Watson formula would be to convince the United Nations that the protection of the global ecosystem should be included in the mandate of the Security Council. As presently constituted, the UN General Assembly has no enforcement powers. Decisions are made by the Security Council, which is composed of fifteen members, five of whom — the United States, China, Russia, France, and the United Kingdom (the currently recognized nuclear powers) — are permanent. The others are elected for two-year terms by the General Assembly. Each permanent Security Council member possesses a veto. With this sort of a setup, it would seem highly unlikely that any of the permanent members would vote to censure *themselves* over an environmental issue, let alone agree to sanctions against themselves or in an extreme situation approve military action against themselves by the others. Since these five nations are among the top abusers of the environment, any UN-focused hopes for ecosalvation would seem futile. However, Article 27 of the UN Charter states that "in decisions under Chapter VI and under paragraph 3 of Article 52, a party to a dispute shall abstain from voting." Also, it remains that the five might at some point decide to act in unison with the other ten members and mobilize against a miscreant country that was, say, cutting and burning down a designated World Heritage rainforest. As we know, when faced with a threat to oil supplies, the UN can project political power militarily in jig time. Since its formation, it has thrown troops, with varying degrees of success, into half a dozen wars and at least one hundred peacekeeping missions.

If there were such a thing as a simple solution, this would be it: adding "environmental protection" to the Security Council's responsibilities. The idea is mind-stretching only to someone who remains blind to the problems piling up in front of us. What is required is that the UN adopt binding agreements in law that the Security Council would have to enforce, giving the UN the power to act without being invited to by the offending nation. Effective and enforceable sanctions would have to be ready for application. A century ago, no one was capable of imagining the routine modern deployment of peacekeeping troops to trouble spots anywhere in the world, assigned either to chase out invaders and mass murderers or to position themselves, arms at the ready, between implacable antagonists. For all its short-comings and failures, the UN's coalition peacekeeping campaigns are one of humanity's greatest overall triumphs, a radical depar-ture from history's horrific litany of might-is-right political rapacity. Why should it be too much to imagine another "radical" metamorphosis from a protector of victims of political injustice and a neutralizer of war-makers to a protector of the environment that ultimately sustains *all* the players?

I'm dreaming aloud, but wouldn't it be nice to see the Coast Guard out there on the high seas saving whales instead of, inevitably, protecting whalers from anyone trying to interfere with a hunt? In fact, this isn't as far-fetched as it might seem. In the high mountains of India's Ladakh region, Indian army officers already patrol the range of the threatened snow leopard, acting as "eyes on the land," on the alert for poachers and with orders to prevent villagers from encroaching on areas that provide habitat for the animal's natural prey. On a similar note, the stated policy of the government of Israel is that every animal in the Bible (except the lion) should once again roam free in wilderness areas of the country. Such species as the desert gazelle, the wolf, the ibex, and the leopard have been reintroduced. Israeli military officers are required to be trained naturalists. Part of their mandate is to protect the 23 percent of Israel's total area that has been set aside as a nature preserve.

In a meeting in Costa Rica in May 2001, military leaders and foreign-policy experts from fourteen countries gathered to consider the environment in the context of "threats to regional security," and while there were predictable and bitter complaints from antiwar spokespersons, my own feeling is that such an appraisal is long overdue. Indeed, how much longer do we have to wait before environmental threats to *global* security are finally looked at seriously?

Robin Rosenberg, deputy director of the North-South Institute, a U.S. foreign-policy think tank, suggested that the military "has a legitimate concern that environmental problems, if left unchecked, will result in avoidable security issues, such as border conflicts, insurrections and economic deterioration," according to the *Tico Times,* May 16, 2001. The talks in San José, Costa Rica, were "the first conference to put the words security and environmental in the same sentence," he added. According to Curtis Bowling, U.S. assistant deputy undersecretary for defense, "Environmental security implies a military peace mission to protect people from environmental threats." In addition to the traditional military task of providing emergency relief following natural disasters, he argued, armed forces must also focus on reducing environmental circumstances that lead to conflict by — get this! — promoting sustainable environmental laws that protect forestry and fisheries, regulate pollutants, and manage natural resources. Added Major General Gary Speer, deputy commander-in-chief of the U.S. Southern Command, "In the same vein that drug-related violence represents a threat to regional security, so too do concerns and conflicts over environmental issues. . . . Militaries must be prepared not only to respond to natural disasters, but also to prevent environmental issues from becoming a source of conflict. . . . The military brings to the table a trained, disciplined force with transportation. We have permanent leadership to execute planned, coordinated and supervised missions in response to natural disasters," the *Times* reported.

Of course, the ultimate step would be to launch missions designed to *head off* man-made "natural disasters," rather than merely to respond after the fact. According to Max Manwaring, a consultant to the U.S. Army War College, "The environment is too big an issue to not use all state and regional resources available. The problem is that a lot of people see this effort in the metaphor of the drug war or fight against communism. But the U.S. is not just looking for a new enemy. In reality, this effort is a recognition that civil society has not been able to address environmental threats, which are not just threats against quality of life, but threats that represent national security risks."

It is not *impossible*, after all, to imagine a time when the IPCC's ongoing work is finally recognized as scientifically irrefutable, and the signatories to the Kyoto Protocol would have to declare a phase-out of the production and release of any more fossil fuels, just as the signatories to the Montreal Protocol were forced on the basis of reason and logic to order the phase-out of CFCs.

If things are left long enough, a fossil-fuel moratorium may have to be declared. The big oil, coal, and gas companies will, no doubt, when compelled by law to abandon climate-destroying fuels, turn their attention to buying up the emerging alternative-energy sector. It will be unfair, and the big guys will remain big through adaptation, vertical integration, and the usual brazen attempts at monopoly for which capitalism is famous — unless, of course, the pace of corporate adaptation to the new reality is simply too brutally slow, and no genuine switch to a green ethic occurs among the shareholders and managers of the world's money machines.

Until such time as the Watson formula of aiding the civilian authority by providing crew and material is adopted by mainstream conservation groups — or, if not them, the civilian authorities themselves — there is a dangerous gap between implementation of existing international treaties and conventions, such as the International Whaling Commission's crumbling moratorium on whaling, and the reality of "scientific whaling" by Japanese and Norwegian whaling interests. Vigilantism won't work, but bringing the existing civilian and/or military authorities into active engagement on the preservation or energy-revolution front makes perfect sense. In the sixties it was fashionable to worry about "being co-opted." Today, I suggest, the only hope is to co-opt the state, that is, to press for robust proenvironment legislation that will set loose the dogs of ecopeacekeeping. All we need to add is a green stripe on the blue helmets.

The concept of intervening to protect the greater good is already well established. If the United Nations General Assembly were to resolve that emissions of the six main greenhouse gases had to be phased out by such and such a date, according to a schedule worked out for each and every nation, no matter how rich and heavily armed or poor and defenseless, and that any country which failed to stick to its quota would be subject to penalties, I predict that movement would begin immediately towards making an emergency "wartime-style" planetary switch to safe fuels. There is no question that it can be done.

But rather than relying on ecoguerrillas to pull our evolutionary bacon out of the fire, I am suggesting that governments everywhere should consider a much harder line against ecological destruction. Much of neoconservative thinking seems to focus on the joys of government–private-sector collaboration. It is not that much of an extension to suggest, if governments are too pressed on other fronts to fulfill their stewardship responsibilities, why not invite in the ecogroups, and let them take on some of the load of monitoring and enforcing? There are many who would be eager to help. Others might be more fastidious about keeping their distance from the dreaded military or police forces. In my view, the more astute hardcore environmentalists will be willing to back the Watson/Ecuadorean approach. Could such an approach be made to the UN by a sufficiently rich coalition of environmental groups to provide the logistical and material support for climate-change agreement enforcement? Of course!

Otherwise, if hardcore guerrilla activity is not moving at a fast enough pace, while the climate continues to take major hits and nation-states seem locked into the ancient tribal pattern of us-against-them, how, exactly, is global change going to be effected in time?

Well, when all else fails, there is still the good old-fashioned sixties idea that "mind-bombs" can be assembled and launched. As a believer, indeed as an advocate of this position, I set out in the fall of 2000 to take direct action against the Carbon Club, in the same way that I had once decided to take direct action against the builders of nuclear weapons. Could "media campaigns" still work after a generation of use and abuse? In the absence of a multimillion-dollar slush fund for an advertising blitz, what hope was there to communicate to the "masses" (i.e., on a big scale) if a good media campaign couldn't still be whipped together? There was still plenty of untapped potential for television-era global street theater, I thought.

STALKING A SUPERTANKER

FOR YEARS, I HAD BEEN THINK-
ing about, writing about, scheming against supertankers. I had
configured them into the flux of geological history as the
equivalent of a fleet of incoming asteroids, each one burning
upon entering the atmosphere. Every time one of these mighty
steel Ultra Large Crude Carriers is drained, its contents distributed, internally combusted, converted into greenhouse
gases, and spewed into the atmosphere from millions of
tailpipes, the Earth experiences the equivalent of another
meteorological bombardment, except that it is coming from
within: energy sucked from the ground and turning into a fire
in the sky.

In my mind, supertankers were a perfect symbol of technology run amok. In a paper commissioned by Greenpeace, completed in March 2000, and rather sweepingly titled "Extreme
Weather Events and Climate Change Response, Scenarios,
Tactics, and Strategy," I had argued in favor of targeting one of
the Brobdingnagian tanker-ships as a way of drawing media
attention to the link between petroleum and climate.

"The climate debate," I wrote,

needs a good stiff jolt of something spectacular. By facing off against mythological-scale supertankers themselves, which are the vital lynchpins holding the oil industry's international delivery system together, we get as close to being able to bump up against an actual instrument or vehicle which, while it may not be the *cause* itself of climate change's *effects*, is without doubt the biggest, most critical link in the chain. Underground or in the air, oil isn't a visible object. It is only in transit that it acquires a shape. We can't physically interfere much with the process of extracting oil from the ground, we can't *see* oil in its liquid form except for brief glimpses as it flows from pumps and hoses, and remains invisible after being burned until it metamorphoses into smog. Inside the hull of a supertanker, however, oil is temporarily captured, contained and bottled up, providing an opportunity for us to engage it, come to grips with it, push against it, trap it.

I could see plenty of excellent reasons for going after a supertanker. But this particular action was one that should be done with a sharp climate-change focus. Tankers were firmly associated with spills, which are actually, in the big picture, a much lesser ecocrime than triggering climate change. The goal, I thought, ought to be to bind supertankers in the public mind just as inextricably to extreme weather disasters as they are tied now to polluted waters. We would intercept a supertanker.

That was the dream.

It had taken half an hour of pounding across a medium chop into stinging rain to get us out far enough to attempt an interception. We'd jumped down into the Zodiacs from the *Arctic Sunrise*, at anchor just outside the breakwater at Long Beach, at 7 a.m., Monday, September 25, 2000. And while I was enjoying the business of charging into battle on high-speed seagoing chariots, not even my wetsuit was enough to cushion the kicking my buttocks were taking as I bounced repeatedly onto the fuel tank. It's always hard to keep yourself from being slammed about like a rag doll in a fast Zodiac in any kind of sea. But in this case, part of the problem was my damned poncho, a Yuppie camper's thing, big enough to be used as a one-man emergency tent, the hood of which kept falling over my eyes. It had also turned into a flapping purple sail, obscuring the view of our bearded young driver, Jesse Reid, who was already having enough trouble seeing past the shapes of his three passengers. "Nice cape," he muttered, politely making his frustration known.

I had another problem: the strap of my Hi-8 video camera, encased in a plastic waterproof casing, had got tangled around my neck, and what with me trying to shoot with one hand and hang on to the safety line with the other, there was no chance, as we bucked along, to straighten the mess out. According to my standard operating procedure, which I had been employing on and off since the dawn of the seventies, I was along for the ride as a reporter to cover what was happening, regardless of whether I had instigated the scenario in the first place.

In this case, I had been on vacation from CITY-TV during the previous week in L.A., so I wasn't in any technical position of conflict as I conspired. Only as of today, when the protest officially started, did I switch back into my reporter mode, to begin covering what went on. Like everybody else, I had the phone number of Greenpeace's lawyer written in felt pen on my forearm, since it was probable that we would *all* be busted, me included, no matter how much I protested that I was just an innocent Canadian journalist. The deal was, sometimes I was media, and sometimes I wasn't.

On this September morning in the first year of the millennium in the waters off Long Beach, we were launched upon a "classic" post–1975 Greenpeace action: Zodiacs skipping toward a ship. Everything had been planned around the objective of getting pictures. We were looking for an "iconic shot," and, in the process, people would take chances on drowning, getting run over, crushed, possibly beaten, arrested for sure, and maybe even murdered. Every effort had been made to minimize risk, and to manage whatever risk inevitably remained when you put people in the way of machines at high speed. But then there has always been this daredevil quality to Greenpeace-style protest. Think. In any period prior to the advent of the little handsheets of gossip and heresy, the first newspapers, there was no point whatsoever in trying to rise up against the oppressor by sticking your neck in the noose or under the guillotine. Yet this was our premise. By endangering ourselves, we somehow attacked the enemy. It was a tactic utterly dependent on media, and more specifically on a free press. It was the reverse of the scientific dilemma, wherein you alter a phenomenon when you observe it, since you are part of the same continuum. In this case, we were a phenomenon trying to alter a continuum by *forcing* the public to observe us.

Accordingly, the most sustained planning, which is to say the most meetings and phone calls and e-mails and faxes, had gone into the question of how to get coverage. For Greenpeace, an action that generated zero coverage was not worth doing. Sentimentality had been weeded out of the organization long ago; otherwise activists would still be out on the ice floes off eastern Canada every spring, fighting the seal hunt. We weren't sure, in the early days, whether we were an animal-rights group as well as pragmatic green political activists. The decision, by the start of the eighties, seemed to have been that Greenpeace was only concerned with issues that could be debated scientifically, e.g., was there an extinction factor? If not, on to other business. Resources, while they had grown from borrowed money to hundreds of millions of dollars a year, were still far from limitless.

Back when I was writing my "Climate Change and Response Scenarios" report, I had envisioned an action that would occur while an extreme weather event — a "freak" weather disaster — was happening somewhere in the world:

> weather disasters guarantee saturation coverage. Disaster is media feedstock, as indeed, is anything to do with weather. By tapping into weather disaster stories, we enter a zone of huge interest to everyone, not just greens . . . [but] we must realize that . . . we can't *compete* with great disaster footage. We should know our place in the news scheme of things. We should aim for a niche, rather than trying to gain stage center. Our claim to be part of the big story can only be justified if we can get our act together *immediately,* or at least while the story is still breaking, before it peaks. If cause and effect linkage is our objective, some measure of it can be achieved through action that occurs simultaneously with the event. Time is our primary link. By synchronizing our action with the event, we establish a coincidental connection, a time parallel, at the very least, which is a step in the right direction. In my opinion, GP's strongest and most coverage-generated response to an extreme weather event would be to attempt to physically pin down and delay at least one ULCC while the extreme weather disaster is still playing on the front pages. This way, we take the immediate weather event's voltage in the media, and connect it to the single most highly visible symbol that exists of multinational Big Oil.

So, the plan had been to hit a supertanker while floods were raging in Europe or mudslides were happening in Venezuela or an ice storm was blasting Canada. Ideally, someone would *weld* themselves into a supertanker's rudder just as it was about to leave a dock, fully loaded, so that it would take a while to remove the activist without burning him or her horribly in front of the cameras. Meanwhile, a truly gigantic banner would be dropped from the supertanker's deck, in effect the biggest drive-in screen ever assembled. From a nearby boat, live-feed broadcasts from the disaster zone would be projected onto the banner, turning the tanker into a massive TV screen, which the TV stations could then record, beaming the images around the world, something that would surely cause Marshall McLuhan to smile in heaven — and which, once and for all, would fuse the cause and effect of pollution and freak weather in the public mind.

Since then, things had been "evolving," as they say in the campaign business. At each step, the grand vision mutated slightly to adapt to the physical, psychological, organizational, ideological, and, indeed, even environmental terrain. First, by September, no high-profile extreme weather disaster had occurred since the Venezuelan mudslides in February. There had been floods in Europe, but not The Flood. The news about the rapid meltdown of the Arctic ice cap had broken, but it wasn't having an effect on anyone except a few polar bears. A record number of forest fires were burning in the American Southwest, but apart from briefly threatening the original Los Alamos nuclear laboratories, with their stockpiles of radioactive waste, the fires — mostly out of sight, out of mind — had been mainly a sidebar story through August. In none of the coverage about them was there a single reference to the possibility of a connection to global warming. There was nothing that you could call a springboard for a big media hit, no "big story" climate event transpiring with which we could "synchronize our actions." So much for my hopes of a "time parallel" to work with. So much for "coincidental connection," "zone of huge interest," "media feedstock," "primary link of timing," moving before the story "peaks." On the back of a beer mat in Amsterdam, a year before, I had written: *Never over-conceptualize.* Too bad I had forgotten my own boozy-but-solid advice.

By the time we hit the water, hope of apocalypse in the background had vanished in the pale purple ground-level ozone haze. No particular context had formed on the media radar that summer, and we had run out of time. We either moved now or forfeited our chance for at least a year.

Now, according to the final, much-simplified plan, I was aboard the smallest, lightest boat in the six-vessel Greenpeace flotilla. We were pounding in a V-formation straight towards the gargantuan tanker on the horizon. Our particular boat had fallen behind the larger, more powerful craft, despite Jesse's best efforts. As he gunned the 60-h.p. Mercury, we hit the crest of a wave and skipped like a stone to the next whitecap, smacking it spine-jarringly, so that we all grunted in unison. Finally my pelvis hit the fuel tank hard enough to loosen the hose. We could suddenly smell gas leaking. A little rainbow-hued slick had formed under my running shoe, so that I couldn't get any traction at all. "That's no good," grunted Jesse, radioing in the scramble mode to the other boats that we were stopping a moment. It took some tugging and shuffling of protest signs, flippers, and waterproof survival packs, but the fuel tank was soon repositioned, the fitting tightened. My ridiculous purple cape came off, and I got the camera strap untangled. The irony of having an oil spill in our own vessel on the way out to do an action against a supertanker was not lost on me. "No way to make these things solar powered?" I yelled to Jesse over the shrieking whine of the Zodiac's engine. He shot me a look that said, "Don't go getting all silly on me."

And now here was the reality of the "mythological-scale" monster itself, emerging from the gray Southern California offshore mist dead ahead: a ship the size of the Empire State Building, as *wide* as most ships are long, the largest mobile object ever built, weighing over three hundred thousand metric tons —

and that before a drop of oil has been poured aboard — a 333-meter (1,000-foot) British Petroleum flag-of-convenience carrier out of Argentina, called, charmingly, the *Pecos*. We had been expecting our target to be coming from the north, from Alaska, but this was entering the harbor from the south, which meant that events were already out of whack with our ideal scenario. It was also coming faster than we had anticipated, because it didn't have to swing around a headland. It was the biggest tanker anybody had seen after weeks of spying. Our intelligence team, listening on the marine band, monitoring with binoculars from positions along the coast, and keeping track of clandestinely obtained shipping schedules, reported that it was "a brute." We had a hard tactical call to make, because, even though it was coming from the wrong direction, too fast, the window of opportunity was starting to close. We had delayed as long as we could, waiting for the right moment. Within days, the Greenpeace mother ship, the *Arctic Sunrise*, would have to head on to her next assignment. The temptation to strike, even if the pace was wrong, was overwhelming, and now that we could see it, something bloated and swollen about the thing cried out: Enemy of Nature, natural enemy! I think of most ships automatically as a *she*, but not this. This was an *it* — although, even from a mile away, it had a face. It came into focus in the lens of my camera in frames as we bucked and skipped across the water and, as it loomed larger, I got the uncomfortable feeling that we were being pulled by its immense gravitational presence into a collision course. Steadily, it began to rise, taking up more and more of the sky and the horizon.

I began to hear the drum roll of displaced, punctured, overturned ocean.

All I had ever seen were aerial shots and diagrams. I knew the incredible statistics. Biggest and longest this and widest and deepest that. Capable of carrying 75 *million* gallons of crude. Ten miles just to stop. In my fantasies, I had seen our attack on a supertanker as something akin to our ancestors cornering a mastodon. Riding our little Zodiacs, we would use our cameras like spears, not wanting merely to kill the beast but to deliberately drive its species to extinction. These things have to be banned and dismantled. In my mind, there is absolutely no doubt about that at all. But its speed was appalling. It heaved its tusks of foam. This was no shambling, wool-covered muppet. What sprang to mind rather, was the Minotaur, the mythic half-man, half-bull, coming up from the depths; only this mutated thing instead was half-man, half-machine.

"Look at that fucking bow-wave, man!" yelled one of the swimmers, Stephanie Hillman, with a tone of awe.

Even though I'd had a good, calm breakfast, my guts suddenly felt empty. I had all the other symptoms of fear, too: dry throat, heart whapping into a high gear. It was there, in the cauldron of white water being cleaved by the bow, that I had hoped we could position ourselves, out of the reach of the Coast Guard when they arrived with their deeper-draft boats. It would be a delicate balancing act, surfing in an inflatable exactly where we should not be, in the hope of slowing the monster down, maybe even stopping it for a few minutes before we were busted. I had based this scheme entirely on the report of an old hippie ecohawk buddy of mine, "Rainbow" Rex Weyler, who had once ridden a craft such as ours under the bow of a supertanker in Puget Sound, and he reported that the experience was like being blessed; he entered a totally unexpected zone of tranquility in front of the bow that was as peaceful as a hot tub. No wonder dolphins loved to play there! Not much more than an arm's length beneath the boiling surface, thrust out like half a submarine fused on the keel, was a great forward bulb, which was ramming a hole through the water. It was right there, above the gargantuan metal bulb and right under the metal cowl of the bow, where my friend had advised me I'd find a kind of pillow wave, where it would be possible to stay afloat at full speed in the cavernous, slavering jaw.

But I could see immediately that there was something wrong. Instead of being buried a yard or so underwater, as predicted, the forward bulb on this baby was dangerously close to the surface. Instead of back eddying, the water above the bulge was a maelstrom of standing waves and exploding upsurges. It would be like riding a following sea on a wave that never breaks. In canoeing terms, we were looking at a horizontal avalanche of Class 5 rapids breaking across the sea at twelve knots.

So much for *that* bright idea.

It wasn't just physical fear that had my teeth on the verge of chattering. It was something larger, a slow-motion psychological blow coming in, that was hitting me not just in the gut, but also in the psyche. The size of the thing was power in itself. If it was, as I had come to believe, an evil power, or at least the engine of an evil power or its manifestation, then we are surely lost. Abandon Planet Earth. Find another dimension or world. Down here at water level, as it loomed toward us, my soul quailed. Too big! Too unassailable. A walled city or fortress in motion, it raced like an entire mesa of steel, plowing across a desert. To go against it was surely to go against a god of some kind. What *could* you do against the intelligence and organization that had created such a vessel? The unholy size of it was a statement in itself about money and greed and technology. Staring at it, I could feel the energy hunger of 6 billion human beings. I could feel the thirst for power of every general and president and dictator. I could hear millions of engines starting. I could sense, in my mind, a searing blast of heat from the future, as though unseen forces were disrupting time and space. A pure embodiment of engineering skills, the supership was somehow as primal as anything I had ever seen outside of natural forces at work. Even in mythology, the heroes never faced anything as big, as ponderous, as heavily armored, and as surely unstoppable as *this*.

I turned my camera on Stephanie as she struggled, the super-

tanker in the background, to pull her wetsuit over her head, and
I glimpsed a certain faraway look in her eye, as though she were
thinking deeply about life and the universe. Her jaw was set. She
wasn't in the mood for any idle chatter. As far as she was concerned, the camera didn't exist. Respecting her space, I panned
past to Suzanne Teachey, our fourth rider, also clad in a wetsuit.
She had her flippers braced against the other side of the Zodiac,
while she clung to the safety line with thick paw-like diver's
mitts. I wanted to say something to both of them about how
much I admired them for what they were about to do, but I
feared sounding corny. I decided not to try to force them to
speak into the camera. What was going on here was too real, too
noble, I felt, to muck it up by playing reporter. Stephanie was
perfectly dignified and composed. It would debase things to try
to coax her into spouting the official campaign message *now*.

As for Suzanne, it would have been grossly intrusive to break
her concentration. Squinted against the spray, her narrowed eyes
were on the supertanker, and I got the impression she was measuring its size against the size of her own resolve. For nothing
less than stopping it was exactly what they intended if everything else failed. To even *contemplate* such a thing, let alone physically place yourself in a Zodiac, psychologically primed for
what could very well turn out to be a kamikaze mission, a person had to be driven by strong passions, maybe even zealotry. Yet
apart from tenuous smiles, I hadn't got too much reaction from
either of them. Stephanie, probably coming up on thirty years
old, had short-cropped curly hair, and until now had sported
gingham dresses and running shoes, a classic Pacific Northwest
vegetarian look. Suzanne, mid-twenties, from Seattle itself,
more a city girl, had straight shoulder-length black hair, dark
eyes, and freckles. She was an intense listener, and always sat or
stood at the back of the room during crew meetings. I had taken
some footage of her last night down in the hold with the action
team, filling in the eight-foot-high letters on a yellow banner

with a green marker. To get a shot of her and the whole banner on my Hi-8, I'd had to back up a dozen steps to see it in full.

OIL FUELS CLIMATE CHAOS

The sight of those blocked-out words should have thrilled me, since I had composed them, and it was the first time in years a slogan I'd written had turned into an actual banner. Four words were all we were going to get to project. And to get down to those four words we had "messaged," as the media team called it. That is, we had fought over the wording — literally for weeks, e-mails spitting back and forth between Amsterdam, Washington, D.C., Vancouver, and Toronto. We had gone through three teleconferences and a weekend meeting before the campaign director, Steve Shallhorn, finally pursed his lips and declared: "We'll run with Bob's version."

Well, I thought, I should hope so. It was annoying to arm-wrestle intellectually with several young "media professionals" (who hadn't been born when I was doing some of my seminal propagandizing) in order to win support for my bright ideas. I tried not to make huffing noises, but I might have lost the gift for working patiently with large groups of dedicated people. I could feel myself behaving in a patriarchal manner, highly out of fashion. Yet in this situation, I was in fact a real-life patriarch.

They were all certainly aware that I had served on the original *Greenpeace* voyage. My mug had showed up in virtually all the photographic histories. And some of them may even have read the book I wrote about the formative years of the organization from 1970 to 1977 entitled *Warriors of the Rainbow,* also published as *The Greenpeace Chronicle.* Not a few viewed me as some sort of Ice Man from a dawn age of ecoactivism, returned from the dead to pace the decks at night and haunt the bar. Several months before, I had been named in *Time* magazine's millennium issue as one of the "Heroes of the Century" for defending the planet.

This placed a ridiculous burden on any relationship with other ecowarriors, whose instinct, if they were true rebels, would be to reject and tear down any form of authority. All this baggage I was carrying meant I was close at least to *looking* as if I had authority, and I guess I did have *some* influence, otherwise the *Arctic Sunrise*—and all these people, for that matter—wouldn't be in Long Beach, ambushing a supertanker.

Alas, the international climate campaign team in Amsterdam, to whom I had sent my report, had been preoccupied. After one teleconference call, in which everyone had seemed to agree to get on with it, the proposal vanished into the bureaucratic depths. That probably would have been the end of it, with me disgruntled and despairing, but Canadian campaign coordinator, Steve Shallhorn, got hold of a copy of my report. Old warrior that he was, he liked the supertanker blockade idea immediately. We had a beer or two at the Rex Hotel on Queen Street in Toronto to discuss the matter. Alas, the Canadian organization for the most part wasn't interested in climate. And that would certainly have been the last gasp of the supertanker action, except that Shallhorn decided, shortly thereafter, to apply for the job of United States campaign coordinator, which had opened up at the time when there was a political void at the top in the Washington, D.C., office. The new American executive director was not yet installed, which meant that Steve would actually be in control for a while. He would be living half the time in Washington, flying all over the place, living out of a suitcase, but it would be worth it. He'd be in charge of a much larger budget than ever before, which meant more power. All he had to do was cope with the incessant, tormented internal politics for which American Greenpeace offices had always been famous.

I thought I'd have an easy time getting things done *my* way, simply because Steve, now the supreme U.S. campaign boss, had brought me in. But that attitude harkened, apparently, back to a more autocratic era. These days not even authorship of a concept was enough to permit one to dictate *anything*. The fierce spirit of antiestablishmentarianism, which had been imprinted in the organization's DNA, was still very much alive. I was not going to get away with single-handedly controlling *anything*.

When I first arrived at the motel in Long Beach, which was our field headquarters, I wanted to put out a press release warning of an "atmospheric Alamo." What the hell, I figured, we're deep in the heart of America. But no, I was advised by the campaign's media team, *that* couldn't possibly be used. It would upset Hispanics. Oh. Shame about that. I bit my tongue.

You don't just suddenly break into a group that's been in action together. Here was a gang of some thirty hardcore activist sea dogs from a half a dozen countries, with everything between them going on in the context of an elaborate subtext. They already spoke a language laced with code words. Once you have shipped together you have bonded for life. These guys were *tight*. It took several days of being aboard, taking meetings, eating canteen fashion, hanging around on deck and in the wheelhouse, and drinking my way through several good late-night sessions in the lounge, to get a rudimentary relationship going with even half the crew, and just to get a handle on the names, some of which were German, Dutch, Swedish, and Chilean. To add to the overload, just the day before we set out from Long Beach, a dozen volunteers arrived whom I'd never seen before — all Americans, mostly from the Seattle area. Introductions all around. Names all gone. They had the wholesome look of campers, almost-Christian zeal. No panic. We'd get to know each other soon enough, especially when we got into a Zodiac together.

It wasn't until late that evening that the final crew meeting was called, while the banner still lay drying on the floor. It was almost impossible to hear anything being said, so we all crowded together in the cavernous hold, the auxiliary engine running, making a perpetual roar so that any spying devices would be unable to pick up what was being said. A lawyer had already

advised us that what we were proposing to do violated several
federal laws, and so we were automatically guilty of conspiracy
if we even discussed the matter. Or at least we could be charged.
So the captain shouted under the roar of the auxiliary as he
pointed out the details on a chart of the harbor. There was a
large purple parallelogram in the middle, a zone designated by
the Coast Guard as being off-limits to everyone except supertankers. We would move out at dawn and head straight out from
the breakwater, running along beside the zone until we got to
the furthermost point, hopefully getting there just as the target
arrived, at which point we would intercept it. The early concept
of having someone weld him or herself onto a rudder had been
rejected when it was learned that, because of the fire hazard,
there are strict rules over activities involving combustion near a
tanker. Anything involving a blowtorch was totally, absolutely
out. Too risky all around. Irresponsible. Kaput.

Instead, the climbers would board the supertanker while it
was in motion, and hang the sacred four-word banner. This
would be done by jamming a Zodiac up against the ship while
people rappelled up the side. The big media outlets in Los
Angeles had been visited by Shallhorn and myself, who tipped
them off that Greenpeace was planning a "big action." They
were on standby with their choppers. And just in case they
missed the "money shot," Greenpeace would have its own
chopper hovering just above the scene, piloted by the legendary
Paula Huckleberry, the person who had flown into the Antarctic
ice-crack and repeatedly placed herself directly in front of a
harpoon. This time, she'd be carrying a still photographer and
a hired video operator, who was strapped into a SteadyCam,
shooting through an open hatch.

But shooting what?

Since all the grand schemes of fantastic timing and gigantic
props and high-tech gimmicks had crumbled one by one, it
seemed we were down to a boarding and a banner-hanging,

hardly revolutionary new-media methods. To add some zest to it, I had got permission to go in with the Zodiac and try to maintain a position right under the bow, out of reach of the Coast Guard. But after that, the only trick anybody could think to inject into the mix was to put swimmers in the water in the tanker's path. This tactic was seen strictly as a last resort, to be undertaken only if the attempt to board the vessel failed or if its captain refused to give way to a Zodiac in his path.

The final decision about whether or not to deploy the swimmers would not be made until the field situation was clear, and certain questions had been answered: How long would the supertanker take to stop at its current speed? How fast could it turn? *Would* it turn? Or would it pretend to be blind — or even *be* blind to anything so small — and rumble right over them? If the Coast Guard showed up on time, could they be counted on to haul the swimmers out of the water rather than let them successfully obstruct a major shipping lane? We hoped. If not — if, for some reason, the Coast Guard boys didn't act responsibly — we'd be standing by to pull them out of there ourselves at the last minute, assuming we were not being prevented from doing so. The U.S. Coast Guard had been hammering protesters lately, running one down and nearly killing her a few months back during an antiwhaling campaign against the Makah Indians off the Washington State coast. To make things worse, Greenpeace activists had been busted as recently as a year ago in Los Angeles harbor next door, and were still facing three-month jail terms as a result. The sea cops, their noses out of joint, might just decide to let the protesters stay put in the water and be run over. In that case, they would disappear like specks gobbled up in a vast broth of foam. Would the wetsuits and lifejackets buoy them up to the surface so they popped free of the stern, or would the props dice them into pieces?

We'd soon find out. Ahead, the tanker had become a *wall*. It made a rumbling, part-piston, part-tidal-wave sound. And of course there was a cowl of black smoke rising like a small volcano from its stack. Black-hulled, with traditional white superstructure, it was, indeed, bigger than most medieval citadels. And it *moved*, displacing swells such as you usually only find deep at sea. As we got close to the starboard beam, I had to pan from one extreme left-shoulder angle to the extreme right in order to get it all in one shot. And it was only by lying back on the Zodiac's deck that I could show the whole structure from waterline to the top of her towering masts. Her deck, of course, would be like a refinery yard, with pipes and tanks and ladder and gantries and cranes and hoses, a place where a man, walking around, would be about the size of an ant upon a truck, but from this far below the radar- and satellite-dish-covered wheelhouse roof, some hundred and fifty feet abeam, I couldn't see above the freeboard. The angle was too steep.

The biggest Zodiac, closer in than ours, slowed for an almost leisurely climb over the swell, then bee-lined across fizzling water for the starboard hull, pulling up parallel, doing about twelve knots. The driver pulled her over hard to the port and bounced a couple of times before seeming to adhere to the plates, even as the inflatable slid up and down like a sponge. A thirty-foot-long plastic coupling hook with the climbing rope inside was jabbed into the air, unfolding telescope-style in reverse, scratching like an awkward space arm — all at high speed in sprays of spitting foam. It was a striking scene: the climbers with their gear and the great bundled banners strapped over their shoulders, crouching as they bounced, as if they were standing up on a motorcycle, poised to grab the rope the moment the grappling hook got a grip up above and to start rappeling up the sheer steel wall as it hurtled forward.

Maybe it looked different from where they were, but from our vantage point further away it became clear immediately that the climbing project didn't have a chance. The hook reached only a quarter to a third of the way to the deck. And far above, a crewman in his Mustang suit looked down, waiting to kick any grappling device overboard. Militarily, I dimly recalled, you needed a ratio of three attackers per defender to take a walled city, and even then only if you had proper siege machines. This ship was as impregnable as Troy and it moved faster than any kind of horse. It had not slowed down a knot.

It was Jesse who finally realized the source of the problem: "She's not full!"

This not only explained why the freeboard was so high, but made sense of the chaos around the bow. The *Pecos*, for some reason, wasn't traveling with a full load of crude, which seemed strange at the time of soaring worldwide gasoline prices. Was that one of the tricks they used to maintain high prices, by keeping supplies low? Had she been full, we would have seen nothing but flat black hull, exposed from the water line up. Instead, the bottom third of the hull was covered with rust-colored anti-fouling paint. She was riding at least thirty feet higher above the sea than normal.

This was plenty enough to totally throw off the calculations that had been applied in the design of the grappling hook the night before in the *Arctic Sunrise*'s hold, but the big Zodiac, looking very small, stayed pressed against the massive hull even after it became clear to all that the hook wasn't getting anywhere. Messages crackled incomprehensibly through the scrambler. The red Greenpeace helicopter, dubbed *Tweetie*, swept over us towards the tanker, banked and swung into a position alongside the Zodiac, while the cameraman strapped into his SteadyCam harness caught the action — or, as it was turning out, the lack of action. The tiny rubber thing nibbling at the ship's side looked futile and pathetic. My only thought was: they should get out of there while they still can, before something goes wrong and they flip and get sucked under. Somebody had the same thought. With a hard bank to the starboard, riding back up and over on the bow swell, the boat was away.

By now, the *Pecos* had cut her speed in half, to barely six knots. I thought it took ten miles for one of these things to stop. Wrong. They are more maneuverable than they let on.

We were all in motion, streaking alongside the shambling supertanker, but tactically the action had stalled. Without climbers aboard the ship to at least hang the banner, we wouldn't be making *any* kind of critical connection in the mass mind between climate and oil. The discontinuity between cause and effect would remain firmly in place. Our goal of linkage would *not* be achieved.

Had we come to the moment, then, when the swimmers would have to make their move? Somebody jabbered something to Jesse over his handheld phone that he could just barely hear above our engine and the roar of the chopper. Leaning forward he yelled, "The captain has radioed he's being boarded and the Coast Guard has called that they're on their way. We're supposed to get in position." He cranked her and our nose went up in the air. We started leaping in great bounds across the water, sheltered from the wind now in the great vessel's lee, racing to overtake her. Stephanie and Suzanne came out of their sitting positions and got their knees braced underneath them. They were really going to go ahead with this.

We were just coming abeam the bow, with a wind and white-caps and drizzle lashing us again, when the black Coast Guard helicopter came beating ponderously out of the sky, and I noticed *Tweetie* veering off and buzzing for the shore, the better to get whatever footage they had back to Long Beach for dubbing and release to the media. When the camera flies, that usually means it's over — although that wasn't quite true this time. Half a dozen other helicopters had materialized over the scene, bearing the logos of various TV stations. So we were still in the game. But there came the opposition cavalry! One, two, three, make those four Coast Guard black-and-orange Zodiacs.

As well, a fifty-foot launch was coming up from the super-tanker's stern, and hard in its wake, a large, formidable cruiser, armed with a fifty-millimeter cannon on the forward deck. They had us matched, boat for boat — and there were two or three more auxiliary inflatables converging on the scene. Out in force, these boys.

"How'd they get here so fast?" Jesse demanded.

"Can you still get us under there?" I asked, pointing to the bow.

"No problem," he replied laconically, and pushed the control stick over. We peeled off the port, coming around in a circle so that we'd cross the bow from that side. From out of nowhere, a Coast Guard Zodiac was right on our tail, no more than fifteen feet behind. We pretended we didn't see them or hear them, even though an officer was thundering over the bullhorn: *"Get back! This is a restricted zone! You don't have authorization!"* Just when it looked like we could outrun them, another red-and-black Zodiac with six SWAT-team-style armed guys wearing flak jackets and sunglasses came sluicing into view from the starboard side of the bow dead ahead. Jesse sheered tightly to the port and booted it, so that it seemed for all intents and purposes we were hightailing it out of there. The Coast Guard boys altered course and kept after us, riding side-by-side. They'd almost overtaken us in a flat-out run when Jesse barked "Hang on!" and executed the tightest turn yet, virtually on a dime. As the two pursuing Zodiacs pirouetted in great explosion of foam, we shot back towards the oncoming bow. It was all I could do to "hang on" while I flopped about on my butt on the Zodiac's floor, swiveling the camera above my head like a football in a desperate attempt to somehow tape what was going on as we closed, engine screaming, and entered the shadow and the maelstrom of white water. The bow of the *Pecos* swung over-head like a cloudbank, and the bulbous anchors passed in orbit like slow-motion asteroids. Then we were clear. Jesse was whooping like a wild man. And the two SWAT teams on our tail swerved off to chase other protest boats.

By now, the *Pecos* was barely crawling. We were instructed over the handheld to regroup with the other boats. As soon as we started to congregate in one spot, the Coast Guard guys settled into positions directly between the tanker and us, completely blocking access.

"No point diving in the water now," Dave, the action co-ordinator, said to the swimmers. "They'll just pull you out."

While we bobbed on the water, thwarted by guys in blue jumpsuits with guns, the supertanker had altered course a mile away and was coming about just outside the seawall, not far from where we had launched our attack a couple of hours before. We could make out the outline of the *Arctic Sunrise* in the haze. Somebody said over the radio that they'd heard a shipping-company spokesman say the tanker never intended to go directly to a dock, anyway, so we had not really caused it to turn or slow down. It was just doing what it had planned to do, with or without a military escort. Its instructions all along had been to lie up outside Long Beach harbor and wait a couple of days for a space to open up. To jump into the water in front of it now would be a *really* futile gesture, since it wasn't going anywhere. As we spoke, one of the truck-sized anchors crashed into the sea.

The *Pecos* had eluded our attempt to render it extinct. Shrugged us off like fleas. Obviously, the Coast Guard had been on alert; otherwise they wouldn't have swarmed us with so much hardware so quickly. It had taken us nearly half an hour to get out here. They were all over us inside ten minutes. So much for any element of surprise. So much for the big media hit. So much for closing the synapse of climate-change discontinuity. Message? What message? As far as anyone, including the media, could tell, we could have been protesting high gas prices.

FEAR OF FURTHER FLYING

FORTY-EIGHT HOURS LATER, Steve Shallhorn and I were squeezing into our seats on an Air Canada L-1011, bound for Toronto from the fabled Los Angeles Airport.

One night, years ago, when I had been down in Hollywood working on a script, a friend had driven me to a place just off the Interstate, where we stood directly underneath the flight path, right up against the hurricane fence, braced ourselves, and looked up. The wheels of the incoming jets were clearing the tops of the passing transports on the highway by a matter of mere yards. From this angle, we could see the lights of the jets all lined up in a row as they glided in, stretching like a truly gigantic bridge over the Sierra Nevada.

For a moment, I could see that the lights were all part of a single stationary structure, the largest causeway ever engineered. But you could only see it at night. We are not just talking metaphor or allegory; the world is linked together by invisible bridges in the sky, structures binding its cities together as surely as the old iron girders and columns of stone that spanned the rivers. Scale! The hard thing to get is the scale! For a second, I had it. I got a glimpse of the true scale of the machine we have

built. Of course, the impact of 150 decibels as the jets yowled
overhead was enough to confuse your senses — louder than
chainsaws or newspaper presses or rock concerts or thunder-
claps. But I had the distinct impression I was seeing the outline
of the real shape of industrial society, the real picture of the
bigness, the sheer density, the mass of human civilization, which
has literally burst out of the bounds of Nature in the last couple
of hundred years. This was something so much more than the
sum of its parts that it was almost beyond our primitive capacity
to see or understand. The techno-supercivilization of the future
is already here, already in place. But mostly we don't see it. We
still *see* like our ancestors. We are good at picking out immediate physical details, differentiating, and extrapolating in order to
take action to survive, but we do not *see* most of what is now
happening all around us. We don't *see* the ozone layer disappearing. We don't *see* the temperature rising. We don't *see* the radiation levels. Mainly, we don't see the *connections,* which is what
this whole largely invisible new civilization is about.

And it is fueled overwhelmingly by oil, of course — geysers
of which are blasted out of the tail of this big Lockheed beauty
we have just boarded.

If a mere puddle of gas that spilled in our Zodiac had struck
me as ironic, what could you say about this? The fact is a mighty
L-1011 burns 3,500 gallons of jet-A fuel *every hour,* and it flies for
an average of ten hours a day. Some of these small-em miracles
of engineering have been airborne for twenty of their expected
thirty-five years of service already. If there is such a thing as a
petroleum karmic debt, which I was coming to believe, one
could not help but add lifetimes of penance to one's cycle of
birth and death by climbing aboard one of these titans of mass
pollution even once, let alone frequently.

But Steve hadn't seen his wife and daughters for nearly a month,
and after just ten days away from my wife, kids, dog, writing
cabin, and waterbed, I was already homesick. Domestication had

taken its toll on my level of dedication. The idea of being off at sea on a mission for three months at a time, as I'd been years before, wasn't something I would seriously contemplate any more — short of an actual United Nations Declaration of a Global Ecological Emergency, with a call for total mobilization. And we were a long way from that. Obviously.

The supertanker campaign had, after all, amounted to little more than routine planetary duty. Certainly, so far as the world was concerned, our action had been an extremely minor media ripple. We did get some coverage — a mention in the *New York Times*, a story with pics in the *L.A. Times*, and an above-the-fold page-one color spread in the *Long Beach Gazette,* with the head-line that blatted: "NOBODY OVERBOARD, Greenpeace *Fails to Block Tanker.*" A couple of big papers in India had picked up the shots of our Zodiac flotilla, augmented by the Coast Guard boats, parading along beside the *Pecos*. What else? The U.K. office reported seeing "some stuff" on the boob tube. CNN had distributed our footage in a business "magazine package" about oil prices and the OPEC meeting. Judging from the Canadian papers we grabbed as we came aboard, absolutely zip had run in the True North.

It was impossible, at the moment, not to feel thoroughly daunted.

The journey from the *Arctic Sunrise*, tied up in Long Beach, through L.A. to the airport had taken only thirty minutes, even though we had covered that many miles, and despite the fact that there was a transit strike. The sky was as gray as the vast cement floodway troughs, but you could make out the silhou-ettes of the high-rises in the various city cores. This made it the equivalent of a clear day. Steve, as it happened, had once worked as a taxi driver. With him at the wheel, we streaked and weaved effortlessly along. This was surely the automobile culture at its apogee. We were taking advantage of one of the great trans-portation achievements of all time. Instead of having collapsed

or been torn apart years ago, as was so often predicted, the Los
Angeles Basin freeway system seemed to be working better than
ever. Earthquakes had become a means of permanent urban
renewal. This was Kerouac's America writ large, projected into
the future: frenetic movement, yet somehow beautiful, despite
its bad press. I had to admit, it was pretty amazing. A sustained
high-speed flow of metal and fiberglass and rubber hurtling *en
masse* like a multicolored insect horde along a nexus of bridges
in the sky, and miraculously not flying off in every direction.

Getting this technostructure up and running, and keeping it
going, was an incredible achievement. Just the intellectual component was worthy of respect, never mind the mathematical
skills it represented. Formidable foes, the builders of industrial
society! You wouldn't want to get on the wrong side of the creatures that had assembled *this*. It had taken life on this planet more
than 4 billion years to get to the point where it could erect a
bafflingly intricate superstructure like this. All powered by ... we
know, we know.

For once, even the car rental system had functioned flawlessly
for us. We got out of the car, handed over the keys, walked a
couple of yards, and climbed into a smoothly whirring bus. A
quick spin around a cloverleaf, a dash down a collector lane, and
we were stepping out of the bus, through automatic glass doors,
up a whispering escalator. We paused for a latte, shuffled down
a tube into the plane, and, just like that, we were trundling out
onto the tarmac, our noses teased by the almost nauseatingly
sweet smell of jet-A fuel. Everything outside the window was
shimmering in the fumes from idling engines, as if we had
started to shift out of phase with matter. It was an alien atmosphere, and the workers we saw down there on the tarmac were
all wearing white masks. It was impossible to get a picture of the
scale of LAX as we humped along the runway beside the terminal, rolling ... and rolling ... and rolling. I tried to keep track
of the number of different logos on the tail fins of the restless,

shuffling suborbital spacecraft we passed, but gave up in favor of just letting the sheer size of the rookery impress itself upon me. Among the stiff-winged birds, the great humpbacked 747s were still kings, after all these years of the Space Age. In my mind, they were the dodos, doomed the moment gas prices pass a certain threshold, but for the moment it was clear they were still the eagles, making a noise like a mini-volcano as they shot into the opaque sky.

Once we had liftoff, the Los Angeles Basin splayed crazily out, and I could see that there was at least as much asphalt down there as rooftops, and *no* parks. Quickly, the ground-level ozone coagulated into a chromatic, dimensionless blur. It was only when we reached the rim of the Sierra Nevada that the bowl of chemicals drained away, and we could see the ground again — except that it was the flinty, scoured Martian desert around Las Vegas. If you would go looking for an image of the future on a heated-up Earth, fly over Death Valley. If you have any doubts that something terrible has already happened, take any flight across North America. Whereas on a normal day as recently as the late sixties, the horizon used to be visible, now, from 35,000 feet, *you never see it.* There is *always* a cataract-colored lens of particulate matter forming a zone of nullity between land and sky.

I am often struck by the thought that I have survived into the future. Certainly the "I" who was me back in the 1950s, reading science fiction and *Popular Mechanics*, would be paralyzed with excitement to be here now in this incredible flying machine, cruising with barely a whisper of thunder on the edge of space. Mass transportation seven miles up, moving at 625 miles an hour! Yes, this is the future. I didn't expect it to arrive here while I was still around. And the template of me which still dwells in the fifties and sees the twenty-first century as a constant source of wonder, goes into a kind of ecstatic trance upon climbing aboard a jetliner. Of all the human generations to live in, I gloat, this is the best! Today, there are said to be 3 million human beings in the

air at any given moment. It is as if our species was starting to lift
off into space, a mass practice session in yogic flying.

Of course, we all profess an utter world-weary distaste for
flying. Airports consume me with ennui, I claim. But the truth
is, I am *addicted* to airports and jets. I savor being up here so far
above the clouds. There is a thrill of power. A superior species?
Hey, look at me; I am a god, or at least a godling. What other
creature can come remotely close to touching me? And it's not
just in the air that this weird sensation of kinky tech-pleasure
and superiority caresses me. I get a blissful junkie fix out of the
background murmur of the airport itself, the eternal-motion
escalators and conveyors, the opulent shops, the little luggage
wheels clicking, the hum of electric carts, everything so deter-
minedly futuristic in design, it is as though I had walked into the
pages of a thirties-era pulp sci-fi magazine — by which, indeed,
airport architects must all surely have been influenced. It shows
in their creations, these scintillating Buck Rogers basilicas of glass
and steel. As a place that inspires awe, airports have long since
replaced churches for me, and the delicate vibration through my
bones and organs as the Rolls-Royce jet engines kick out tens of
thousands of horsepower worth of thrust is pure technological
eroticism. It pains me to the depths of my would-be spacefarer
soul that these *Wunderflugzeugen* should turn out to be atmos-
phere-wreckers, causing massive damage to the very chemistry
of the skies they have come so quickly to rule.

But the fact is, these jets are incinerators fixed with wings and
sent catapulting back and forth across the sky, blasting their toxins
directly into the thin reaches of the upper lower atmosphere,
where they now form a global outer onion skin of opaqueness.
Of course there is a direct correlation between the methane and
carbon dioxide and benzene and formaldehyde bursting from
our engines and the dying, phlegm-colored sky all around.
Supertankers might play a pivotal role in the transmutation of oil
into heat-trapping emissions, making them the greatest pollution

machines of all time, but this enormous rocket is a close second: a veritable flame-thrower of CO_2, nitrogen oxides, and volatile organics. If the goal is to cut down on greenhouse gases, what better place to start than by grounding the jets until they can find some clean way to propel them? Any pretense that jet flight involved somehow treading more lightly on the Earth died in the autumn of 1999, when the first study came in, showing that each passenger in a jetliner is using the same amount of fossil fuel as any given yahoo down below driving an SUV. You can't be green and fly in a polluting machine.

Yet for ecoactivists to try to conduct campaigns without actually traveling to the scene of the action would be worse than tying both arms behind your back before going into battle. Until the art of holographic projection and reception is perfected, warriors — of all stripes — will still have to take to the field. It may seem *impure* that the arch-foes of petroleum should use petroleum to fight petroleum, but what else is there to do? Sailboats can't keep up. Zodiacs aren't solar-powered. And campaigners have to be moved around fast. Still, I can't help wondering, if even *we* can't escape dependency on the stuff, are we asking too much from everyone else? Are we caught in an irreconcilable contradiction? I think so. Because, no matter what tactical rationale we offer for being on board this ultrapig of a machine, Steve and I should be traveling cleanly, in hydrogen-fuel-cell magnetically levitated airships. And we're not. We tell ourselves we are involved in a guerrilla war, and you can't give up mobility when fighting an overwhelmingly powerful adversary. But there is a certain inevitable decay of our integrity. Our L-1011 binds us like junkies, even as it allows us to leap over entire continents to confront an enemy in mere hours, instead of taking weeks or even months to engage him. Militarily, who could deny themselves such a capability?

Surely, I thought, this line of brooding was just campaign postpartum blues, because we didn't save the universe in one blow. I should be too wise and experienced at this stage in life to mistake every battle for the war, thereby letting minor setbacks grind me under. I should, in fact, be modeling myself after Shallhorn. Even though the evidence of imminent doom was all around us, and he saw it just as clearly as I did, Steve had a small, beatific smile on his face. He seemed aglow with an inner-Buddha-light, if you buy into that, and sometimes I do. At this moment, he was radiant. He was heading home after a long absence, of course, but he also had the look of a man who was pleased with the work he had done. And why not be pleased? At least somewhere in the world for a couple of hours, Big Oil was under attack. It was only a media attack. But it made a ripple, and that was something. Later, another ripple would be set in motion. And another. Someday . . .

"You gotta keep it in perspective," he offered, sensing my gloom.

Steve knew whereof he spoke. He had been working for Greenpeace for something like seventeen years, which is time enough to acquire perspective galore. He was a student radical who started out, like so many, opposing American nuclear testing. At various times Shallhorn got involved in actions to stop Trident submarines, interfere with nuke tests in Nevada, prevent reactors from being built, blockade shipments of plutonium and radioactive waste, harass nuclear-powered and -armed warships. Most recently, he had been the coordinator of a mission to put a Greenpeace ship in the target zone of a Star Wars missile test out in the Pacific.

Steve is a big man, but there didn't seem to be an intimidating bone in his body. Even among Canadians, he is an abnormally nice, polite, sweet guy. You'd never suspect, looking at him in his Blue Jays T-shirt and baseball cap and shorts and running shoes, glasses low on his nose, that the FBI, the CIA, Interpol, the RCMP, and the Canadian Security Intelligence Service have bulging files on him. They probably have him tagged as some kind of "professional agitator." And, of course, that's what he does. He agitates for a living. He gets paid to do it. He's part of an incredible phenomenon, namely the emergence of non-governmental organizations as a new tier of global power. As campaign coordinator for Canada for nearly a decade, he has flown back and forth to Amsterdam for meetings more times than he can remember. In the next couple of weeks, he will be winging off to Amsterdam again — this time in the capacity of campaign boss for the U.S. office, which means only, he says modestly, that he has a bigger budget. But for all his soft-spoken, laid-back, good-buddy demeanor, Steve is a wily political survivor and operative, who has learned a few things along the way.

The madness of the past few weeks, as he bore the main responsibility for keeping the campaign on track and in motion, worrying about all the logistics, tactics, politics, and finances, does not seem to have drained him in any way. If anything, it has given him new strength. Having been in the driver's seat for a while, he has got used to making decisions, trusting his instincts, using his brain. He is more capable of certainty, put it that way. And maybe he has seen something I haven't.

"Mind if I ask, why are you so *up*?"

He chuckled, and there was a mischievous glint in his eye: "For a minute there, we had 'em surrounded."

It is such an incongruous image, measured against the reality of the giant *Pecos* and our flotilla of gnats, that I had to start laughing too.

"Well, cheers," he said a few minutes late, over a Bloody Mary. "Here's to a not bad campaign."

But looking out the window at the chemical-laced sky, I soon sank back into despair. It's not like we were talking about a disaster in the future. We were talking about a disaster that had already begun. What I was seeing around us was the dust stirred up in the present moment by the first shock waves of the mighty collapse as it gathers momentum.

"We're not going to be able to pull out of this in time," I declared in full prophetic mode, meaning *we*, the human race.

Steve didn't ask the obvious, namely, who was almighty I to know the future with such finality? But he was too gentle to slap me down. Instead, he pondered, and I gave him time. He has read the same papers and books and studies and reports as I have. He has been to meetings and seminars and rallies, and sat on committees, face-to-face with the scientists whose works we've read. He has been through all the stages in the last decade, as global warming went from being an issue on the exotic ecofringe to something all but a handful of the most archconservative editorial writers acknowledge as real. The climate disaster has form, he knows perfectly well. If there is a metaphor that fits us right now, it's two old salts standing in a wheelhouse, surrounded by navigational and communications gear like radio, radar, sonar, sounder, Loran, and SatNav, with the biggest computers in history running simulations for us twenty-four hours a day, and through the mist and fog of a bit of Time we can see the mountainous outline of the monster wave coming in. Our senses reel and we look for mistakes in the computer models, but there's no mistaking it any longer; there is a tsunami coming towards us.

"We are *so* fucked," I groaned.

"Maybe we are," Steve finally admitted. "Maybe it's too late to do anything." He gave a quintessentially Canadian shrug. "But we might as well try. I'm sure there's a lot of forgiveness built into the system."

A pause. He added: "It *is* billions of years old."

Of course. Perspective, again.

"Besides, what else are you going to do with your life? Sit around and whine?"

There it was: as much of a rationale for action as you could reasonably ask for. And a very Greenpeaceful response, too. Steve could look unblinkingly into the nightmare ahead, and somehow maintain an essential optimism. He was officially fanatical, but in practice, displayed an almost laissez-faire approach to revolution. We can do this; we've got the tools and the know-how. It's just a matter of time, organization, focus, proper planning, and effective messaging.

"Gaia won't be saved in a day," Steve added lightly. "It'll take at least a week." His adamant refusal to be let down was infectious. I had to giggle.

Having fixed my mood up a bit, he buried himself in a magazine, still beaming. It's a very good thing there are stalwarts, uncrushable souls like him around, just as it is an excellent evolutionary thing that nongovernmental organizations such as Greenpeace have come into existence to give him the wherewithal to get on with his revolutionary work. And perhaps it is still possible that, with a sufficient degree of organization and shrewdness and luck, they can kick-start the awakening of the global body politic to the crisis it faces, possibly even in time for us to take collective emergency evasive action.

But maybe not.

That's my dark, persistent fear. Of course, I don't want to think too hard about the worst-case scenario because it drives me crazy. We would very easily be kidding ourselves about there being any hope left upon which to base rational action. Maybe, having been set in motion, the trend-line of climate transformation is already unalterable, in which case, it is unsurprising that after all these years I am being driven back into the embrace of a smothering sense of futility.

Probably the era of the worst defeatism was back in the fifties, when we used to be marched out of school while the air-raid sirens howled, only to be instructed to line up in rows on the cinder of the racetrack, so that, when we became cinders ourselves, we'd fit right in with the landscape. That was about the only reason I could see for anything so stupid and suicidal as standing out in the open, waiting for a nuclear weapon to go off in the sky. I dropped out of school, convinced The End Was

Near. I had recurring nightmares of being the only survivor in the rubble of a nuked city. Like all kids who learn they are terminal, I wanted to grow up fast, get out, run around free, smoke, drink, travel, and make love while I could. It was a *given* that humanity was toast. Previous generations had had to contend with the concept of Armageddon, all right, but it was as a Biblical prophecy with an indeterminate time frame, not a plausible physical reality just the touch of a finger on a red button away. Mine was the first generation to actually find themselves facing a *real* Armageddon, with a radioactive half-life of thousands of years. My initial unoriginal personal response was to retreat into hopelessness. Then, like an unpredicted summer storm, a mass peace movement rose around the world. The seventies and eighties were a whirlwind of spinoff activism at every front, with environmentalists in the front lines. We experienced an unprecedented explosion of hope and energy, a flourishing of democracy, a green political awakening, and even some good and useful legislation. But it all seemed to have plateaued in the nineties, as conservatives, funded by big business, consolidated power under an assortment of political disguises, and the tide of ecoreform ran up against high, thick stone walls of staggering geopolitical self-interest. Indeed, it seems we are drifting backward even as the macrowave comes marching towards us.

As Steve and I descended into Toronto's Pearson International Airport, the CN Tower was barely visible through the ground-level ozone. I still felt suffocated under my sense — my *rational* sense, this is the worst part of it — of oncoming, unstoppable ruination. My mother used to warn me against taking the weight of the world on my shoulders. Yet, in our time, the most critical, pivotal moment of history, anyone who isn't taking the weight on becomes part of the burden. Time is the primary resource we are in danger of running out of.

As we taxied . . . and taxied . . . and taxied, bumping over a tarmac surface that probably covered at least as much ground as ancient Rome, something mountainous climbed into view above the sprawling shell of the present Terminal One. The new shape had been just a forest of rust-colored girders emerging out of a newly dug quarry when I left ten days ago. Now a scallop-shaped roof had appeared, giving it the look of some immense coliseum. Soon it will all be glassed in with smart extensor nodules being offered like nipples to still-shrieking, empty-bellied birds. The airport, already the biggest in Canada, will soon be able to handle *double* the number of passengers, which means twice as many jets taxiing and lifting off and thundering down, spewing methane. It means hundreds of millions of pounds of more volatile organic compounds, nitrogen oxides, and CO_2.

Yet the atmosphere won't be getting any deeper or wider to absorb all those extra emissions. It is like this at more than half the big airports in the world. Each of them already emits more toxic chemicals than a large factory. Why are they being allowed to expand like this? Who needs the greenhouse gases? So that more people might take vacations abroad? What happens when those people include a new middle class in China, all wanting to climb aboard 747s to go look at the Acropolis? The airport authorities around the world are building as though there was some kind of subspace race on, and, indeed, that's exactly what is happening. All the economic projections that point to and depend on growth are planned to justify expansions. Airports catalyze growth. Airplanes sustain it. Air terminals are the great portals of trade and passage, midway through the evolution from sheltered harbors to space stations. Again, I am in awe of the audacity of the Megamachine's builders. These are guys who honestly believe they have overtaken Nature as masters of the world. At the very least, they have succeeded in replacing nature with something unnatural. Not man-made, but very definitely man-altered. Like the tainted curry of air roiling above the tarmac.

Out on Highway 401 later, I noticed there were more trucks

on the road here than down in Southern California, which shouldn't surprise me, even though L.A. has more *cars* per capita than anywhere else. Since the 1950s, Canada has been busy dismantling its once universally hailed railway system, shunting more and more freight into trucks and planes. The 401 is, after all, the country's widest, deadliest stretch of superhighway. I know this, but it was not until I was out in the midst of the buffalo jump of monster rigs that the *scale* of the insatiable Canadian energy appetite manifested itself tangibly. It is not just that Canadians per capita are more mobile than any people in history; it is the way we ship our goods and equipment around that takes us over the top. Whereas trucks used to stand out on the highway, now they blur one into another, just like the planes forming the sky-bridge into L.A.

These Canadian trucks carry *everything*. A giant crane wedded to a flatbed overtook me. I was engulfed by the shadow of a load of great steel container tubes, each big enough for me to stand up in. A rig came up beside me bearing empty pallets stacked eight feet high. A backhoe was chained behind the next rig like a captured beast on display. Slabs of concrete hurtled by, leaning against each other like dominoes. The skins of tarps slapped and thrummed, stretched over every industrial shape imaginable. Battered and chipped blue dumpsters rattled along. There were rigs without a load that looked like disembodied robot heads. A red tow truck so big it must have been built in a different gravity field dragged a yellow school bus like a fresh-caught marlin. Green armored garbage trucks charged forward with forks folded like praying-mantis forelegs. I lost track of the number of double-tanked chemical carriers and dusty gravel trucks with screens over their loads. I was overtaken by an empty car-carrier like a squashed Ferris wheel. I found myself pacing a steel death-trap filled with blue-eyed pigs struggling to stay on their feet. A twenty-four-wheeler *vroomed* by with diesel exhaust pipes thrust up like the horns of a fighting bull in the instant it tossed a matador. Although most of the shapes were as basic as boxes and barrels and bins, they were ornately festooned with ladders, cat-walks, lifts, gangways, winches, chutes, platforms, clasps, latches, handles, roll bars, air conditioners, ramps, funnels, scoops, buckets, pods, blowers, antennas, mirrors, reflectors, guards, drums, spouts, and the ubiquitous mudguards. The whole rumbling, shambling horde moved at an impossible speed. With the corrugated soundproofing walls on either side of the freeway hemming us in, the blur of asphalt below, smog above, this felt more like a gun barrel than a road — everybody inside cartridges being *shot* along. Again, despite the fact that these were all mass-produced machines, there was a sense of something as primal as a tidal surge at work. Like the supertanker and sky-bridges, the midday traffic on the 401 seemed part of some unstoppable wave.

We dropped Steve off downtown. He was still aglow, carry-on bag over his shoulder, wearing a kind of showboat California hat as he hailed a cab beneath the spectacular glass cliff-walls of the banks and insurance companies. There was certainty in his body language, a small cat-smile on his lips. I was convinced one more time that he sees something, and draws strength from it, that I don't see, and therefore can't tap into. Maybe he's a purer soul. Maybe it's just that he's less wounded philosophically — or, put another way, he's stronger. Ah, face it, maybe he's just younger. In any event, it dawned on me that Steve was, in fact, a soldier on leave at the moment from a very long war that will, when you think about it, have to go on forever. When we began to venture down the path of environmental activism back in the late sixties, we thought it would be just like every other cause, something that was winnable, with fixed goalposts, and when it was won, it would be over. But the humans, you see, never quit. You no sooner preserve a wilderness, than it comes under renewed pressure. You save a species, and somebody else comes

after it. You enact a law, and someone breaks it. You ban a substance and someone smuggles it.

Just as we once aspired to conquer Nature, now we must
tame man. Steve's war, like mine, is not with Nature. We war
against our own species. And what better-armed, more cunning
and dangerous creature could there be, unless it comes from
another solar system?

I was glad that Steve could still smile, because I myself felt
close to panic. And it was partially because I was a Canadian and,
beyond that, a North American. I *knew* the enemy all too well.

THE ENERGY MAMMOTHS

IT IS TIME TO STOP FRETTING about the Americanization of the world. What truly ought to be feared is the *Canadianization* of the world. In terms of energy use, that would be the American Way of Life plus 15 percent. On a per capita basis, according to a report published May 26, 2001, by the *Toronto Star*, Canadians use that much more energy than the famously hyperindulgent and wasteful neighbors to the south. Data from the Organization of Economic Cooperation and Development (OECD) and the U.S. Department of Energy show that Canada consumes more than 400 million British Thermal Units per citizen, which means that we Jolly Canucks burn through more BTUs than even Americans, whose appetite was pegged most recently by the Census Bureau at 346 BTUs each. The voracious consumption level of Canadians gives us the dubious distinction of being individually the Number One energy drains on the planet. We consume *72 percent* more energy per person than the G7 average. With only .5 percent of the world's population, we generate 3 percent of the world's greenhouse gases. To put this in another perspective, Germany, despite having the world's third-largest economy and a population of 82 million, accounts for only 4 percent of the world's energy consumption. Out of the top ranks of the industrial nations, therefore, the Canadian incandescent-lit, coal-burning, SUV-trucking culture has surged far out in front, leaving everybody else in its exhaust cloud, with the United States a close second.

So, as a Canuck, I am in no position to criticize *anyone*. When the first stone is thrown, it will hit my greenhouse glass house before any other. It remains, however, that the United States of America, in aggregate, is the energy Beaste of Beastes among nations, its output of pollutants — like its economy and its military — far outstripping any competitors. If you were looking for a huge lost piece of a puzzle in order to complete the picture, you would be looking at America.

With just 4 percent of the Earth's population at the dawn of the third millennium, the U.S. produces 25 percent of its greenhouse gases.

With a population of 288 million people, the Land of the Free and the Brave spews more greenhouse gases than most of the developing coutries in Asia, South and Central America, and Africa together. That is, it takes ten times the number of people in the U.S. — we're talking about 2.6 billion human — to emit an equal amount of climate-smashing chemicals. Or, put another way, according to a report by the National Environmental Trust entitled "First in Emissions, Behind in Solutions," the U.S. emits more CO_2 than India and China, which have the highest emissions of the developing countries, combined.

And it is not just the nation as a whole that has a gigantic impact. Individual states emit more carbon dioxide than entire clusters of developing countries. The emissions from Texas alone (the highest in the country) "exceed the combined emissions of 119 developing countries with an aggregate population of over one billion people," the report states. "Forty-two of the 50 U.S. states individually emit more carbon than 50 developing countries combined, and five states separately emit more carbon than 100 developing countries. Even Wyoming, the least populated state with 495,000 people, emits more carbon dioxide than 72 developing countries having a combined population of nearly 318 million. Wyoming's per capita emissions are nearly 650 times greater than those of the 72 developing countries."

These are nearly quantum differences, as though human beings inhabited entirely different energy universes, and hence different pollution environments. When one-quarter of the pollutants in the planet's atmosphere come from a single nation, and a relatively sparsely populated one at that, something is seriously out of whack.

To appreciate the scale of the damage we cause in the process of all this energy burning and consumption, we North Americans have to start thinking of ourselves as abnormally *big*. In terms of impact on the biosphere and the gobbling up of nonrenewable resources, the difference between someone living well in any industrialized country — the U.S. and Canada in particular — and someone still plowing a field with a cow in Nepal is staggering. The total amount of CO_2 exhaled into the atmosphere every year around the world is reported to be slightly above one metric ton per person, but that average gives a completely false impression that this is somehow "everyone's" fault. There are too many people. That must be it! We blame the poor as much as ourselves, a stance that derives from the fallacious argument that overpopulation is to blame for the world's main ecological woes. The reality is that a fraction of the world's population sucks up and spews out more stuff than the rest of humanity combined. We are *not* equal. It is grotesque to argue that the passing of one North American energy behemoth through the biosphere doesn't create more havoc, cause more damage, suck things drier, and leave more of a scar than the passing of a Nepalese living at the very bottom rung of the energy-consumption scale. At issue, more than human numbers, is the human *load*. According to sociologist William Catton, writing in *Overshoot: The Ecological Basis of Revolutionary*

Change, the world is being required "to accommodate not just more people, but effectively 'larger' people" — especially in the industrialized countries.

We need to stop thinking of ourselves purely in political, cultural, and social terms and start perceiving ourselves in terms of energy use, which, in the case of North Americans, is without precedent. And to get a truly accurate picture of the size of these superconsuming mutants, we would have to measure their appetite against the average energy and resource use by human beings throughout history, at which point our monster morphs into something even *bigger.*

Another way of looking at the relative "size" of North Americans is by employing the Ecological Footprint tool developed by Professor William Rees and elaborated on by Mathis Wackernagel of the University of British Columbia. "EF analysis," as it is known, accounts for the flow of energy and matter to and from any defined economy and converts these into the corresponding land/water area required from nature to support these flows. The authors of *Our Ecological Footprint: Reducing Human Impact on the Earth* work from the premise "that the human enterprise cannot be separated from the natural world even in our minds because there is no such separation in nature. In terms of energy and material flows there is simply no *out there* — the human economy is a fully dependent subsystem of the ecosphere. This means that we should study humanity's role in nature in much the same way we would study that of any other large consumer organism."

In *Our Ecological Footprint,* they further explain:

> The premise that *human society is a subsystem of the ecosphere,* that human beings are embedded in nature, is so simple that it is generally overlooked or dismissed as too obvious to be relevant. However, taking this "obvious" insight seriously leads to some profound conclusions. The

policy implications of this ecological reality run much deeper than pressing for improved pollution control and better environmental protection, both of which maintain the myth of separation. If humans are part of nature's fabric, the "environment" is no mere scenic backdrop but becomes the play itself. The ecosphere is where we live; humanity is dependent on nature, not the reverse. Sustainability requires that our emphasis shift from "managing resources" to managing *ourselves* that we learn to live as part of nature. Economics at last becomes human ecology.

Basically, EF analysis is an accounting tool that enables us to estimate the resource consumption and waste-assimilation requirements of a defined population or economy in terms of corresponding productive land area. The question is asked: how big would a glass or plastic hemisphere that let in light but prevented material things of any kind from entering or leaving need to be so that a city underneath it could be sustained indefinitely? The total ecosystem area that is essential for the continued existence of the city becomes its de facto Ecological Footprint on the Earth. This way of measuring the amount of land required to support a typical individual's present level of consumption is proportional both to population and to per capita material and energy consumption. More formally, the EF of a specified population or economy can be defined as the area of ecologically productive land and water in various categories — such as forests, pastures, croplands — that would be required on a continuous basis in order to provide all the energy and material resources and to absorb all the wastes discharged as a result of consumption.

This might be just an interesting new way of quantifying wealth in terms of ecological capital, but the EF analysis goes a considerable step further. It notes that sustainability requires we live within the productive capacity of nature. Put another way, humanity must learn to live on the income generated by remaining natural capital stocks. By "natural capital," the authors mean not only all the natural resources and waste sinks needed to support human economic activity, "but also those biophysical processes and relationships among components of the ecosphere that provide essential life-support." Technology notwithstanding, human beings remain in a state of "obligate dependence" on nature's productivity and life-support "services." While both human population and average consumption are increasing, the total area of productive land and natural capital stocks are fixed or in decline. Moreover, in a global economy, no region exists in isolation. Especially in the industrialized countries, we draw on resources from all over the world.

The North American experience is a perfect illustration of the overspending of natural capital, yet this kind of economy, based largely on trade, is generally lauded as a good thing. Trade, it is argued, can overcome any regional limits to growth caused by local shortages. In the short term, this is obviously true. Yet, being finite, the planet can only sustain so much of a total load before the natural capital has been spent. "Load pressure relative to carrying capacity is rising much faster than is implied by mere population increases," Rees and Wackernagel write. By "measuring the population's total load rather than the number of people, we recognize that people have an impact somewhere even if it is obscured by trade and technology. Indeed, to the extent that trade seems to increase local carrying capacity, *it reduces it somewhere else*." So long as adequate productive land remains somewhere on Earth, local consumption that exceeds local productivity can be sustained by importing the surplus from elsewhere — until the point at which we go beyond carrying capacity.

According to the core EF analysis, we have already reached this point:

What is the present aggregate demand by people on the ecosphere? A rough assessment based on four major human requirements shows that current appropriations of natural resources and services already exceed Earth's long-term carrying capacity. Agriculture occupies 1.5 billion hectares of cropland and 3.3 billion hectares of pasture. Sustainable production of the current roundwood harvest (including firewood) would require a productive forest area of 1.7 billion hectares. To sequester the excess CO_2 released by fossil fuel combustion, an additional 3.0 billion hectares of carbon sink lands would have to be set aside. This adds up to a requirement of 9.6 billion hectares compared to the 7.4 billion hectares of ecologically productive land actually available for such purposes. In other words, these four functions alone exceed available carrying capacity by close to 30 percent. Even if all 8.9 billion hectares of ecologically active land were included, present "overshoot" exceeds 10 percent. . . . Thus, to accommodate *sustainably* the anticipated increase in population and economic output of the next four decades we would need six to twelve additional planets.

According to UN figures, the billion people who live in affluence consume over three-quarters of the world's total output. The remaining 5 billion people — 80 percent of the population — survive on less than a quarter of world output. In terms of EF, consumption by the rich billion alone claims more than the carrying capacity of the planet. The total amount of land on Earth is 51 billion hectares (197 million square miles), of which only 13.1 billion hectares (51 million square miles) are not covered by either ice or fresh water. As population has mounted though this century, the available per capita ecological space has been shrinking from about 5 hectares (12.4 acres) per person to only 1.5 hectares (3.7 acres). Bucking this trend, the affluent in the industrialized countries have *expanded* their Footprint.

The Ecological Footprint of an average North American works out to between 4 and 5 hectares (10 and 12.5 acres), roughly comparable to three large city blocks squared. That's to keep *one* North American living in the style to which he/she has become accustomed! Compare this to the .38 hectares (.94 acres) that sustain one person in India. While the overall difference isn't as great as the gap between levels of energy use by the two peoples, one North American still needs roughly twelve times as much land to sustain his/her lavish petroleum-based lifestyle. We are dealing here, of course, in averages. In fact, the Footprint of the poorer half of India's population registers at .2 hectares (.5 acres). And if we adjust the EF of North Americans so that we are looking at the top 20-percent income earners — those with four cars, a heated swimming pool, central air-conditioning — the Footprint expands to an incredible 12 hectares (29.6 acres) per capita!

This has to be measured against what Professor Rees calls a "current fair Earthshare," defined as the amount of ecologically productive land available per person on Earth. By 1996, this amounted to 1.5 hectares (3.7 acres). Of that, only .25 hectares (.62 acres) were arable. A North American "drawing down" 12 hectares (29.6 acres) of ecologically productive land thus leaves a Footprint *forty-eight times larger* than his fair share.

Another useful method of measuring energy profile is to employ the Climate Change Calculator, a CD-ROM program provided by the Women's Health Network of the City of Toronto (www.climcalc.net/eng/Intro_1.html) that allows you to estimate your own personal CO_2 emissions, while providing comparisons with national averages. You answer questions about your energy use — how often you fill up the tank with gasoline, how much natural gas you burn at home, what kind of a lawnmower do you use, what do you leave running, how much do you travel, and do you fly often? Basically, the program puts together a CO_2 profile of the user. The average Ontario resident in the year 2001, it turned out, produced 4.2 metric tons of CO_2 annually. For New York State residents, the average was 5.8 metric tons. In my case (sorry, Dexter) it worked out to *9.2 metric tons* — all those flights, all those days of driving around Toronto as a reporter, coming in and out from the suburbs . . . how swiftly and enormously it added up! I could see it now, a blue-black cloud rising above me, following me everywhere like a trailing cowl. It is not difficult to imagine this 9.2-metric-ton death-cloud. It is a concentration of the air that hovers all summer and well into winter over the Toronto megalopolis. My own personal cloud, my CO_2 shadow, is so enormous it could be dispersed above the three large city blocks it takes to sustain me and it would *still be visible* as a dark nimbus. *That* is my outline against the horizon. Of course, the cloud that is my totality of emissions emerges from dozens of different throats, from tailpipes, chimneys, vents, and leaks. It foams volcanically from the coal-burning smokestacks of Lakeview Generating Station. It wavers like a heat wave over the Don Valley Parkway and the 401. It fuses with the pall over suburbia. If we compress my contribution to all this until it matches its own weight in flesh, we are looking at a mass of greenhouse gases equal in size to a fully grown woolly mammoth. Except that *this* creature is a demon of carbon released from the depths, loose on the Earth, ultimately wreaking havoc on everything around him.

Belching poisonous fumes, the Great North American Energy Mammoth leaves a deep track and refuses to look up to see what will happen if it continues to overgraze.

We are *not* clean. We have it all, yet we want more. We want to maintain our exorbitant high-tech lifestyles. In fact, give us *more* toys! If we are ever going to outgrow this kind of adolescence, we have to find a way to look at ourselves in some mirror other than the one held up by growth-dominated capitalism. To see our ecoshadow as it falls hugely across the tortured landscape is a good, sobering start.

Finally, as we grope towards a new, ecologically realistic assessment of what it means to be a North American in the twenty-first century, we have to face the implications of the fact that one of the ways Americans get to be energy hogs is by sucking at the Canadian fossil-fuel teat. Assuming a continuance of the American policy of Manifest Pollution Destiny, annual U.S. demand for natural gas is expected to grow from 603 billion cubic meters in 1999 to 794 billion cubic meters by 2010, a 32-percent increase. Guess where this will mainly come from?

If the United States did not have easy access to Canadian fossil-fuel resources, is there a chance the American lifestyle might have been modified by now? Certainly, back in the time of Jimmy Carter, just after the first OPEC shock wave, there was a moment when the American energy juggernaut actually paused for a moment, shaking its head and looking around in dull surprise. Carter sat by the fireside in a cardigan sweater and spoke of conservation in pastoral tones as "the moral equivalent of war." A generation later, George W. Bush says, "We've got to make sure that gas comes — flows freely out of Canada into the United States."

In his Depression-era masterpiece, *The Road to Wigan Pier*, George Orwell wrote that "in order that England may live in comparative comfort, a hundred million Indians must live on the verge of starvation — an evil state of affairs, but you acquiesce in it every time you step in a taxi or eat a plate of strawberries and cream." The modern moral conundrum can be graphed in similar terms, using EF analysis. So that North Americans may maintain their current climate-raping lifestyle, billions upon billions of people around the world are going to have to endure drought, floods, storms, starvation, and exodus. And who knows for how many generations? The difference between the "evil state of affairs" in imperial England and modern-day corporate America is that the ecological evil done by us will have a conical effect as it reverberates across time, spreading out in widening circles of impact. Our share of damages to the biosphere will not end with the passing of the North American energy empire. The effects of a 330-million-strong herd of over-evolved energy beasts rumbling back and forth across the land will be felt forever.

We have to ask: what kind of a people would drive single-occupancy SUVs when they *knew* the suffering it was going to cause others down the road? For all intents and purposes, we might as well be running our own grandchildren down, and our neighbors' as well. Those tons of emissions trailing behind us may disappear from view eventually, but they reach into the future. Our heirs and descendants become roadkill as surely as if we'd crushed them under our Goodyears. (Maybe you'll see it this way, Dexter: the Good Years we enjoyed, unfortunately leaving you to pay the price of the Bad Years that followed.) It is not just that my generation sucks energy hard, using up resources like candy and wasting an incredible amount of every-thing, we have by default left control of our destiny — which is very much shaped by climate - - in the hands of the likes of the Saudi princes, Albertan oil execs, Carbon Club lobbyists, and the backroom West Virginia coal interests who delivered their state for George W. Bush.

In most ethical systems, abdication of responsibility is considered a crime in itself. For people dwelling in unrivaled decadent energy luxury, like Americans and Canadians, the abdication of responsibility for energy use and sales and the fallout is all the more reprehensible. On an individual basis, because we chew up more turf and spit out more garbage than anyone else, ours is the worst-case offense. Among the looters of the planet, we take a bigger haul than any other people. We dig a deeper hole. We level more trees. We drain more water. We spew more contaminants. We spill more poisons. We cast larger, darker ecological shadows.

One thing the climate debate has lacked so far is any display of moral leadership in this area. Desperate people, such as members of threatened island states, can make impassioned speeches against global warming, but there is no particular vision involved in being caught in the pathway of disaster. It is just plain bad luck. In the great climate game, the strategic interests of individual countries have so far been the only things that count. It is clear that the petrotyrannies, including the Arab states, will continue to oppose any limitations on production, no matter how much scientific evidence is amassed. Without a free press or democratic opposition, there is zero chance of this changing. As for the large corporate offenders, they can be counted upon to exert every ounce of muscle to fend off alternative energy strategies. Even the so-called "green" oil companies continue to expand operations. In Russia, Gazprom muzzles the media. The developing countries, far from preparing to cut emissions, are building and buying cars at record levels, with indicators pointing to 2.3 billion cars on the roads by 2030, mostly due to growth in Asia. Only the EU countries — conspicuously lacking in oil deposits, except in the North Sea — have shown any quasiserious willingness to cut emissions. For them, reducing dependency on a resource they don't have only makes sense. They are also structurally less dependent on the car than North Americans.

And then, of course, there are the Juice Cans, whose *realpolitik* style of putting their high-end lifestyles first and risks to planetary ecological security a distant second has made them pariahs in any sense of political morality. Indeed, the Juice Cans' collective behavior has been immoral in the extreme. From a classical geopolitical point of view, there is no surprise here. Unfortunately, traditional strategies of national self-interest aren't going to work in the face of a true global threat. Post-IPCC, it should be clear to everyone that the ultimate self-interest of each state is to be found in preservation of a stable biosphere. It should be, but as yet there is little sign of a shift in the ancient human style of looking after number one. Nowhere has this found more perfect expression than in the attitude of President George W. Bush, defender of the American Way.

Yet while generalized international loathing has tended to focus on the Americans for ostentatious hyperconsumption, the even-more-scandalous wastefulness and hucksterism of the Canadians tend to be overlooked. Among devious, selfish materialists, Canadians are the *worst*, especially when we wrap ourselves in sanctimony. Peacekeepers — not warmongers! Meanwhile, behind the scenes, it's: "Hey Yankee, wanna buy some really crude oil?"

STEPPING BACK

W$_{\text{ITH ALL THE CONTAMINANTS}}$ in the world ultimately mixing together in the biosphere, the linkage between human destinies has never been greater. What the Brazilians do to the Amazon (once about as faraway a location as you could imagine) now affects me. What Oregonians do to West Coast rainforests affects me too, through the medium of deforestation and the desequestering of carbon. My own CO_2 cloud moves slowly upward, mingling somewhere above the big oceanic thermals with CO_2 from Bangkok and Rome and Mexico City and proceeds to reinforce, to thicken, to *enhance* the greenhouse pane, while everything stirs and writhes below, as if caught between a magnifying glass and the sun. Meanwhile, deep under the surface of the North Atlantic, thermohaline circulation falters under the impact of a surge of fresh water due to shrinking Arctic ice sheets. Collectively, we are stirring the planet from the extreme heights of the biosphere to its depths. And there is the operative word. It is as a *collective* that humanity is having its impact on climate. Until now, ecological catastrophes have been local, and — at worst — regional. We have never had a true global ecocrisis. But now the climate crisis is already well in motion.

The fundamental difference between the climate issue and previous archetypal environmental crises is that, in order to "save the climate," we have no choice but to push for an energy revolution, which also just happens to be a technological revolution. Wonder of wonders, this puts ecology and technology on the same side. The underlying issue — energy choice — involves everyone, not just a few industries. It has a staggeringly complex geopolitical component, which can't be ignored. In dealing with climate, we are in fact dealing with energy. Climate change is caused by bad energy calls. Ergo, we are face to face with the energy question, which we *must* answer.

The fact that we *have* answers is critically important; otherwise we would be in the position of fighting against our own civilization, loyal to the planet perhaps, but traitors to the human race. On the downside, the energy issue seems almost too awesomely intractable to untangle. On the plus side, a technology-driven energy revolution is already in the works. If higher efficiencies can be achieved in any production, the new method will ultimately prevail. This is the wind at our backs. There is no point at this late juncture in adopting a purist position, in saying "No deals with demon technology!" If a desperate species looking for a way out of an awful dilemma ever needed help from fancy space gadgets, it's us and it's now. Between them, the supercomputers and fuel cells and solar panels and wind turbines might just be enough to keep us viable through the age of fire or ice to come.

The climate-change issue, seen as an energy issue, forces an inherently proactive agenda upon us. Unlike nukes, or bad industrial practices like ocean dumping or clear-cutting, we cannot stop the climate-change juggernaut without a systems-wide transformation. The simple shutting down of petroleum-based civilization is not going to be permitted, not even by ultraliberals. Like it or not, we cannot tackle fossil fuels without pushing something forward in their place. This essentially involves a revolution.

The intellectual beauty, as it were, of climate change as an issue is that the solution is built into the very structure of the problem. Activists are perforce the agents of sun and wind and water, involved in a great, historic world-energy revolution. Rather than simply wanting to stop, slow down, or phase out fossil fuels, we want to *start*, *speed up*, and *phase in* solar panels, wind turbines, etc. For a change, activists aren't in the "anti-" position. We are in favor of something! This is especially important, because nearly everyone thinks that without oil and coal and gas and nukes the world will be hurled right back to the Dark Ages. They need to know that the highest of the high tech is with us. In the case of climate change, ecofreaks are fighting on substantially different terrain than usual. Instead of beating against the headwinds of tradition and technology, we have the wind literally in our favor.

If someone had the power, the changes could be made starting tomorrow. The technology is available. The knowledge that we are assaulting our own descendants is staring us in the face. But no one has the power. Apart from the top dozen industrialized states, the most formidable organized forces on the planet are the multinational corporations, few of which have shown much inclination to stop steering in the direction of profitability just because of the specter of a smashed biosphere. Nongovernmental organizations are multiplying and spreading, and they will no doubt move up to positions of greater influence as the crisis progresses and the predictions of the IPCC continue to come true, thus discrediting the Carbon Club's apologists.

If someone had the power . . . Power! What a rare match of meanings in one word! We mean the forces of human will that determine the political relationships between people, and we also mean the forces of nature we tap to serve that will. Nature and politics: two fundamental concepts, fused — and, moreover, given physical shape right before my eyes. The electrification that comes with industrialization has put an awesome pool of power at the fingertips of ordinary mortals. What happens when I reach out and turn on the power? Everything! The lights come on. The furnace kicks in. The air conditioner. The TV. The microwave. The computer. The garage door lifts. With each additional flick of a switch or touch of a button or tap of a pad, a program nudges the output at a nuclear reactor or a coal-fired generating station up just a fraction of a gigajoule. Huge and seemingly distant from radioactive holding tanks, the CO_2-caked chimneys are actually extensions of me. As I hit this computer key I suck manufactured energy. When I climb into my car and hit the ignition, I start kicking out hydrocarbons. In the sense that McLuhan would have meant it, I *wear* my energy environment. Without it, I am naked. And my energy environment wears *me*. I am a symbiotic part of the energy field, its Footstep, its Shadow. I am the causative factor. Without me, it happens less. It is a slightly smaller field, with a smaller anthropogenic greenhouse effect. Some 9.2 metric tons of gases per year less, in fact. If I were to die tomorrow, it would be a matter of a great energy mammoth falling over, its mighty cowl of carbon dioxide dissipating. Over sixty years, had my carbon load been as consistently heavy as it is today, I'd have pounded 552 metric tons of greenhouse gases into the atmosphere.

This is the supercreature I have become.

Anything that large has some degree of power, of course: the power, if nothing else, of self-control. The prevention of the birth of more of us would spare the biosphere the burden of more energy behemoths lurching to their feet, squalling for fuel. Better yet, a move towards a *smaller* population would mean subtracting large amounts of climate-changing substances from the total load. Population control in North America thus delivers a better payoff in terms of emissions reductions than in Sudan, and perhaps should be pursued more aggressively, although no one dares suggest such a thing. The idea of stepping *back* from growth or even stabilization is still very much an esoteric concept in a world where freeways continue to stride across urban landscapes, airports and suburbs spread out across farmlands, and sales of gas-powered lawn mowers and leaf blowers soar. The meaning of "overshoot" (or even "finite") has definitely not registered.

Here is what *could* be done: individuals living at the apex of the fossil-fuel economies could voluntarily step back. As the shadow of Thermageddon falls upon us, it is the first thing you'd think we would do: back away. *Use less energy. Don't feed the fire.* It is so obvious that it sounds patronizing to say it. Gandhi advocated "voluntary simplicity," and never has the concept had more validity than in the context of climate change. The idea is for people to deliberately reduce their demands and even their possessions in order to live sustainably upon the land. If sustainability is our goal — giving our species a chance to "live long and prosper" — no better way can be found than to switch personally to alternative energies. Cutting back and reducing wastage, these are good solid steps that any ethical person, or even mere loving grandparent or parent, ought to consider themselves obliged to undertake on behalf of their descendants.

Yes, but *how do we make the change?* Is change, on the scale that is apparently necessary, even possible in time?

It's too bad there isn't a gigantic "solar waterfall" somewhere that could be tapped by environmental groups in exactly the way petrotyrants skim off their royalties from oil. It would seem right now that money buys political power at the highest levels, with the Carbon Club being able to throw tens of millions of dollars into advanced mass-brainwashing programs to sway public opinion at critical political moments. In countries where the media is controlled by the state (or by the oil industry, as in Russia for instance), such programs are the norm.

The power of modern advertising techniques is not be underestimated. And the firepower is all on the other side. While the larger established enviro groups get off a blast of paid opinion in the pages of newspapers and sometimes even on television from time to time, they can't hope to match the sustained saturation advertising done by the carbon boyos virtually at will. Otherwise, environmentalists must risk their lives (or at least their reputations) to get a moment or two of news coverage. Make no mistake, the budgets of environmental groups are still minimal compared to the resources that can be deployed by Big Oil using the tool of mass advertising — and more to the point, exercising direct hands-on power at the political level.

Is this how control is exercised today on the big freedom-loving continent between the Atlantic, Pacific, and Arctic? One would have to be a Pollyanna not to see it. And at the moment, with pitifully few exceptions, all the nation-states' guns are pointed *against* environmentalism. And almost all the advertising, all but a fraction of 1 percent, is aimed directly at the stimulation of material appetite, insecurities, consumerism — in a word, growth. This is inherently an antienvironmental position, no matter how it is glossed. To continue buying, spending, accumulating, driving, flying exactly as we have been doing for so long, when we *know*, like the Newfoundland skipper, it can't go on, shifts from being a "crime against the environment/future generations" to being a *premeditated* crime. This is what I call it when you say, "to hell with everyone and everything," and go ahead and take what you want, do what you want, regardless of the damage to current ecosystems and uncounted legions of humans presumably to come.

No one fines me, charges me, or arrests me for driving to work. The idea is absurd — *now*. But when the day comes that the human race finally awakens to its dilemma and begins to thrash about desperately, trying belatedly to extricate itself from ecohell, it will not be absurd at all. Climate damage can now be clearly pinned on the six deadliest greenhouse gases. What hasn't been clearly pinned, legally, is the issue of causation. Nobody has been able to establish causation between the damage itself and the manufacturers of the gases; so they continue to enjoy immunity from any significant threats of litigation. This is a systems-wide problem. Witness the fact that, as part of our petroleum-saturated society, it turns out *all* of my neighbors use pesticides to keep their wide swaths of front lawn green and dandelion-free, even though many of them have small children and grandchildren. If, back in 1962, after I had read Rachel Carson's *Silent Spring,* you'd told me that we would still allow the spraying of carcinogenic petrochemicals in the suburbs or *anywhere* by the time we got to the twenty-first century, I would have shaken my head at your lack of faith in our power to change.

Yet patently we have not advanced very far at all after a whole generation of activism on the chemical front. In that time, using advertising budgets that, if anything, surpass those of the oil, coal, and gas people, the petrochemical industries have mounted such a storm of advertising that most consumers experience warm and fuzzy feelings at the mere sight of their logos. The offshore peddling of herbicides and pesticides and toxic waste, as well as their manufacture and shipment, is overlooked almost entirely, so that the corporate players continue to hold their great heads aloft, as though they had nothing to hide, and their Lilliputian opponents seem powerless to prevent them from continuing to attack the surviving biosphere — a rainforest is torn off like a limb over here, an estuary gouged wide open over there. The speed at which it is happening is dizzying, which helps explain perhaps the *numbness* so many feel when the specter of this sort of thing is raised.

It is high time we started considering, at all levels, the morality and ethics of continuing to burn fossil fuels when we have scientific evidence that they are upsetting the balance of nature in a dangerous way. Oronto Douglas, leader of the No More Oil Campaign, has asserted in *Earth Island Journal,* "It is simply immoral to carry on with an outmoded product such as oil.

Petroleum is poisonous for the Earth's climate and has been the cause of so much suffering. The quest for more must end now."

But so long as industrial-growth policies remain the economic bedrock of developed and developing countries alike, the idea of *stepping back* is heresy, or lunacy. To even suggest a steady-state economic system is to court ridicule. To advocate a rollback in consumption, energy production, and development is considered a hopelessly radical position. Yet recycling itself was considered pretty radical a mere thirty years ago, and today waste diversion is the theme at official municipal, provincial, and sometimes federal levels. Who would have predicted at the height of the Cold War that a unified Germany would announce the phase-out of its nuclear program by the summer of 2001? Is this a rollback? Absolutely! By making a smart about-face and resolutely marching the other way toward green alternatives, the Germans have displayed the kind of moral leadership that has so far been lacking in the climate debate. To see the Germans make a decision of this magnitude, while still fully intending to abide by, if not exceed, the Kyoto agreement, is a reminder to disheartened Americans and Canadians that federal governments *can* be a source of good. All you need is a system of proportional representation, which alas was elbowed aside somewhere along North America's political evolutionary path. By the time we manage to reform our winner-take-all system, the point of no return on climate change will likely long since have come and gone. So, to seek salvation via the route of conventional party politics in the United States, the United Kingdom, or Canada, is a much longer shot than it is in Europe.

The only way I can imagine the industrialized countries suddenly getting serious about clamping down on emissions is if an "optimal disaster" occurs, something dramatic enough for a clear link to be seared into the minds of a sufficient majority. It would have to be overwhelming, given the imperviousness of the system to public opinion, to open the way for political action. Yet we have already seen record-breaking forest fires; in Canada, we've endured an ice-storm disaster and the worst smog season ever. The permafrost in Alaska is definitely melting, and so is the Arctic ice cap. But still there is the dislocation of cause and effect. Would it take a tidal wave, caused by some sort of thermohaline reaction? A tornado hitting Wall Street? Yellowstone National Park burning to the rock? As it is, current news stories about forest fires uniformly fail to answer *why*? Nobody in the mainstream media connects the thousands of acres of fires flaring along the edge of the Rockies, April heat waves in New York and the Middle West, and yet another snowless winter with the mighty pink-and-brown cloud hovering over such places as the Syncrude and Suncor oil-sands sites on the Athabasca River. What does the loss of trees matter anyway, compared to the profits and royalties to be extracted from the ground? Nobody thinks to order the shutting down of the tarsands projects, or of the coal-fired plants that provide the power for the refining — which would be the sane thing to do. Nobody in office above the municipal level even *suggests* requiring or encouraging reductions in energy use. No one dares to utter the words "carbon" and "tax" in the same breath (or gasp). No one suggests freezing the development of any more airports until the airline fleets can be retrofitted to use alternatives like hydrogen or fuel cells, which is another sane thing to do. In both Canada and the United States, the situation is stunningly out of alignment with the reality of climate crash. Our leadership turns in circles, even if every once in a while it gives a sign that it, too, can hear the wind blowing harder. No one — at *any* level — talks about fines for single-occupancy vehicle use. Squeegee kids were chased off the streets, but the vehicles themselves — whose crime is nothing less than the corruption of our atmosphere — remain, and multiply. No one is demanding conversion to natural gas, electric, or propane cars, trucks, and buses. Why has fuel-cell technology (invented in 1839) taken so long to come to market?

Cigarette smoking, which has virtually no impact on the natural environment (except at the growing end, which involves pesticides), is banned indoors, but cars are allowed to smoke outside all they want, and *that's* ridiculous! Urban sprawl continues virtually unchecked, with thousands of acres of Class-A farmland being gobbled up around big cities every year, forcing, through lack of adequate mass transit, the use of yet *more* single-passenger cars.

In due course, all this can be changed. A few substantial efforts to legislate ecological morality, like Ontario's famous Blue Box recycling program and a similar one in Seattle, have proven successful, so long as they are in harmony with the public's perception of a need or even a duty. In Canada, there are even faint signs that a green dimension is establishing itself in the spectrum of political life. In British Columbia, during the 2001 provincial election, the Green Party rose tantalizingly in the polls above the former governing socialist party in Vancouver, attaining 15 percent of the popular vote. Under a system of proportional representation, that would have translated into several seats in the legislature, but under the current system this simply meant that not a single Green was elected. In the United States, there are no Green Party representatives in either the Congress or the state legislatures. How many political generations will it take for a true greening — an ecological maturing — to occur? In the meantime, as one wag observed, "for the first time the glaciers are moving faster than climate negotiations," and the United States and Canada, with their insistence on dodging real change, are still ranked among the worst offenders when it comes to causing a traffic jam on the road to a workable, useful protocol.

A scaling-down of our energy-opulent lifestyle is logically the best starting point for any climate crusade. One American or Canadian cutting his or her emissions by one-third is the equivalent of a dozen Indians shutting down completely. If we North Americans were somehow to be motivated in large enough

numbers to pledge individual reductions on a scale commensurate with what the IPCC is now calling for — in the 70-percent
range — we might set enough of an example that public opinion
might push for a much more proactive political agenda. In terms
of global percentages, a reduction in emissions on that scale
among high-end energy users in any major city in North
America would amount to a measurable reduction in global GHG
levels, depending on how widespread such a movement could
become. I am suggesting the establishment of a "Step Back"
organization, whose members would pledge to reduce personal
emissions according to the schedule recommended by the IPCC,
not the minuscule compromise steps being promoted under
Kyoto.

I also propose measuring our "carbon load" in the atmosphere
and turning it into a resource, through the introduction of a
global carbon tax. For the moment, let me refer to it as a system
of "Petro Karma Points." Beginning, say, next year, each person
could be debited one Petro Karma Point per kilogram of greenhouse gases emitted, based on current Ecological Footprints. As
we approach 7 billion metric tons of GHG per year, the number
of kilograms per person would start to reflect our actual draw-
downs of energy as well as the load factor. Someone like myself,
racking up 9.2 metric tons of CO_2 alone, would enter the new
era carrying an enormous debt of Petro Karma Points. Instead
of talking about emissions-trading schemes between corporations, perhaps we should be discussing emissions trading
between individuals. Or is this a dangerous thought? A "user
pays" system makes as much sense as anything else. According
to this notion, someone with 9.2 metric tons worth of Petro
Karma Points, like me, would pay a much higher carbon tax
than someone blowing off one one-thousandth of that in Sudan.
It would be a way of redistributing some wealth from the North
to the South, a real step in the direction of fostering cooperation on climate change.

The first step in the curing of any addiction is recognition by the junkie that he's hooked. This book has hopefully contributed to that. What should not be overlooked, however, is the possibility that we North Americans might recast ourselves in the big human picture as good guys, instead of the conniving, obdurate energy gluttons we are seen by ecologists as being — and indeed *are*. All we would have to do, for openers, is redirect federal loans and grants from fossil fuels to solar, wind, wave, tidal, small-scale hydro, biomass, and geothermal power. Energy-efficiency programs would have to be put in place, too, subsidizing retrofits, or offering some other kind of tax incentive. Why not mandate or subsidize the development of hybrid cars using self-charging batteries? A freeze on further development of dirty fuels is well within the powers of the federal authority in both the United States and Canada. A freeze on the building of any more highways may even be achievable. Their dismantling can at least be imagined. To envision such an extreme green program actually being implemented, you have to simultaneously imagine electric, solar, or fuel-cell-driven monorails rising from the rubble of asphalt, whisking hundreds along at the energy cost of a family van being used by one person. Bans on automotive traffic in the downtown core of *every* city will be voted in sooner or later. On the issue of smog, the health community has been allied with environmentalists for at least a decade. It was the weight of medical authority in the form of the American Medical Association that finally tipped the scales against the tobacco companies, and, as the doctors gain a clearer understanding of the long-term health implications of climate change, they can be expected to join more actively in the fray. The Red Cross has already added its voice to the chorus calling for an about-face on energy policy, saying that the signs of global warming are already here, accounting for most of the world's refugees.

Writing back in 1982, at the height of the Cold War,

American author Jonathan Schell took on the task of describing the consequences of nuclear war in language that brought the full horror of such an eventuality home to many who had simply avoided thinking about it. In *The Fate of the Earth,* he took our imaginations beyond the brink and made us look at the consequences of an all-out Soviet–American nuclear exchange, which would turn the world into a "republic of insects and grass." No such vividly detailed picture of the aftermath of Thermageddon has yet been sketched, but it is uncanny the way Schell's description of the psychological state induced by the threat of nuclear annihilation speaks to our mental and emotional condition now in the face of climate crash:

> At present, most of us do nothing. We look away. We remain calm. We are silent. We take refuge in the hope that the holocaust won't happen, and turn back to our individual concerns. We deny the truth that is all around us. Indifferent to the future of our kind, we grow indifferent to one another. We drift apart. We grow cold. We drowse our way toward the end of the world. But if once we shook off our lethargy and fatigue and began to act, the climate would change. Just as inertia produces despair — a despair often so deep that it does not even know itself as despair — arousal and action would give us access to hope, and life would start to mend: not just life in its entirety but daily life, every individual life. At that point, we would begin to withdraw from our role as both the victims and the perpetrators of mass murder. We would no longer be the destroyers of mankind but, rather, the gateway through which the future generations would enter the world. Then the passion and will that we need to save ourselves would flood into our lives.

I have always been a "nature freak." That is, from somewhere in my late childhood, when I first went out camping as a Boy Scout and started experiencing "being outdoors," I found my own form of worship. It was the intricateness of nature that first caught my attention. No matter what I looked at or probed with my pocketknife or cut into pieces, the closer I looked the more complex it became. Then came a moment when the play of light on a loose sheet of blinding-white birch bark caught my eye, mesmerizing me. It was like a lock opening in my heart. Suddenly, everything I saw or sniffed was overwhelmingly beautiful. I remember reaching out to touch the parchment of bark as though it was the greatest treasure ever found. There was nothing special about it at all. It was the moment. I could see my breath, there was a slight glaze of frost on the bark, the smell of damp fallen leaves burning somewhere, and as I touched the bark I tingled and shivered. The bark was almost agonizingly real yet so *holy* at the same time that I stood until my feet grew cold, caressing it with my fingertips, watching my breath, astonished, amazed, awestruck by the world I was really noticing for the first time. Until then, I had been a Catholic who thought miracles were weird zaps coming from Above or from outside the universe (which is the closest I could figure to where God must be). But this was coming from the middle of things. The bark was alive, like skin. The tree was alive. The *ground* was alive. The Miracle of Nature came from *inside* the universe, not outside. I started going camping as often as possible, frequently by myself. To this day, I enjoy nothing more than a good canoe trip, which never fails to put me back in touch with the sense of the miraculous, which is to say the *unaccountable* beauty of nature. This is the difference: I can admire a masterpiece of architecture but I know the region from which it emerged, so to speak. The architect imagined the thing. I too have an imagination and have pulled ideas and even pictures up from its depths. I have a sense of connection with the dimension of human creativity, which means I can marvel at the works of my fellow humans, but there is no awe because it is all quite explainable in terms of engineering and mathematics. The white bark of the tree, like the tree itself, however, is the product of some kind of magic emanating from inner space. For a "nature freak," the fact that the atmosphere of the whole planet has been chemically altered is like a Christian witnessing the invasion of Heaven. We are born out of wildness, exactly like the other animals (and plants), and civilization is only there to help us after the fact. Polluting the wildness is a way of making it unwild, of breaking it, squeezing it by sheer force until it mutates. As we begin to own and control it, we lose it, because it is no longer the same thing: its independence is gone, the magic is covered with soot.

Eden has been contaminated, and is now withering before our eyes. It's not the Fall of Man we are talking about any longer: it's the Fall of Eden.

What a waste if we continue the plunge into the chaos and suffering of a world aflame or flooded or crushed under ice! What a waste of an excellent planet and a species with greatness in it! Scientists calculate that life on Earth is about 4 billion years old. At the rate the Sun is heating up, it will be impossible to reduce the greenhouse effect sufficiently to maintain life beyond another 1 billion years. In other words, we find ourselves four-fifths of the way through life on Earth. Everything from here on in will be shaped by what we do now. Nonsense, you say. A million years from now, who will know that we existed? The trouble is that a million years from now the planet could be emerging from a millennial climate shift triggered in a brief spurt of carbonization just before the end of the Holocene. In the worst-case scenario, nothing will remain but the contours of naked mountains and the basins of dried-up seabeds, which is all we have found on either Mars or Venus. With a dead planet orbiting on both sides of us, you would think we would be wary about what we did to our own precious, downright weirdly stable atmosphere.

The Bush–Cheney administration may be the worst acci
dent to have befallen humanity, their Carbon Club–backed
political victory coming at a time — the very moment! —
when the political figure the world most needed was former
vice president Al Gore, who foresaw the climate crisis perfectly.
He knew the file like the back of his hand. Insofar as anything
published or spoken was concerned, Gore was far out ahead of
his fellow politicians and journalists. He would have been a
perfect American president for the current planetary emergency.
He could have been the Franklin Roosevelt of the climate wars.
The decision by American environmentalists to shun Gore in
favor of the doomed Ralph Nader will go down in history as one
of the most self-defeating moves by a green constituency anywhere. In any event, this is what we are left with in North
America: an ecofreak's worst nightmare! Vice President Dick
Cheney has called for the construction of two thousand more
coal-fired power plants in the next twenty years (which would
work out to an average of one new power plant every week for
that entire period). He also called for the easing of regulations
governing power-plant construction, to make them cheaper to
build, and, of course, dirtier to operate. He proposed lowering
federal pollution standards to make this permissible. As part of a
"comprehensive energy plan," federal funding for energy conservation and alternative-energy programs was to be chopped.
Drilling in the Arctic National Wildlife Refuge and off the
Florida pan-handle was to be allowed until both projects ran into
political trouble at the congressional and state levels. The U.S.
federal budget for 2002 pledged to cut research into geothermal,
hydrogen, solar, and wind energy by half, while research into
cleaner coal technology got a $2-billion infusion. And in the
wake of the September 11 attacks on the World Trade Center
towers and the Pentagon, George W. Bush, as commander-in-
chief fighting a war against terrorism, saw his popularity surge to
record highs. Who could stand against him without being

branded unpatriotic? Accordingly, the United States obstinately remains outside the Kyoto Protocol. In North America, Big Oil holds sway. Not only do American, Canadian, and Mexican financial institutions remain silent about global warming because they have connections with the energy corporations, but the oil industry has an enormous workforce that can be effectively mobilized to lobby politicians. Oil companies account for the top nine of the leading twenty-five American corporations, and almost a third of the next tier of highest earners.

Thus, American delegates were absent from the historic meeting in Marrakesh, Morocco, in November 2001, where environment and energy ministers from around the world finally signed a badly watered-down version of the Kyoto Protocol. The deal committed the developed countries — *sans* America — to a reduction of greenhouse gases by 5 percent from 1990 levels by 2012 — nowhere near the required 70 percent cut called for by the IPCC. Yet, even with such a measly reduction involved, Canada, Australia, Japan, and Russia obfuscated to the bitter end, trying to get everything they could out of it through the sale of carbon credits on the international market. For the time being, the developing countries get to forge ahead with petroleum-based industrialization exactly according to the old Western model, with its famously disastrous environmental consequences. To come into effect, the pact has to be signed by fifty-five countries, including those that emitted 55 percent of the polluting gases in 1990, the baseline year. Even if America had signed, the treaty would have been feeble to the point of uselessness. Without the United States, it is barely more than ceremonial. And the great danger is that an awakening public might slump back into incomprehension, thinking that the "climate problem" has been solved, when all that has happened is that a very low bar has been set.

Nevertheless, despite a vigorous program to dismantle as many environmental protection regulations as possible, it seemed for a moment, in early June 2002, that the Bushites had actually come around on climate change. Headlines flared across the country and around the world on the basis of a story saying the Bush administration had "admitted" in a submission to the United Nations that not only was global warming real but it would cause "lasting and substantial changes" to the U.S. landscape "within decades." The submission, titled "U.S. Climate Action Report," had in fact been released by the Environmental Protection Agency, under the administration of Christie Whitman, and it was stunningly detailed and definitive in its portrayal of the effects of global warming on America. Moreover, it went the distance and stated categorically that the heating is largely a man-made problem.

Among the impacts predicted by the EPA:

- The coastal Southeastern states can expect rising sea levels to compromise wastewater, groundwater, and storm water systems;

- Georgia, North Carolina, and South Carolina can expect more intense wind speeds and rain during hurricanes;

- The worsening intensity of hurricanes could result in "complete devastation" for coastal communities in Florida and Louisiana;

- Drought on the Great Plains and in the Midwest is expected to continue, reducing groundwater supplies crucial to irrigation;

- Colorado and Wyoming could lose entire ecosystems as alpine meadows disappear and the snowpack shrinks;

- Periods of severe drought are expected to produce continued severe wildfire conditions, as witnessed in the summer of 2002, and the diminished spring melt could lower stream and river levels;

- On the Pacific coast, saltwater intrusions will compromise groundwater supplies and impact on farming.

This was indeed sensational political stuff, since the EPA's ultimate boss, President Bush, had been holding steadfastly to his claim that nothing serious was happening at all on the climate front. The media generally took the release of the EPA report as evidence that President Bush was "distancing himself" from his hard-line Carbon Club buddies, and bowing in the direction of the greenies and scientists. Democrats saw a slick effort to preempt global warming as an issue, undercutting Al Gore's signature position, while conservatives, utility industry mouthpieces, and right-wing talk show hosts like Rush Limbaugh saw it as a betrayal and a flip-flop. The oil industry's favorite son was suddenly accused of "environmental extremism."

No so. Within twenty-four hours, the White House was in full denial mode. "I read the report put out by the bureaucrats," sniffed President Bush. It wasn't going to change his mind about staying outside of the Kyoto Protocol. His plan was to call for strictly voluntary measures by industry, a scheme that analysts say would allow emissions to continue to rise, but at slower rates — eventually — than business as usual today.

Whether Bush embraced the report or rejected it made little difference in practical terms, because there were no recommendations for action. The report failed utterly to suggest doing anything more than lying down and "adapting." There was no suggestion of a response other than a fatalistic acceptance. "Because of the momentum in the climate system and natural climate variability, adapting to a changing climate is inevitable. The question is whether we adapt poorly or well." This was an oddly supine position for an administration that was vigorously fighting a war on terror, yet couldn't imagine that ecological terror has far greater long-term consequences than any attack mounted by political and religious zealots. Entire ecosystems are disappearing from the continent, precipitating drought, floods, fire, and superhurricanes — and the great United States of America can only roll over and whimper about putting up with things as they get worse? Adapt! Surely the call for adaptation to climate change will be seen someday as the equivalent of the policy of appeasement that, a generation earlier, led to the Second World War.

Part of George W. Bush's take on adaptation was to dump Dr. Robert Watson from his position as chairman of the IPCC, making sure this key office would go to a rival from India with a much more conservative stance. Dr. Watson's crime was to be too much of an advocate for action on climate. Even if he had made some bad calls along the way, such as urging his fellow scientists in the early days of the IPCC not to freak out politicians and the public by revealing how bad things could get, Bob Watson had served tirelessly and articulately. He was one of the human reasons the Kyoto Protocol had been dragged kicking and screaming into existence. Not surprisingly, he had acquired enemies along the way, including energy giant ExxonMobil, which successfully lobbied Vice President Cheney to have the crusading scientist replaced.

Shortly after Dr. Watson's departure, the United Nations Department for Economic and Social Affairs released a report as part of the buildup to the Johannesburg World Summit on Sustainable Development, known as the Rio Plus 10 meeting, that confirmed the deposed IPCC leader's worst fears. Forests are indeed being destroyed, droughts are indeed becoming more intense, agricultural production really is failing to keep up with the demand for food, sea levels actually are rising, species are going extinct at an unprecedented rate, and the lives of billions

of people are at risk, with 800 million already chronically under-
nourished, as a result of environmental devastation. There was
nothing particularly *new* in the report, but it drew on data from
the UN and various international organizations to quantify what
headlines called "a gloomy picture of the planet."

This was not enough to galvanize George W. Bush to attend
the Johannesburg meeting at the end of the summer of 2002,
which by July was well on its way to establishing a record as
the second hottest year on Planet Earth in a thousand years, after
2001. At Johannesburg, the Western nations collectively shrank
from taking on any more responsibility to alleviate the sufferings
of the Third World, while admitting they had done nothing to
combat global warming — most of them having slid backwards — since Rio. While 170 nations had agreed to lower emissions by the year 2000, fossil-fuel consumption had actually risen
in all of them by 9 percent. The one ray of light: activists did
manage to move the Kyoto ball ahead a few precious political
inches. Japan had already ratified by June. India announced soon
after the meeting that she would join the international effort.
Mighty China was next to declare in favor of ratification.

And finally, on December 10, 2002, Canada's parliament
voted by a three-to-one margin to ratify the pact, thereby joining
98 other nations in a concerted effort to tackle the climate threat.
A multimillion-dollar anti-Kyoto campaign launched by the
Alberta government and the Oil Patch put a dent in the nation-
wide support, but not enough to derail the push by Prime
Minister Jean Chrétien and his tough, activist environment minister, David Anderson. Both men stood up, in the end, to pressure from western Canada, the U.S., and of course big business.
From an environmental point of view, it was Canada's finest
hour, and a genuine legacy to Chrétien's — and Anderson's —
terms of office. After a weak start, the Liberals had redeemed
themselves.

The Canadian vote came the same week that scientists

revealed the melting of the Greenland glaciers over 265,000 square miles, 9 percent more than the previous maximum melt area. In September, ice coverage in the Arctic Ocean dipped to 2 million square miles, less than at any time since records began. The same week as the Canadian vote, the American Geophysical Union was told by Penn State geophysicist Dr. Richard Alley that the message climate-change scientists ought to be sending to governments should not be that greenhouse gases are slowly changing the atmosphere, but rather that the Earth is being pushed close to "a breaking point, after which calamitous change will be unavoidable."

To a lot of people's astonishment, after the Johannesburg meeting even Russia had announced its intention to ratify by year's end — a clear sign, if there ever was one, that the scientific evidence of a speeded-up warming in the far north has become overwhelming — but it failed to follow through. Once the Russian Duma does vote to ratify, the accord will come into effect, reaching the magic number of 55 percent of the world's emissions as well as fifty-five countries minimum.

Meanwhile, coal-producing Australia has reneged on its original commitment to sign the protocol and joined the United States as a rogue environmental state. This left a torn patchwork quilt of a treaty — not much, but much better than nothing, and perhaps with just enough muscle to start changing course. It is just possible that the accord has been forged in time to be effective. At least now a foundation for a rational phase-out of fossil fuels has been laid. As the climate cataclysm kicks in, humanity will have an international agreement in place to start taking on the awesome task of doing nothing less than *managing the climate from here on.*

And doing it without America — unless the only superpower decides to stop acting as a drag on the rest of the world's best and only chance to avoid disaster.

CHAPTER 13

A PLEDGE

My admission of my failure to prevent the crunching of the great ship of climate on the rocks will be of little comfort to you, Dexter. I just want you to know that I tried. I hope that these pages will be the subject of much merriment by the time you reach my age. Boy, wasn't the old man *down!* He didn't have a clue what was coming, did he? I admit, there is always the chance that the perfect nonpolluting source of energy will be smoothly trundled in to replace our primitive forms of power generation. A starship fleet could also have arrived from anywhere. A World Federation might be established, too. It's *all* possible. But the *likelihood* right now is that you will have inherited a world so pulverized it might as well have been besieged by aliens.

What I might as well further admit is that, for a full decade after I first heard the distant rumbling of the approaching eco-storm, I carried on life absolutely as usual. As the years passed, and further editions of the IPCC reports came out, scientists stepped up to the microphones one after another, by the thousands, to proclaim: "It's coming!" I read the articles, followed the debate, and interviewed many of the players, including scientists whose warnings grew noticeably less cautious as the magnitude of the coming event began to hit them. It surprised me, in the early years, how almost zombie-like climate scientists became when they tried to answer questions. Later, they came out of it (or some of them did) and found their human voices. In retrospect, I can see they were in a state of shock. With climate change an event that was still 99 percent in the future, the shock of what they had glimpsed had not had time to wear off. A psychologist has suggested that environmentalists frequently show symptoms of suffering from the equivalent of post-traumatic stress disorder. They have been soldiers in the front lines fighting against one thing or another for so long — and *losing* — that they suffer a high rate of "burnout." Similarly, the climate scientists have been in the emotional trenches, facing a nightmare that until recently the broad masses gave no thought to at all. The idea of our planet being mutilated touches a deep chord in our natures. So I think the scientists adopt the mental stance of doctors, distancing themselves emotionally from their subject.

As both an environmentalist and somebody covering the climate story as a journalist, I started doing the same thing. I compartmentalized what I was learning and what I knew, tucked it away with the information generally labeled Something Going On Far, Far Away. After years of living on a farm surrounded by coniferous trees and on a boat surrounded by coastal mountains, I settled deliberately into a middle-class suburban existence in Canada's biggest city. If you must live in a city, a third-of-an-acre yard with a cedar hedge around it so you can't see your neighbors is not to be disparaged. You were too young to remember the pool, Dexter, but we had an executive-size swimming pool with a heater we used until Halloween. You won't remember the sauna or the hot tub or the steam shower in the cabana, either, because they have been converted into a darkroom and storage area. But at one point, they were all running. Bubbles and steam and an electrical heater going twenty-four hours a day through the long winter nights — all that in addition to the rest of the

house, my wife's van, my car. Soon our children would be ready
to drive, so we kept the previous van and car, fully expecting to
become a four-car household. There were floodlights mounted
around the yard to throw beams on the undersides of the trees,
making lovely silhouettes. The bulbs were the size of headlights.
We'd leave these on all evening so we could see how pretty
everything was through the two walls of the living room, which
were mainly glass. I have a cabin to write in, equipped with an
air conditioner and electrical heater.

Until this year, I continued driving my car to work, refusing
to take the subway, on the grounds that it was "too inconve-
nient." I did not even get around to applying weather stripping
around the doors and windows to keep the heat from escaping,
because these kinds of irritating manual tasks kept slipping to the
back of my to-do list. Subconsciously, I was going along with the
prevailing Canadian energy ethic — it's cheap and plentiful, why
worry about it? Just like the skipper from Newfoundland, I knew
what I was doing, I knew it was *bad* for the environment, but the
damage was already done. No sense being silly or romantic
about this. The hydro dams were built. Enough of the nukes
were still clunking along, so we didn't have brownouts, and
sooner or later they'd be closed down. As for the coal-burning
plants, well, the nearest one was way on the other side of town.
I also flew, as I have confessed, a lot. In all, so far, I estimate I
have traveled 889,000 miles. This may turn out to be nothing
compared to the distances you might cover, Dexter, especially
if you were to fulfill your grandpa's dream of becoming an
astronaut.

The point is that even *I*, an old-style whale-loving anti-
nuker, spent a decade in a state of paralysis in the face of the
incoming climate tidal wave. *Frozen on the spot.* It wasn't until
long after I knew there was a problem that I actually began to
change my behavior, and it is only now that I can see so clearly
what to do.

There is no point me assembling this picture of the political gridlock we face in my time, the lust for gain, the utter lack of pity for the future, if all it comes down to is an elaborate effort to distance myself from my fellow mammoths. See, Dexter? It was *them*. It is so easy to make yourself look good, or at least better than the sordid truth. He who writes history bends it. I won't try to get away with that. The sordid truth is that I *pigged* on a big scale. I was like the people Jonathan Schell wrote about — looking away, remaining calm and silent, and growing cold, indifferent to the future of our kind, while the holocaust gathered.

I had two conscious rationales for utterly ignoring the environmental consequences of my lifestyle. First, I argued, any changes I undertook personally would amount to such minuscule spots in the big picture that it would not make any difference. It didn't *matter*. Second, that we were doomed, period. Might as well live, love, laugh, and be happy, as an old song suggested. I had been to Los Angeles before. I was in London during the last great Killer Smog in 1962. I once looked out from the Empire State Building and could barely make out *anything* in the copper haze. At night, I saw a river burning in Minneapolis–St. Paul. I saw detergent foam reach up ten stories to the top of the Red River locks. I drove in a *tuk-tuk* through Bangkok, and gave up trying to quit smoking. In Mexico City, I spent a week wearing paper breathing masks in *El Tráfico*. From 35,000 feet I looked out over Europe, over North America, over Japan, over Brazil, over the North Pole, for God's sake! And everywhere I had seen a soup of petrochemicals like gauze separating me from the world below. The world was truly *enveloped*. I felt suffocated. And more than a little terrified if I let myself think about it too much. The thing has gone too far. It's too big, I thought. There are too many people, too many machines. I'd been in the rush-hour subways in Tokyo and Hong Kong. I looked across the endless *barrio*-covered hills around Rio. Rather than filling me with the excitement I had expected, or raising my spirits, my travels left me feeling overwhelmed, defeated. Futility and pessimism: these were my excuses for personal inaction. *I gave up.* It hadn't always been that way, and maybe middle age had sapped my outrage, but I found myself paying a lot of attention to my garden. I grew vegetables and flowers. It was a way to keep my head down, appreciate the Earth, without looking up too much or listening too hard. Just carrying on as usual. Car. Big house. Pool. Plane trips. Leave the saving of the planet to the smart young professionals, the adventurers, and those on karmic quests.

This was uncharacteristic behavior, this stage of paralysis. For half my life I had been involved, at least intellectually, in the mass green consciousness–change that came swirling out of the sixties. I was accused of being the Chicken Little of Canadian Journalism *back then.* I merely considered myself observant enough to have noticed that there were an awful lot of nuclear weapons being piled up to the north and south of where I lived, and I reasoned that this was bad. Reason aside, along with millions of others around the world, I awakened to a peril that had been considered too remote to really worry about. Nuclear war was a subject for science fiction until the peace movement came along. My very private journey was taking place within an emerging electronic global culture, however, and my opinions came to be amazingly in line with mainstream ecological thinking. We were all learning about it at the same time. My journey, I like to think, continues to be a private matter, yet I am surely just as much the child of a common worldview as ever. The ecological issues I perceived to be of paramount urgency in the sixties and seventies were indeed urgent, and needed to be addressed by as many thinking people as possible. My sources of information were the same as those of my peers. That remains the case today. We are all tapping into the same body of data. The sky did *not* fall during the Cold War, but that doesn't mean it isn't falling now.

I have not heard the term "climate movement" yet, perhaps because climate is still seen as a "new" issue, a latecomer of an ecodisaster, which has not had much time to imprint itself in the public mind, unlike oil spills and logging. There are no "charismatic megafauna" to aim cameras at, either. What has to happen now is for climate to take the leap that the nuclear issue did at a certain time. Climate stands as such a towering issue it threatens to swallow all other green concerns. It has an impact on everything.

It was not until I was nearly finished writing this book, Dexter, that the breakthrough finally came for me. It was caused by a combination of things, but mainly a re-realization, only deeper and clearer, that my separate existence is an illusion — something I had learned to appreciate at the height of the sixties, but had largely forgotten as I sank further into isolation. Ecology is flow. You and I are most definitely part of the flow. Everything I do affects the flow and everything the flow does affects me. It was the image of a fully grown mammoth that finally drove it home to me that I *am* an energy monster, and if nobody is going to rein me in, I had better start doing it myself. A couple of years before, I had learned the trick of quitting smoking, which (for me anyway) was to attack the addiction as if it were an enemy. I practiced old karate exercises with the tobacco demon in mind. Now the trick is to learn to withdraw from my dependency on fossil fuels. To that end, I have taken several small steps and one big one.

The small ones amount to common-sense options like setting a lamp up on the kitchen counter to be turned on instead of using the wall switch which ignites no fewer than *nine* light bulbs; disconnecting the garage door from the remote control; picking dandelions by hand instead of using pesticides; shutting down the hot tub and sauna. The one big step thus far has been to abandon my car at the Light Rapid Transit parking lot, a five-minute drive from home, and go in to work by LRT and subway.

I quickly found myself enjoying the extra time for reading, and especially appreciated the fact that I could arrive at work feeling relatively unruffled, compared to the stressed-out road-rage case I was a year ago. By my calculations, I should be able to shave 20 percent off my energy consumption level before even having to put any money out. An energy audit is next, with a chance to cut back by at least another 20 percent through orthodox efficiency measures. And then, to get serious, I start bringing in the solar-panel experts. The goal is to reduce my own emissions by as much as the IPCC has urged — 70 percent relative to 1990 emissions. If government stalls on action, that's no reason for individuals to throw in the towel, or absolve themselves of any further responsibility.

Nor can we dismiss the possibility of a "self-structuring hierarchical jump," as biophysicist John R. Platt described "deep" revolutions. In an article entitled "What We Must Do," in *Science*, November 28, 1969, he described the sudden transition of flow systems from one self-maintaining integrated system to another. His thesis was that serious change occurs when a collective restructuring is triggered by the accumulation of data which doesn't fit the old patterns, pressure building up in isolated situations that begin to converge, precipitating a clash between old and new systems. Then change, when it comes, moves with the speed of lightning. No one individual or group controls it. No one can predict it. He cites the Reformation and the Industrial Revolution, changes that

> go deeper than ordinary political revolutions because they are not simply an exchange of power from one group to another, but a thoroughgoing change in philosophy, personal attitudes and ways of work and economic organization in every part of society. . . . The largest of all these changes, in its speed and scale and its long-range evolutionary implications, is the world transformation through

which all humanity is now passing. . . . It is no distortion
to speak of this world reorganization of all our patterns as
a "quantum jump," or as a sudden collective change of
awareness or flash of understanding for the human race.

Platt wrote this long before the Berlin Wall vanished, catching
everyone by surprise.

"The reason for the speed of the change," which he compared to crystals rearranging suddenly,

> is that it is prepared for everywhere at once. Even though
> individual elements of reform seem weak, when they
> reach a certain critical density and begin to join forces, the
> old order finds itself overwhelmed from without and
> betrayed from within, from directions it never guessed.
> The new self-maintaining patterns, like new vortex pat-
> terns, are self-reinforcing to each other as soon as they
> touch, because they can form the beginnings of a better-
> integrated system with a speed of understanding and
> communications and economics that the old malfunc-
> tioning system cannot match.

Prophetic words! A description of the nascent climate movement if I have ever heard it.

My own experience of the anti-nuke and anti-whaling/anti-
sealing campaigns is that they were global consciousness-altering
phenomena. After hesitant, futility-haunted beginnings, they
spread through the body politic of the Western world with
incredible speed. Television alone couldn't account for this. They
touched that deep chord of feeling we have for the fate of the
planet. Once the realization sets in that the climate *is* crashing,
taking a lot of biota, if not everything, down with it, there is
surely bound to be a surge of genuine mass grief and anger. How
it plays out politically remains to be seen, but all the elements of

one of Platt's self-structuring hierarchical leaps to a new level of stability are in place. If humanity is able to make another leap like the one into the Industrial Age, only this time *out* of it, we might stand at the dawn of a Golden Age instead of the Fall of Eden. As the challenge has become more global, the solutions become more global. When the Change comes, oil and coal might find themselves suddenly outlawed everywhere, in the same way that nukes are being shut down in many parts of Europe.

There is no lack of possible solutions, Dexter. I have only to turn to the World Wide Web, or, more to my liking, walk into a bookstore. Entire sections are devoted to energy and conservation. The search for answers took a quantum jump in 2001 with the publication of *Stormy Weather: 101 Solutions to Global Climate Change*, by Guy Dauncey with Patrick Mazza, which compiles a list of the available off-the-shelf green technologies, plus a huge range of proposals for developing distributed grids, building solar capacity, shifting taxes, burying carbon dioxide, building sustainable transportation systems, and stopping sprawl. The concepts, the knowledge, the equipment, and the tools, they are all readily available. After the intransigence of the fossil-fuel industry and its allies, the most frustrating thing about our dilemma is the tantalizing closeness of an eco-paradise. We *could* be logically, intelligently, rationally, wisely going about the business of converting to sustainable energy sources. The wind turbines could be growing like forests. Solar panels could cover every rooftop. Trains and planes powered by fuel cells could be whizzing along. There would go electric cars instead of gasoline guzzlers. Heat pumps. Geothermal. Tidal power. We could be harnessing it all. We have the gear. We could be halfway there by now if the technology had been deployed when it could have been. Instead, as an international community, we sometimes seem a jumbled riot of shouting, bumping, stumbling, and door-slamming. But that's not entirely fair, because there are powerful environmental movements at work all over the world, and progressive governments here and there are starting to listen. It has been said that a new paradigm can't take hold until the people who personify the old one die off, but that is an unhappy thought, since the current president of the United States is younger than *me*.

But wait, what if I *am* the old paradigm? It doesn't really matter what I read or think or write. It is what I *do* that counts. It has dawned on me, Dexter, it is not my species I must oppose in defense of nature, it is *myself*. Gandhi said there was no such thing as an enemy. In the context of the man-made Holocene climate crash, there is indeed an enemy: it is I, the user.

If I fail to change, I invite you to spit on this book. Just as I invite your friends to spit on *their* grandparents' pictures if it turns out they did nothing, carried on as usual, even *after* they found out what was happening to the atmosphere. I mark the year 2000, the year of your birth, the year we found out the Arctic ice cap was 40 percent gone, as the point where history will say the greenhouse "fingerprint" became visible enough for policy changes to begin, for someone, somewhere, to start changing course.

Me! For *me* to change course.

The climate crisis isn't out there somewhere. Its causes are close at hand, literally, as close as the night-lamp switch. I hold them in my hand when I dig the keys out of my pocket to start the car. Don't judge me by my words, which are many, someone said, but by my actions, which are few. And that should be said about all of us here, now, in the belly of the beast, mainlining coal and oil. My vow to you, Dexter, is that I am coming off the stuff as fast as I can. It took me years to learn to stop smoking. It will take a while to learn to stop climate-wrecking.

SELECTED READING

(Reference is to the latest available edition.)

Abbey, Edward. *The Monkey Wrench Gang.* New York: Harper Perennial, 2000.

Athanasiou, Tom. *Divided Planet: The Ecology of Rich and Poor.* Athens, GA: University of Georgia Press, 1998.

Bacher, John. *Petrotyranny.* Toronto: Science 4 Peace/Samuel Stevens, 2000.

Bell, Art, and Whitney Strieber. *The Coming Global Superstorm.* New York: Simon & Schuster (Pocket Books), 2000.

Benarde, Melvin A. *Global Warning — Global Warming.* New York: John Wiley and Sons, 1992.

Carson, Rachel. *Silent Spring.* Boston: Mariner Books, 1994.

Catton, William. *Overshoot: The Ecological Basis of Revolutionary Change.* Champaign, IL: University of Illinois Press, 1980.

Christianson, Dale E. *Greenhouse: The 200-Year Story of Global Warming.* New York: Walker & Company, 1999.

Collinson, Helen, ed. *Green Guerrillas: Environmental Conflicts and Initiatives in Latin America and the Caribbean.* Buffalo, NY: Black Rose Books, 1997.

Dauncey, Guy, and Patrick Mazza. *Stormy Weather: 101 Solutions to Global Climate Change.* Gabriola Island, BC: New Society Publishers, 2001.

Doos, B. A., and Annika Nilsson. *Greenhouse Earth.* New York: John Wiley and Sons, 1992.

Dotto, Lydia. *Storm Warning: Gambling with the Climate of Our Planet*. Toronto: Random House of Canada, 2000.

Earth Island Institute. *Earth Island Journal* 13:4 (Fall 1998).

Earth Report: The Essential Guide to Global Ecological Issues. Los Angeles: Price Stern Sloan, Inc., 1988.

Foley, Dermott. *Fuelling the Climate Crisis: The Continental Energy Plan*. Toronto: David Suzuki Foundation, 2001.

Foreman, Dave, and Bill Haywood. *Ecodefense: A Field Guide to Monkeywrenching*. Chico, CA: Abbzug Press, 1993.

Gelbspan, Ross. *The Heat Is On: The Climate Crisis, the Cover-up, the Prescription*. New York: Perseus Books, 1998.

Gore, Al. *Earth in the Balance: Ecology and the Human Spirit*. New York: Plume, 1993.

Grady, Wayne. *The Quiet Limit of the World: A Journey to the North Pole to Investigate Global Warming*. Toronto: McFarlane, Walter and Ross, 1997.

Hunter, Robert. *Red Blood*. Toronto: McClelland & Stewart, 1999.

———*Warriors of the Rainbow: A Chronicle of the Greenpeace Movement*. New York: Henry Holt, 1979.

Hunter, Robert, and Robert Keziere. *Greenpeace*. Toronto: McClelland & Stewart, 1972.

Hunter, Robert, and David McTaggart. *Greenpeace III: Journey into the Bomb*. New York: William Morrow & Company, 1979.

Hunter, Robert, and Rex Weyler. *To Save a Whale: The Voyages of Greenpeace*. Vancouver: Douglas & McIntyre, 1978.

Intergovernmental Panel on Climate Change. *Climate Change Impacts on the United States: Overview Report*. National Assessment Synthesis Team, ed. New York: Cambridge University Press, 2001.

———*Climate Change 2001: Impacts, Adaptation, and Vulnerability: Contribution of the Working Group II to the Third Assessment Report of the Intergovernmental Panel on Climate Change*. James J. McCarthy et al., eds. New York: Cambridge University Press, 2001.

————*Climate Change 2001: Mitigation: Contribution of the Working Group III to the Third Assessment Report of the Intergovernmental Panel on Climate Change.* Bert Metz et al., eds. New York: Cambridge University Press, 2001.

————*Climate Change 2001: The Scientific Basis: Contribution of the Working Group I to the Third Assessment Report of the Intergovernmental Panel on Climate Change.* J. T. Houghton et al., eds. New York: Cambridge University Press, 2001.

————*Climate Change 2001: Synthesis Report: Third Assessment Report of the Intergovernmental Panel on Climate Change.* Robert T. Watson et al., eds. New York: Cambridge University Press, 2001.

Leggett, Jeremy. *The Carbon War: Global Warming and the End of the Oil Era.* New York: Routledge, 2001.

Leggett, Jeremy, ed. *Global Warming: The Greenpeace Report.* New York: Oxford University Press, 1990.

Leopold, Aldo. *A Sand County Almanac.* New York: Ballantine Books, 1990.

Manes, Christopher. *Green Rage: Radical Environmentalism and the Unmaking of Civilization.* Boston: Little, Brown and Company (Back Bay Books), 1991.

McKibben, Bill. *The End of Nature* (10th anniversary edition). New York: Anchor, 1999.

McNeill, J. R. *Something New under the Sun: An Environmental History of the Twentieth-Century World.* New York: W. W. Norton, 2001.

Meadows, Donella H. *Limits to Growth: A Report for the Club of Rome's Project on the Predicament of Mankind.* New York: New American Library, 1977.

Meadows, Donella H., Dennis L. Meadows, and Jørgen Randers. *Beyond the Limits: Confronting Global Collapse, Envisioning a Sustainable Future.* White River Junction, VT: Chelsea Green

Publishing Company, 1993.

Mungall, Constance, and Digby McLaren, eds. *Planet under Stress: The Challenge of Global Change.* New York: Oxford University Press, 1990.

Platt, John R. "What We Must Do," *Science* (November 28, 1969).

Ramphal, Shridath. *Our Country, the Planet: Forging a Partnership for Survival.* Washington, D.C.: Island Press, 1992.

Rees, William, and Mathis Wackernagel. *Our Ecological Footprint: Reducing Human Impact on the Earth.* Gabriola Island, BC: New Society Publishers, 1995.

Schell, Jonathan. *The Fate of the Earth.* Palo Alto, CA: Stanford University Press, 2000.

Schneider, Stephen H. *Laboratory Earth: The Planetary Gamble We Can't Afford to Lose.* New York: Basic Books, 1997.

Somerville, Richard C. J. *The Forgiving Air.* Berkeley: University of California Press, 1998.

Strong, Maurice. *Where on Earth Are We Going?* New York: Texere, 2001.

World Commission on Environment and Development. *Our Common Future.* New York: Oxford University Press, 1987.

Zielinski, Sue, and Gordon Laird, eds. *Beyond the Car: Essays on Auto Culture.* Toronto: Steel Rail Publishing, 1995.